AUCKLAND CLASSICAL ESSAYS

AUCKLAND CLASSICAL ESSAYS

PRESENTED TO E. M. BLAIKLOCK

———

EDITED BY B. F. HARRIS

1970

AUCKLAND UNIVERSITY PRESS

OXFORD UNIVERSITY PRESS

First published 1970
© Contributors as named

Printed in New Zealand by
John McIndoe Limited, Dunedin

EDVARDO MVSGRAVE BLAIKLOCK
IN VNIVERSITATE AVCKLANDENSI ANNOS XLII
LITTERARVM GRAECARVM LATINARVMQVE
PRAECEPTORI
HVNC LIBRVM
D D D
DISCIPVLI COLLEGAE AMICI

CONTENTS

INTRODUCTION

These Essays are the first tangible evidence within a single volume of a classical tradition in the University of Auckland which continues to flourish. Anyone who reads the earlier history of the Department becomes aware that sound foundations were laid at the very beginning. T. G. Tucker, the first Professor who was at Auckland from 1883 to 1885 before transferring to Melbourne, was at pains to point out publicly that classical scholars do not represent their subject as 'a necessity of intellectual culture', but adds 'that a good classical education is one of the very greatest factors thereto, is admitted by the best talent of generations'.

Tucker's immediate successors, H. M. Posnett, C. A. M. Pond, and H. A. Talbot-Tubbs, all taught the Classics as 'literae humaniores', and the Department was consolidated under the longer careers of H. S. Dettmann, A. C. Paterson and C. G. Cooper. While all of these men had their fields of special competence, their lecturing covered a broad range, with emphasis on good exegesis of the Greek and Latin authors selected for study. There was no substitute for an accurate and sympathetic understanding of the texts. Within the Auckland Department—and this would be typical in Australia and New Zealand—the range of teaching undertaken by each staff member continued to be broad, and although the limitations of this method were obvious, there were also major compensations both for lecturers and students. However, in the last two decades a considerably increased staff has allowed specialization in teaching and the opportunity for research, and it is now possible to work mainly in one of the fields of literature, history, philosophy or philology.

There is still a popular notion, even within the universities, that classicists have largely become a self-perpetuating community. This is far from the truth, as a casual glance at the careers of Auckland classical graduates will show. Some have gone into the diplomatic and civil services, others have attained eminence in politics, law, and the church, others again have become leaders in the teaching profession. Of those who have entered other academic disciplines in the universities of the Commonwealth and beyond, many are now working in English language and literature, in a wide group of modern languages, and in schools of law.

This volume of essays brings together a number of Auckland graduates who have remained in the university classical field. Their diverse interests will immediately be apparent, with the proportion of historians notably high. A particular link between them is that all have at various times been pupils of E. M. Blaiklock, to whom this book is dedicated. Dr Blaiklock in 1968 completed the longest teaching career in the Department's history, with forty-two years' service, the last nineteen as Professor. He has been a dedicated classicist, who learned his skills chiefly from A. C. Paterson and whose lectures on the Greek tragedians, and on Vergil, Horace, and Catullus, have perhaps been the most memorable in a very wide range. Without doubt literature has been his first love, but his interest in classical history has also been lively and has stimulated many in their formative years. We wish Dr Blaiklock an active and enjoyable retirement.

The grant from the Sir Perceval Maitland Laurence Fund III by the Faculty Board of Classics at Cambridge University, for the publication of plates to accompany Mr Nicholls's essay, is gratefully acknowledged. The lines on p. 150 are quoted by permission of Professor C. K. Stead. I wish also to express my thanks to my former colleagues Professor W. K. Lacey and Mr W. F. Richardson of Auckland, also to Dr Agathe Thornton of the University of Otago, for their assistance in preparing the book for the press; to Professor E. A. Judge of Macquarie University; to the Auckland Editor of Publications, Mr R. D. McEldowney; and finally to the University of Auckland for sponsoring this enterprise.

B. F. HARRIS

Macquarie University, Sydney
May, 1970

Frontispiece

Eretria Museum, terracotta centaur from Lefkandi in Euboea, late
tenth century B.C. (p. 37)

GREEK VOTIVE STATUETTES AND RELIGIOUS CONTINUITY, *c.* 1200 - 700 B.C.

R. V. Nicholls

This study is devoted to one of the humblest of all periods of Greek art, not from any convictions as to its aesthetic merits, which are scant enough in all honesty, but for the real challenges it presents to our knowledge—broad challenges of a kind that it is hoped Professor Blaiklock will feel it well worth our trying to meet, incomplete though the evidence yet is. The study itself deals with the crude statuettes of clay or bronze dedicated in shrines or graves during that Dark Age that followed the collapse of the Minoan and Mycenaean cultures and preceded the start of the new upsurge that led ultimately to Archaic art.[1] The time-span covered is from about the twelfth to the eighth centuries B.C., with a few related developments that are slightly earlier or later included for completeness. Whatever their artistic limitations, these figures deserve reappraisal for two reasons. They constitute the main surviving evidence for Greek religious practices over this ill-known period, and they afford the chief hope for any further light on just what preceded early Greek sculpture as we now know it.

It is now over forty years since Nilsson first published his *Minoan-Mycenaean Religion*,[2] postulating Bronze Age origins for many of the cults and beliefs of Greece in historical times. This hypothesis has been widely accepted and seems partly confirmed by the divine names since read on certain of the Linear B tablets.[3] But relatively little attention has been given to the meagre evidence of the intervening five hundred years to be considered here and whether or not it confirms this concept of religious continuity. The most notable recent exception has been that of Desborough who, in a masterly study of the earlier part of this period, has discussed each of the main known Mycenaean shrines from this point of view.[4] In the great majority of cases, his conclusions as to whether they show

continuity of worship into the immediately succeeding periods are
cautiously negative. Here we are going to tackle the problem rather
differently by trying to trace through this whole period the history
of the practice of dedicating statuettes to the gods, dealing first with
the figures of terracotta and then with those of bronze. Before beginning, however, it may be helpful to glance at the history of the
end of the Bronze Age as it emerges from the archaeological evidence as analysed by Desborough and others.

The centralized Mycenaean power with control, direct or indirect,
over much of the Greek mainland and islands had fought and won
the Trojan War, most probably in about the third quarter of the
thirteenth century B.C. In about 1200 B.C. it suffered a major
calamity, seemingly partly the result of a great land-borne raid of
northern barbarians, evidence for which has also been adduced from
the sudden impact of Mycenaean metalwork and similar crafts on
the northern Balkans as the invaders withdrew again.[5] Vital areas
such as the southern Peloponnese were largely depopulated from
about this period on, possibly because of drought and probably because of the widespread emigration occurring at this date.[6] This
apparently involved not only movement of population in Greece
itself, but also the colonization of territories such as Cyprus and
possibly also Greek participation in the great waves of invading 'Sea
Peoples' that overthrew the Hittite Empire, swept down through
Syria and Palestine and were defeated on the frontiers of Egypt in
1191 B.C. by Ramesses III.[7] Henceforward Mycenaean culture
seems broken up into small local units. A further disaster in about
the middle or third quarter of the twelfth century B.C. brought the
final destruction of the citadel at Mycenae and a fresh wave of emigration from the Mycenaean heartland.[8] But the Dorian penetration
into the eastern and southern Peloponnese and the southern Aegean
islands may have begun rather later than implied by Thucydides,[9]
starting in about the mid eleventh century B.C. on Desborough's
interpretation, although Styrenius' views seem to allow a rather
earlier date.[10] In any case it was apparently a gradual process continuing on into the tenth century B.C.

To turn now to the terracotta statuettes themselves, it is to be
observed that Crete seems to have been subject to mainland Greek
rule since the fifteenth century B.C., but in votive figurines, as in
other things, her own older and more accomplished Minoan tradition showed a remarkable tenacity. The impact of the different religious beliefs of the island's new masters is, as we shall see later,
something rather harder to evaluate. Although there is some evi-

dence of Cretan influence on the mainland statuettes from the time
that they started to evolve in the later fifteenth century B.C.,[11] the
Mycenaean figurines themselves that emerged were only very rarely
imported into Crete.[12] The most characteristic Mycenaean statuettes
of the fourteenth to twelfth centuries B.C. are small handmade
female figures that have been quaintly but usefully classified as 'φ-',
'τ-' and 'ψ-types', according to the resemblances existing between
those letters and the way they hold their arms.[13] The few natural-
istically rendered examples suggest that the 'φ-type' has its upper
arms lowered with its hands held near each other on the midriff or
between the breasts, whilst the 'τ-type' seems to have its elbows
raised horizontally with its fists brought back against the top of the
chest. If correctly interpreted, both of these postures are old traditional ones adopted by Minoan bronze and terracotta figures apparently mainly representing votaries or worshippers; it thus seems
possible that both types may be ultimately of Cretan inspiration,
although the highly schematic forms that they regularly adopt are
wholly a mainland Mycenaean contribution.[14] Whether they represent goddesses or mortal women is a vexed question.[15] Although
they may have mortal antecedents, it seems that the minds of their
dedicators may have been as confused and inconsistent on this point
as were those of their much later successors offering terracotta
statuettes at archaic and classical temples. The 'τ-' and 'ψ-varieties'
are regularly provided with flaring head-dresses, possibly of divine
type, and it will be seen below that there are other grounds for
regarding the 'ψ-figures' as representing goddesses. All these figures
have been found in graves, shrines and general habitation sites and
this range of use makes them an uncertain criterion for identifying
early sanctuaries. Isolated fragments may not of themselves suffice,
e.g., to identify the Mycenaean building under the archaic Teles-
terion at Eleusis as a public temple.[16] But very large concentrations
of them, even divorced from building remains, may well indicate a
public cult, as, e.g., by the Temple of Athena Pronaia at Delphi.[17]
The various other varieties of handmade Mycenaean statuettes have
usefully been listed by Higgins.[18] Here it will suffice to cite the two
commonest because of their significance in what follows: small
statuettes of animals, especially cattle, and highly stylized render-
ings of two-horse chariots.[19]

Much larger human figures of terracotta were fashioned hollow
on the potter's wheel in the fourteenth and thirteenth centuries B.C.,
in a technique probably also learnt from Crete although handled in
a distinctively Mycenaean style. The largest of these, several of

them about two feet high, have been found in a shrine at Mycenae destroyed in the thirteenth century B.C.[20] The figures themselves are from a storeroom and may be somewhat earlier, perhaps of about the late fourteenth century B.C. One approximates to the 'φ-posture' and others seem to have had the right arm raised and the left bent forward across the body—a stance possibly related to one met with on Cretan bronze statuettes of worshippers.[21] This type also seems well represented among the wheelmade figures of intermediate size known from several parts of Greece over the fourteenth and thirteenth centuries B.C. and which, in their final stages, occasionally acquire a cylindrical head-dress, or *polos* (Plate 2a), possibly suggesting divinity.[22]

Of the handmade human figures, only the 'τ-' and 'ψ-types' continued to be made in the twelfth century B.C. and it is the 'ψ-variety', which then preponderates, that is mainly of concern here. Stripped of its elements of Mycenaean stylization, this appears to consist of a female figure with its upper arms extended sideways and its forearms held vertically. Although not universally so accepted, this seems indeed to be a local version of the pose regarded in Crete as representing the epiphany of a deity, most commonly the so-called 'house-' or 'palace-goddess'.[23] Both in Crete and on the mainland terracotta statuettes of goddesses in this pose became widespread from the thirteenth century B.C. on. The Cretan examples include not only small handmade figures but also others that are much larger and more sophisticated (e.g., Plate 1a), to which an important study has been devoted by Alexiou.[24] These are sometimes quite big, several being between two and three feet in height,[25] and fashioned hollow on the potter's wheel, a technique of great antiquity in Cretan statuettes, but here used much more ambitiously. These larger examples are made up of wheelmade cylinders, etc., of gritty clay, worked into a more human shape while still pliant and joined together so that they freely intercommunicate for ventilation in firing, with a main vent commonly provided in the top of the head. Small holes are also not infrequently pierced through the centres of the ears. There is no technical necessity for these and it can only be assumed that their rôle is simply 'all the better to hear with'.[26] It would thus seem that prayers may have been addressed to these idols, although one may hesitate in accepting the common view that they are cult images rather than private dedications, if only because of the way that numbers of them tend with time to accumulate together in a single shrine. The shrines themselves are indoor affairs, usually in the form of a rectangular room with a low bench against one wall to carry the idols and certain of the ritual vessels.[27] The most remarkable of these last are the so-called 'snake-tubes', tall, drainpipe-like, handled pottery stands or recipients for libations, sometimes with snakes modelled on them.[28] The idols themselves show a measure of schematization, unlike the natural forms associated with earlier Cretan work, doubtless partly due to the exigencies of the technique and partly to the different spirit of the age. Some bear interesting attributes, e.g., the poppy-heads at the shrine at Gazi mentioned below.[29]

Alexiou has dated the oldest of the Cretan idols of this kind to the early thirteenth century B.C. But, as the characteristic pose of the goddess also appears much earlier in Cretan representations in other materials,[30] there has been a tendency to try to revise the chronology of some of these terracotta figures. Dates as early as the fifteenth century B.C. have been proposed for the idols from a villa at Mitropolis, near Gortyn,[31] and at least as early as the fourteenth century B.C. for a figure from Sakhtouria,[32] although in neither case does the style seem to indicate so early a period. There are, however, some idols whose style may possibly favour a date slightly before 1300 B.C., although it is impossible to be sure because local conservatism is hard to evaluate. A head from the Dictaean Cave already showing the pierced ears characteristic of these figures might just possibly still belong to the fourteenth century B.C., to judge from its style and quality.[33] And the idols from a site in the Amari valley published by Alexiou might possibly span not only the earlier thirteenth century but also the later fourteenth, on the facial types and head-dresses shown by some of them.[34] Alexiou has probably rightly assigned the Pankalokhori statuette to the thirteenth century B.C.,[35] although it still retains faint echoes of the Amari figures, and the idols from the sanctuary at Gournia[36] and from the Shrine of the Double Axes at Knossos[37] seem soundly dated to the thirteenth century. The Mitropolis and Sakhtouria examples mentioned above presumably likewise belong to about the thirteenth or earlier twelfth centuries B.C. The Gazi idols have been assigned to about the twelfth century B.C.[38] and the Prinias figures variously ascribed to the twelfth or eleventh centuries B.C.,[39] the Kisamos statuette being probably contemporary,[40] whilst the Karphi idols (e.g., Plate 1a) are dated to the eleventh century B.C.,[41] these later works being often the most elaborate of their class. In the Cretan Protogeometric Period of the tenth and ninth centuries B.C. there may have been some decline in quality, but the tradition remained alive, as witness the wheelmade head from such a figure found at Kalokhorio in the Pedhiadha Plain[42] and various humbler statuettes such as those from Phaistos.[43] Before turning to the counterparts of these idols in Greece proper, it may be useful to recall yet again that they seem to have been evolved in a Crete under mainland Greek control and that the strength of the island's local artistic traditions may mask the extent to which they expressed the beliefs of a rather mixed population, part native and part Achaean.[44]

Seen against these Cretan figures, the most interesting mainland find is that of the hollow wheelmade head of such an idol (Plate 1c) from a sanctuary of the twelfth century B.C. at Asine in the Argolid.[45] It shows the same pierced ears as many of the Cretan examples.[46] But the shrine where it was found seems only to have been in use for a very short period in the twelfth century B.C. and Alexiou's attempt to link it with the later Cretan example from Kalokhorio mentioned above seems as impossible chronologically as it is unconvincing stylistically.[47] Like its Cretan equivalents, the shrine was rectangular, with a low bench along one wall. But, before postulating it as the work of Minoan immigrants, it may be well to recall that simple rectangular sanctuary buildings seem also to have been erected by the Mycenaeans, e.g., in a relatively untroubled part of the world such as Delos[48] and, indeed, that this kind of shrine, complete with bench, seems to have flourished there and in Rhodes as late as the Archaic Period.[49] The Asine head, anyway, does not seem to be a Cretan import, but a local Mycenaean product possibly showing some Cretan influence in its ear treatment. In style it resembles the stucco head from Mycenae of about the thirteenth century B.C.[50] and, in terracotta, it is extremely close to an only slightly smaller hollow wheelmade head from Tiryns (Plate 1b) showing the same treatment of the eyes and the same painting of the hair.[51] This is wholly Mycenaean in technique and lacks the pierced ears. It also still dates from the thirteenth century B.C.[52] One should expect the Asine head to be contemporary and it seems important to note that no fragments from the body of this statue were found at Asine. Perhaps it was originally set up elsewhere in a shrine of the later thirteenth century B.C. and damaged in the disaster of *c.* 1200 B.C. It is also only possible to offer a very tentative suggestion as to what function the head fulfilled in its second rôle as the main cult object in the humble twelfth-century shrine at Asine. If its hollow neck were placed over the top of a thin wooden stake set vertically in the ground, with a shorter horizontal rod secured to it below the neck, and the resultant schematic shoulders and body heavily draped, the product would be a plausible cult figure, in function perhaps not unlike some of the primitive herm-like wooden images known from literary sources.[53] Another analogous instance is attested archaeologically, although in this case the synthetic 'body', in the form of a hollow terracotta cylinder, is preserved and is so short as to give the effect of a bust rather than a statue. This was at a sanctuary at Ayia Irini in Keos, in later times dedicated to Dionysos.[54] This was apparently originally established under Minoan control or inspiration and acquired a remarkable range of female terracotta sculptures, probably mostly datable to about the sixteenth century B.C., but was destroyed in the fifteenth century B.C., possibly in the natural calamities caused by the Theran eruptions that seem also to have wrecked the Minoan Thalassocracy. The shrine was subsequently revived by the Mycenaeans and the cult seems to have continued through the Dark Age, so that a head from one of the statues of the sixteenth century B.C. was found set in the synthetic cylindrical 'body' mentioned above and apparently still serving as a cult image in the eighth century B.C.[55]

Apart from the Asine and Tiryns heads, there are various other hollow wheelmade Mycenaean figures of a goddess with raised arms. These seem to develop from the earlier wheelmade idols of the mainland already discussed,[56] as witness a rather provincial example from the Menelaion near Sparta.[57] But they seem to emerge at a relatively late stage and may mainly have flourished in the later thirteenth century B.C. They are also attested from the Temple of Aphaia in Aegina[58] and arms possibly from such figures are also known from Melos[59] and Chios.[60] A few degenerate examples (e.g., Plate 2*b*) may be as late as the twelfth century B.C.,[61] but in most areas their brief history may have stopped with the calamity of *c*. 1200 B.C. In the twelfth century, as in the thirteenth, by far the most numerous divine representations of this kind seem to have been the small handmade 'ψ-figures' already dealt with.[62] But at this late stage their divinity seems to have existed essentially in their posture and when this was deliberately modified, e.g., to the traditional gesture of lamentation with the hands to the head, the figure itself seems to have been transformed to that of a mortal woman in mourning.[63] Even the 'ψ-statuettes', along with the last of the other handmade Mycenaean figures, seem to have ceased to be made by the end of the twelfth century B.C. The remarkable revival of such representations at the end of the Dark Age will be discussed later.[64]

The worship of Nilsson's 'house-' or 'place-goddess' seems in origin to have been a form of domestic cult.[65] In addition, in Crete there were a number of major public cults, commonly centred on rather remote holy places on the tops of mountains or in sacred caves.[66] In Mycenaean Greece such public cults, as distinct from those of palace, house, or tomb, seem to have developed more gradually, but when they emerged they flourished in the middle of towns as well as in remote sacred places. In addition to the more especially handmade Mycenaean figures discussed above, they are often associated with large terracotta statuettes of animals, initially mainly of bulls, although these are soon joined by those of horses and other creatures.[67] Like the larger goddess figures just dealt with, they are fashioned hollow on the potter's wheel, the body consisting of a cylinder with sealed ends like a barrel. On the larger animals, legs, neck and head are also shaped from hollow cylinders, intercommunicating for ventilation in firing and with external vents provided at mouth, chest, rump or feet. The practice of dedicating such large figures of bulls and other creatures spread also to Crete and Cyprus, as will be seen below. If one may generalize somewhat on the basis of the more adequately documented sanctuaries, the shrines associated with them seem to have been open to the sky and to have centred around an open-air altar, near or around which the large votive animals appear often to have been placed. In a few instances there is evidence also of subsidiary buildings to house a cult image, sacred vessels or other votive offerings. Large wheelmade terracotta statuettes of animals or vases in animal form are attested rather earlier in Anatolia and Syria among the Hittites and their neighbours and predecessors[68] and rather later in northern and central Persia.[69] But in neither case is there any clear evidence of direct links with the Greek statuettes just described. These seem rather to have evolved from local Aegean ritual vessels, the rhyta in the shape of bulls, which have a history dating back to the start of the second millennium B.C. in Crete,[70] and were normally made on the potter's wheel in the same way as the later large bull statuettes.[71] In actual fact the Minoans employed not only the vessels just mentioned in the shape of a standing bull, but also rhyta in the form of animals' heads, both those of bulls and of other creatures.[72] For use as rhyta, it had been these animal-head vessels that had also been copied by the Mycenaeans, but with a slightly greater preference for the bovine.[73]. But there is some evidence that the Cretan rhyta in the form of complete figures of standing cattle had also been adopted in the Cyclades by the close of the Minoan

Thalassocracy[74] and a later wheelmade bull statuette of the kind discussed here from Phylakopi in Melos still retains a tiny vestigial rhyton orifice on the top of its head.[75] At this distance in time it is hardly possible to gauge the ritual function of the animal rhyton[76] or whether libations of wine poured from its mouth were regarded as magically transformed into the blood of sacrificial victims. But the wheelmade bull statuettes, on the other hand, are commonly associated with an altar at which burnt offerings were made and may well originally have commemorated such sacrifices or been substitutes for them, later becoming acceptable offerings in their own right, as suggested by the less appropriate creatures also represented.

Few of the large bull statuettes are from reliably dated contexts, but they are usually assigned to the twelfth century B.C. as indicated by graves in Rhodes of that date yielding figures of much the same style and technique showing mules or similar animals carrying jars.[77] But several considerations seem to show that the large bull statuettes had in fact already started by the late thirteenth century B.C. Thus, they feature in certain sanctuaries in Cyprus immediately following the Mycenaean colonization of c. 1200 B.C., e.g., at Pigadhes and Ayia Irini,[78] both themselves subsequently destroyed in the mid twelfth century B.C.,[79] and later at Idalion.[80] This would suggest that their use was already current among the new Mycenaean immigrants and it is interesting to observe how the local bull rhyta in the native 'base-ring' ware of the thirteenth century B.C. and earlier were adapted into statuettes in the early to mid twelfth century to meet the new fashion.[81] To return to Greece proper, it is to be noted that the decoration of several of these bulls could be either of the thirteenth or of the twelfth centuries B.C. An isolated example from Delphi (Plate 3a),[82] still modest in scale and with clumsily overgenerous provision for ventilation, helps establish the characteristics of the early examples, since the 'rock pattern' decorating its rump can hardly be later than the thirteenth century B.C.[83] It shows a scale pattern on its flanks, which may possibly reflect the net pattern occurring from time to time on the Cretan rhyta.[84] Other such wheelmade animals have been reported from Thebes.[85]

The Athenian examples are mainly from the slopes immediately under the Acropolis.[86] Two wheelmade bulls from the north slope, some fragments of which appear in Plate 3b, show early features and may be of the late thirteenth or early twelfth centuries B.C.,[87] whilst the head of another in Plate 3b is from a context of the early twelfth century.[88] Other fragments from the north and north-west slopes, shown on Plate 3*b*, seem assignable to the twelfth century B.C., as also a rather similar complete bull in Berlin, reputedly from Athens.[89] A bull from the south slope of the Acropolis, now in Heidelberg, seems of the late twelfth or early eleventh centuries, with its decoration of dotted semi-circles.[90] Its shape is quite distinctive, with the body cylinder generous in diameter but greatly reduced in length and slightly constricted in the middle. More harshly angular is another fragment from the same vicinity (Plate 3*c*), seemingly from a she-ass carrying pots.[91] This is not reliably datable, having lost its decoration, but its leg treatment seems later, mid-way to that of the tenth-century stag from the Kerameikos (Plate 2*c*) which will be considered below.[92]

Similar wheelmade bulls, etc., are well represented from a sanctuary on the site of the later shrine of Apollo at Amyclae, near Sparta.[93] Some of these show that, despite the general depopulation of the area after *c.* 1200 B.C., the cult continued to flourish through the twelfth century B.C.[94] One, of about the early eleventh century B.C. (Plate 2*d*), shows degenerate ornament and a more extreme form of the proportions displayed by the Heidelberg bull from Athens.[95] The tradition may have continued some time beyond this, to judge from fragments from the succeeding level showing Protogeometric ornament.[96] In the Argolid, late Mycenaean wheelmade bulls of about the late thirteenth or twelfth centuries B.C. are attested from the early excavations on the Acropolis at Mycenae itself,[97] and from the Argive Heraeum,[98] Asine,[99] Tiryns[100] and from a hill shrine near Epidaurus, later dedicated to Apollo Maleatas.[101]

These wheelmade votive bulls are also abundant at certain Cretan sanctuaries at the end of the Bronze Age. With much of the material as yet unpublished, it is hazardous to generalize in the negative, but it does seem that the earlier stages shown by their mainland counterparts are hardly represented, even though there does seem to be continuity at the cave- and peak-sanctuaries in offerings of quite small bronze bulls, etc.[102] Indeed, if one accepts Desborough's argument for a late start for the Late Minoan III.C Period,[103] it seems that the Cretan wheelmade terracotta votive animals may not have begun much before the twelfth century B.C. On the other hand, a Cretan bull rhyton of about the thirteenth century B.C., such as that from the Dictaean Cave,[104] is already approaching the votive statuettes in style and technique, although clearly somewhat earlier, whilst a fragment from Mitropolis, described as probably from a rhyton,[105] already shows the eye-treatment of the twelfth-century votives. It thus seems possible that, although the mainland wheelmade animals were apparently inspired ultimately by the Cretan rhyta, the new religious usages that they represented may not have made much impact on Crete, any more than on Cyprus, until they were introduced by fresh waves of immigrants from the mainland in the twelfth century B.C.

Some of the finest Cretan animal figures of this kind have been found at Phaistos.[106] They include large bulls and a mule carrying jars and appear to date from the twelfth and eleventh centuries B.C., but little has yet been published about how they were found. More information is available about a deposit of rather similar date at Ayia Triadha.[107] Here there was earlier a shrine of the 'house-goddess', with 'snake-tubes' in its first phase and possibly also to be associated with fragments of goddesses with raised arms of about the thirteenth century B.C., but this was eventually abandoned.[108] In the twelfth century a new open-air sanctuary came into prominence nearby, associated with wheelmade votive bulls and similar creatures[109] and flanked on one side by a building of mainland megaron-type. Statuettes of men also occurred, including fragments of figures of some size, though whether of worshippers or deities remains uncertain.[110] The most interesting of these larger fragments is a leg,[111] shown as wearing sandals, greaves and a short tunic, presumably under a breastplate, much as the figures on the warrior vase from Mycenae.[112] Also remarkable are some large wheelmade statuettes that are only part human, quadrupeds with the heads sometimes apparently of women and sometimes certainly of men and tentatively identified as sphinxes, which remains as likely an interpretation as any.[113] Their ears are sometimes pierced, like those of the 'house-goddesses' discussed above.[114] Karageorghis, who prefers to describe them as centaurs,[115] has remarked on the resemblance between them and wheelmade terracotta quadrupeds of much the same date but with two human heads from Enkomi in Cyprus.[116] He argues for direct Minoan influence on Cyprus. But it seems equally possible to suppose that the fresh wave of Mycenaean immigrants to Cyprus that arrived after the destruction of Mycenae in about the third quarter of the twelfth century B.C., and that apparently produced the Enkomi figure, may have been connected with those arriving from the same area in parts of Crete at about the same time and that these related communities may have remained in contact for some while thereafter.[117] Degenerate sphinxes apparently dating from the eleventh century B.C. were also found in the Spring Chamber at Knossos, again in association with material showing links with the mainland.[118] Other terracotta offerings at Ayia Triadha include 'horns of consecration', occasionally topped with human heads,[119] and animals on wheels,[120] not unlike those from Attica.[121]

The cave-sanctuary at Patsos has produced a number of wheel-made horses, bulls, etc., of about the twelfth to tenth centuries B.C.[122] and others have been found at Tylissos.[123] They seem rather less frequent where the 'house-goddess" still held sway, although Prinias has yielded an exceptionally large head from such a bull[124] and a house at Karphi an oddly proportioned horse.[125] Isolated examples of this date are attested from the Dictaean Cave, along with a number of others dating from near the close of the Dark Age.[126] More consistently of the ninth and eighth centuries B.C. are the bulls and other animals apparently from the remains of sanctuaries at Kavousi[127] and Vrokastro,[128] and the evidence is carried forward from the latter part of this period into historical times by shrines near Lato[129] and on the Acropolis at Gortyn.[130]

In Crete it is not only these large animals that show an unbroken tradition through the Dark Age. The handmade statuettes also have checkered survivals and the large wheelmade human figures seem to reveal clear continuity. They have already been traced down to about the ninth century B.C.[131] and the rest of the story is simply told by three fragmentary statuettes of moderate size from Vrokastro. The earliest of these is still in the broadly Subminoan tradition of the idols already considered[132] and the others reveal the degree of schematization reached by the eighth century B.C.[133] They may well represent votaries rather than deities.[134] In the Eteocretan region of eastern Crete, votive material is rather scant[135] until somewhat before the close of our period, as at Mrs Hawes's shrine at Kavousi,[136] or somewhat after, as at Praisos.[137] Within these limitations, it seems worthy of remark that there is little evidence for a local late survival of the goddess with raised arms and that Mycenaean votive bulls were eventually as readily adopted here as elsewhere. The individual style of Eteocretan wheelmade terracottas and the skill shown in large-scale terracotta sculpture are features of the succeeding periods.

Cyprus reveals a similar continuity in the dedication of wheel-made terracotta votive bulls throughout the Dark Age. The finds of the twelfth and eleventh centuries B.C. at sanctuaries at Pigadhes, Ayia Irini, Enkomi and Idalion have already been touched on.[138] The remainder of the development is best seen in the stratified contents of the open-air sanctuary at Ayia Irini,[139] with suitable modifications to the excavators' chronology,[140] supplemented by similar finds from other sites, such as Idalion,[141] Pigadhes[142] and Kourion.[143] As pointed out by Karageorghis, the type of quadruped with two human heads at Enkomi seems to have developed, not as much into centaurs, as into the Cypriot bull-men, seemingly of mixed Greek and oriental inspiration.[144] Human figures also occur, including small goddesses with raised arms.[145] Karageorghis' proposal to see direct Cretan influence in these may take too little account of a legacy common to the whole Aegean world.[146] Figures of worshippers, chariot groups, etc., became much commoner in the eighth century B.C.

This continuity in votive terracottas in Crete and Cyprus is an inescapable fact. But in Greece proper the situation is far more obscure. Higgins has argued for a complete interruption for most of the eleventh and tenth centuries B.C. and a subsequent relearning of the necessary skills from Crete.[147] This seems refuted by the finds from this period, meagre though they are as yet, and the way that the wheelmade terracotta animals seem to continue the trends of the end of the Mycenaean Period without reference to contemporary developments in Crete. But, what with the calamities that marked the closing stages of the Mycenaean Period and the widespread changes of population that followed, this continuity may have been by no means universal. It is perhaps significant that it seems as yet only clearly attested in Attica, which had traditionally retained its identity throughout these troubled times, and East Greece, whose colonization by the displaced Ionians after their temporary sojourn in Attica had apparently already begun by the mid eleventh century B.C.[148] Both are areas where Mycenaean traditions could be expected to be kept alive.

In Athens there is the added difficulty that no large votive deposits of early date have yet been found intact and, as in Late Mycenaean times, one has to rely on scattered finds apparently from disturbed deposits of this kind, supplemented by related material from tombs or habitation areas. The wheelmade animals, already traced down to the eleventh century,[149] seem to have continued on. The next significant item is a wheelmade stag (Plate 2c) from a grave of the later tenth century B.C. in the Kerameikos.[150] It was certainly never a scent bottle, as has been claimed,[151] but it is possible that its legs may once have been attached to some form of plinth. The body is still short and broad, but the modelling is more realistic—a tendency carried further by the next item (Plate 3d), three fragments from the Acropolis of a wheelmade horse mounted on a rectangular platform that originally ran on four wheels.[152] This is dated by its decoration to the first years of the ninth century B.C. Wheels for such models are attested even earlier in Athens, one example still being Mycenaean[153] and others being dated to the late eleventh[154] and tenth centuries B.C.[155] and they continue through the following centuries. They may not only have been used on these wheeled animals, a late Attic version of the schematic handmade Mycenaean chariot-groups being apparently equipped to run on four such wheels, too.[156] Part of another wheelmade horse like that from the Acropolis, this time perhaps of the later ninth century B.C., was found below on the north slope.[157] From the tenth century B.C.[158] to about the early eighth century[159] there are also smaller handmade horses, possibly toys, equipped to run on wheels without a plinth. As the eighth century developed, handmade terracottas preponderated, but one class of Attic animal figures that consistently retained the wheelmade technique were the donkeys or mules carrying jars, now also set on four wheels.[160] These continued on through the seventh and early sixth centuries B.C.[161] and had much earlier antecedents.[162] Also set on four wheels were the rectangular or T-shaped plinths of a class of handmade four-horse chariot groups that had developed by the mid eighth century[163] and continued on into the seventh century B.C.[164] By the late eighth century the handmade terracottas were becoming quite numerous and covered a wide range of animals and birds and human figures in various postures, including, it seems, a group of a man and woman riding in a cart.[165]

With the Attic material as incomplete as it is, it is difficult to generalize. But it does seem that the emphasis on bull figures, so marked elsewhere, may have dwindled quite early in Athens. It is hard to gauge how far the strange array of wheeled models were also toys, but it does seem to emerge that they were associated as well with the graves of adults and dedicated at shrines.

East Greece was far more conservative. Two sites have produced particularly helpful material, a small sanctuary of Athena at Emborio in Chios and the Temple of Hera in Samos. At Emborio the main Mycenaean occupation was apparently of the twelfth century B.C. and, after a long gap, Greek settlement seems to have been resumed again in the mid eighth century B.C.[166] The shrine has yielded the arm of a human idol of about the late thirteenth century B.C.[167] and part of a wheelmade animal of about the twelfth century B.C.[168] But it is hard to follow the excavators in assigning their most remarkable find to the eighth century B.C. This is a

Plate 1

a

b

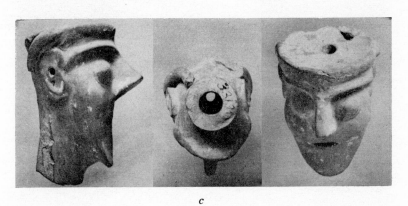

c

a Heraklion Museum, from Karphi (pp. 4-5); *b* Nauplia Museum 8460, from Tiryns (p. 6); *c* Nauplia Museum 3313, from Asine (pp. 6-7)

Plate 2

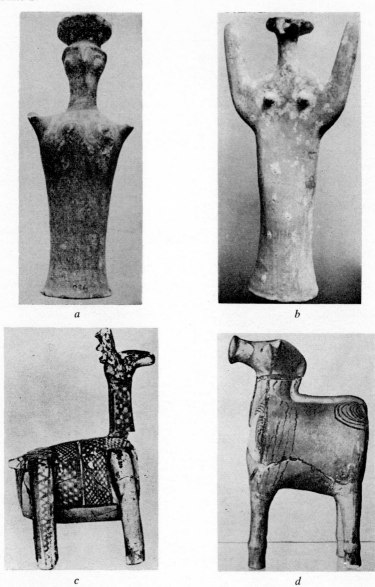

a Aegina Museum 936, from Aegina (p. 4); b Munich, Museum antiker Kleinkunst 7607, from Rhodes (p. 7); c Athens, Kerameikos Museum, from the Kerameikos (p. 13); d Athens, National Museum 15123, from Amyclae (p. 10)

wheelmade horse, in shape and decoration still very close to the twelfth century B.C., described as attached to part of a flanged lid.[169] If it is to be related to the Attic material at all, it is to a yet earlier stage in the evolution of the wheelmade animals on plinths mentioned above. From the mid eighth century on, the terracottas are fairly abundant and overlap with those from Samos.[170] Their main importance lies in identifying the later stages in the rather slow sequence of development in Samos.

The Samian finds are associated with a succession of open-air altars and with the earliest of the great temples.[171] They are at first predominantly of wheelmade animals, especially bulls, and have been well published by Ohly,[172] although recently his arguments for complete continuity throughout the Dark Age, from the close of the Mycenaean Period on, have tended to be set on one side,[173] partly because of the need for some revision in the dating of the later associated pottery found with some of them,[174] more because of the dearth of early published vases as a whole.[175] Meantime, the excavators have convinced themselves that the cult goes back to late Mycenaean times.[176] Ohly had recognized that some of the earliest wheelmade animals from Samos showed the same short, full bodies, pinched in at the middle, as the bulls of the end of the twelfth and early eleventh centuries B.C. from Athens and Amyclae.[177] These early animals are associated with a relatively clear banded ornament that may have lasted quite long, sometimes quite Mycenaean in appearance,[178] but also sometimes developing Mycenaean motifs into something more Geometric in spirit.[179] There is no break at the end of this stage, as the animal shapes carry straight over into the next two decorative phases. These are an overall close ornament, e.g., of framed checkers, cross-hatching, etc., as on the Kerameikos stag,[180] and a plain black over the whole surface,[181] occasionally with small reserved areas of decoration. These plain black bulls may also have had quite a long life, finally degenerating into a coarse, unpainted class, overlapping with the handmade animals, both plain and decorated, and with the late eighth-century finds from Chios. The wheeled animals, so popular in Athens, are rare.[182] Small handmade statuettes and rather larger human figures fashioned on the potter's wheel seem well attested in the eighth century B.C.[183] At this stage it seems difficult not to accept Ohly's hypothesis of an unbroken local tradition. It is also, on other accounts, desirable to have the Samian sequence begin early enough for it to overlap with a period when wheelmade votive bulls were still popular in Attica.

We shall now touch on certain other classes of terracottas from the Dark Age outside of this main stream of development. In Greece proper some of the earliest human figures of the Iron Age are of women with bell-shaped bodies and jointed legs, intended to be hung up by their heads and to jiggle in the wind. Their counterparts of the fifth and fourth centuries B.C. represent dancing girls, and so may these despite their more matronly build.[184] Their development has been aptly traced by Higgins, from Athens in the late tenth century to Rhodes in the ninth century, Kos in the early and mid eighth century and Boeotia in the later eighth and early seventh centuries B.C.[185] Their bodies are wheelmade, apart from the Attic examples which are in a curious handmade ware of obscure ethnic significance.[186] Terracotta models of shoes occur in Attic graves, both in Mycenaean times and in the ninth century B.C. But the Mycenaean shoes are of an oriental variety with curled toes,[187] known also in much earlier terracotta models from Anatolia and in much later ones from Etruria; indeed, if the painting on one has been rightly interpreted as showing wings, they may have heroic or even divine associations. By contrast, the ninth-century shoes from Athens[188] and Eleusis[189] are good, heavy artisans' boots. Being vases, the so-called 'duck askoi' are of less direct concern here, but may be mentioned for the way that they seem already to complement the sequence and distribution of the wheelmade votive bulls. Their bodies were also shaped on the potter's wheel, but initially in the form of an open bowl, with the rim subsequently pinched together to form a sort of spine down the back of the creature.[190] They are commonly in the form of three-legged birds, but occasionally acquire animal or even human characteristics.[191] They are already attested in the twelfth century B.C.[192] and, although many gaps remain to be filled, they are widely represented over the succeeding centuries.[193]

In Greece proper, terracotta models of houses or temples only seem to start to appear as dedications at sanctuaries towards the end of the Dark Age.[194] On the other hand, models of round granaries with trapdoors at the top occur in Attic graves of both the ninth and eighth centuries B.C.[195] They may simply have served to ensure a magical food supply for the dead, but one may equally wonder whether they may not actually have contained grain as a symbol of resurrection. Other rather similar models of round buildings occur in Crete, more especially in the twelfth and eleventh centuries B.C., but with a door in the side and, in some cases, a knob-like projection on top of the roof.[196] Very occasionally they contain figures of the goddess with raised arms and they are usually interpreted as shrines, although no round buildings seem to be known in actual Cretan sanctuaries of this date. The latest and most elaborate of these models, dating from the later ninth century B.C., may yield further clues as to their function.[197] There the goddess seems to have had a thin stem threaded through her right hand (possibly an actual germinating grain or small ear of wheat ?). The projection on the roof is shown as a chimney-like trap, with two men looking down through it and possibly throwing something down on to the goddess. Round granaries are soundly attested in Crete[198] and it seems at least possible that these models from sanctuaries and tombs are also to be linked with them—certainly a more plausible interpretation than the other suggestion advanced that they represent subterranean tombs.[199] More in the shape of a shrine, with its low bench against one wall, is another Cretan model of similar date from Knossos,[200] representing a rectangular one-roomed building with an elaborate doorway with a window above after the Minoan tradition and of a kind in evidence on early Cretan temples.[201]

It has already been suggested that the sequences in votive terracottas indicated for Attica and East Greece may have been by no means universal in Greece proper through the Dark Age. In so far as the practice of dedicating them was interrupted in any area—and the total material is as yet too slight for negative evidence to be safely invoked—it seems to have been acquired again at various stages from neighbours who had maintained an unbroken local tradition. At the close of our period, small votive terracottas were well on their way to becoming universal throughout Greece once more and larger wheelmade work in the old technique is in evidence, e.g., in mainland Dorian areas where a break in the tradition might perhaps be expected—as witness, e.g., the fine heads from Amyclae[202] and the grotesque masks from Tiryns.[203] By the seventh century B.C. female votive figures had reclaimed their preponderant rôle. Here we are concerned with one remarkable associated phenomenon, the re-appearance of the goddess with raised arms. The Cypriot evidence assembled by Karageorghis has been touched on above.[204] Alexiou has grouped the Cretan examples of about this date.[205] They tend to be from Dorian or Achaean areas, rather than Eteocretan. In Greece proper large wheelmade figures of this kind are attested, e.g., from Samos,[206] Rhodes,[207] Boeotia[208] and even non-Greek Lemnos (Plate 4d).[209] Such a goddess is represented on a seventh-century votive plaque from Athens (Plate 4c)[210] where, indeed, small, cheap handmade terracottas of this form became for a time almost as common as they had ever been in the Bronze Age.[211] How this strange revival might have come about will be considered after a brief discussion of the votive statuettes of bronze.[212]

Although, at their best, they attain a much higher standard aesthetically, the bronze statuettes dedicated at shrines from the twelfth to the eighth centuries B.C. show but little of the complex pattern of survivals revealed by the terracottas and so can be dealt with rather more briefly here. Sound external grounds for dating are much less readily available and chronology becomes a much more subjective matter as a result. There seem to be three local traditions to be considered—a Cretan one, already old and in slow decline, but which nevertheless probably continued well into this period, a Cypriot one that flourished in the twelfth century B.C. but seems to have died out thereafter, and the widespread development of votive bronze statuettes in Greece and Crete in the closing stages of the Dark Age.

The Cretan bronze statuettes of the close of the Bronze Age cover a rather different range of types from the main run of contemporary terracotta figures.[213] They tend instead still to mirror the varieties that had been current several centuries earlier in both bronze and terracotta at the peak- and cave-sanctuaries. The richest finds are again from the open-air sanctuary at Ayia Triadha[214] and from the Dictaean Cave,[215] as well as from other cave-shrines such as those at Patsos[216] and Phaneromeni.[217] The most distinctive figures are those of men and women worshipping, most often with the right arm raised by the head in salutation and the left by the side or, more rarely, bent forward across the body; but other poses are also represented, including those approximating to the mainland 'φ-' and 'τ-figures',[218] although statuettes with both arms raised are rare.[219] There is a wide range of small animal statuettes which are even more abundant, cattle being by far the commonest subject. Both human and animal figures apparently continued on down through the twelfth and eleventh centuries B.C. and possibly through the tenth century as well, there being relatively few chronological controls by which their development can be measured.[220] Exceptionally, distinctive contemporary terracotta types are copied as well, such as sphinxes (e.g., Plate 4*b*)[221] and a possibly related Pegasos (Plate 4*a*).[222] A later class of human figures has been recognized with flat-topped heads of distinctive shape, long necks and, usually, bent knees, but whether these date from the middle of the Dark Age, as suggested by Miss Lamb, or near its close, as proposed by Boardman, is far from clear.[223] There are also numerous other extremely coarse statuettes, some of them quite undatable and some of them apparently assignable to the eighth century B.C., thus overlapping with the much more remarkable work to be detailed below. It is thus possible, but by no means certain, that there may have been continuity in the making of bronze statuettes in Crete throughout the Dark Age, but if there was, this local tradition eventually sank to so humble a level that it probably had little influence on later developments.

The Cypro-Mycenaean bronze statuettes have been studied by Catling,[224] along with the related bronze tripods and stands.[225] Statuettes were apparently already being produced under Syrian influence in the fourteenth and thirteenth centuries B.C., but the main developments occurred under the impetus of fresh Mycenaean colonization in the twelfth century B.C. Small human and animal votive figures were made in moderate numbers, but the real masterpieces are two very much larger statuettes of gods found in two different shrines at Enkomi, where they had apparently served as cult images.[226] But, so far as can be judged at present, this local skill in producing bronze figures passed into eclipse in the eleventh century B.C.

The Mycenaean mainland seems to have manifested little corresponding interest in the making of bronze statuettes and such figures as are found are mostly imports, more especially from the two centres just described and from Anatolia and Syria.[227] Votive wheels apparently of the twelfth and early eleventh centuries B.C. from Mycenae[228] and Argos[229] have been regarded as of northern origin, which need not surprise, in view of the apparent incursion of c. 1200 B.C., although it is interesting also to compare the Cretan wheels from Gournia[230] and on the model from the Dictaean Cave.[231] In the light of all this, it is difficult to follow the theories that see Mycenaean survivals in the later mainland bronze statuettes of the Iron Age and seek correspondingly high datings for some of them.[232] The artistic climate in Greece changed considerably in the ninth and eighth centuries B.C. under the stimulus of heightened trade with the orient, carried out both by the Phoenicians and by the Greeks themselves, who had established their trading stations at Al Mina and Tell Sukas in Syria by the later ninth century B.C.[233] Oriental craftsmen from the vicinity of Syria and Phoenicia seem also to have begun to establish themselves in Greece itself to help meet the demand for new luxury articles, producing gold jewellery, ivory carvings and vessels and armour of beaten bronze. This phenomenon is well seen in Crete, which lay astride the trade route between the east and west Mediterranean.[234] And it is here we find it first having an impact on bronze sculpture. Some remarkable large statuettes of a god and goddesses were found at a temple of the second half of the eighth century B.C. at Dreros in Crete.[235] They are of beaten bronze over a wooden core (now decayed) and may possibly have served as cult images. As a result of Boardman's penetrating analysis of their style, it emerges that they are probably as old as the temple itself and thus some of the earliest known Greek sculpture of an 'orientalizing' character.[236]

But the bronze statuettes that flooded Greek sanctuaries in the eighth century B.C. were usually of quite a different kind, being cast solid in a style that seems almost wholly native,[237] although some of their poses might owe something to the orient, the pudic nude female figures to Astarte and the warrior statuettes brandishing a weapon to Baal or Reshef. Whether there was any debt also to the bronzes of continental Europe to the north rests somewhat obscure.[238] The dating of these Greek figures depends heavily on analogies with painted scenes on vases and with terracotta statuettes[239] and, in this connection, it is to be noted that there is quite a wide correspondence in type as between these bronzes and the small handmade terracottas of the eighth century B.C.[240] The different areas tended to manifest distinctive local styles.[241] In subject, there is a wide range of animals and birds, with horses and bulls being the most popular, and also of human figures, the latter being only very rarely clearly marked out as divine.[242] More complex groups comprising several figures together were also produced, the most popular consisting of manned chariots. Many of the types of figures also occur as embellishments on the Greek tripod-cauldrons, which had been growing in size and elaboration as they acquired a symbolic rôle as prizes at the great festivals.[243] The earliest of these figurine attachments seem to have been in the form of bulls' heads and a rough guide as to their date is perhaps provided by an Attic pottery pyxis of about the late ninth century B.C. with a rather similar bull's head attachment.[244] Thus the bronze statuettes, also, may well span the later ninth as well as the eighth centuries B.C., although they do not seem to have reached maturity until towards the middle of the eighth century B.C.

It now remains to summarize certain trends that seem to emerge in the religious use of these humble figures as a whole. The main turning point seems to be the calamity that struck mainland Greece in *c.* 1200 B.C. and broke the unity of the Mycenaean world. Up to that point there seems to have been a steady and progressive development in the varieties of votive figures, but after *c.* 1200 B.C. this development becomes curiously fixed and frozen. Thus the wheelmade terracotta votive bulls that seem to constitute the main innovation of the later thirteenth century B.C. persist with relatively little change for the next five hundred years in areas such as Crete, Cyprus, and East Greece to which they seem to have been carried by emigrants leaving the mainland as a direct result of this and subsequent disasters. On the mainland, after the upheavals it had undergone, the survival of these figures seems to have been somewhat more checkered. And here it is worth stressing that, while their presence provides good evidence for continuity of worship, their absence, of itself, does not necessarily prove discontinuity. The kind of public altar-cult with which votive figures such as these are associated seems possibly to have increased in importance initially as the centralized Mycenaean power waned and perhaps as royal authority in religious matters itself declined as well. But the emergence of the true Greek temple from these simple open-air sanctuaries was a slow and gradual process, although the pace quickened considerably in the eighth century B.C. under foreign stimuli and growing prosperity and as increasing emphasis was placed on the building housing the cult image itself.

Only a tiny number of the human figures considered here themselves functioned as cult images. But many of the votive statuettes seem to have portrayed deities, particularly a goddess with raised arms, and it is not improbable that these may also approximate to the appearance of contemporary cult figures of this type, probably most usually of wood, the traditional material for early images of this kind in Greece and one that has but poor chances of survival down to our own time in the Greek climate. At least, this seems the only simple explanation that will account for the way in which, in later times, figures of this type kept reappearing spontaneously in widely separated parts of the country without any direct continuity that can be traced among the votive statuettes themselves. Something much more than an archaeological zeal on the part of the faithful needs to be invoked to explain this! If one may presume that early cult images of this primitive type continued in use in certain shrines, then an occasional later copying of their forms in votive statuettes dedicated locally is only to be expected. This explanation has already been invoked by others to explain an even later phenomenon, the appearance of statues of this and related types in scenes on Attic and Italiote vases of the fifth and fourth centuries B.C. showing primitive cult images.[245] Indeed, wooden cult figures of remarkable antiquity and crudity seem to have survived even down to Pausanias' day.[246] A few might indeed have been works of late Mycenaean times, as tradition in some cases suggests, but, from what has been seen of the remarkable conservatism shown by the votive statuettes of the centuries immediately following the collapse of the Mycenaean power, the new images of this period also would still very probably have followed the forms of their predecessors; others, again, may have been even later still. The goddess with raised arms can only have been one of a number of types current among these images, but she is one that has a considerable fascination for modern archaeologists and apparently had an even stronger appeal for the dedicants of the humble statuettes that form the subject of this study.

NOTES

1. This article has grown out of a paper read at the Warburg Institute on 13 December 1966. The plates have been financed by the Faculty Board of Classics, Cambridge, from the Sir Perceval Maitland Laurence Fund III and Mr E. E. Jones has helped enormously in preparing them. Plate 3*a* is by Mrs Mary Eliot and the photographs for Plate 4*a, b* and *c* have been supplied by courtesy, respectively, of the Syndics of the Fitzwilliam Museum, the Trustees of the British Museum and the Direction of the American Excavations in the Athenian Agora. The following abbreviations are used, in addition to those specified in *L'Année philologique:*

CVA	*Corpus Vasorum Antiquorum*
Ergon	Τὸ "Εργον τῆς 'Αρχαιολογικῆς 'Εταιρείας (Athens, 1954 f.)
KCh	Κρητικὰ Χρονικά (Heraklion, 1947 f.)
MMR[2]	M. P. Nilsson, *The Minoan-Mycenaean Religion and its Survival in Greek Religion,* 2nd ed. (Lund, 1950)
PM	Sir Arthur Evans, *The Palace of Minos at Knossos* (London, 1921-36)
SCE	E. Gjerstad and others, *The Swedish Cyprus Expedition, Finds and Results of the Excavations in Cyprus, 1927-31* (Stockholm, 1934 f.)

2. 1st ed., Lund, 1927 ; 2nd ed. here cited, as given in n. 1. Cf. also idem, *The Mycenaean Origin of Greek Mythology* (Cambridge, Mass., 1932, Sather Classical Lectures viii) and idem, *Geschichte der griechischen Religion,* Vol. i (Munich, 1941, Handbuch der Altertumswissenschaft V. 2 i), pp. 237-359.

3. J. Chadwick, *The Decipherment of Linear B,* 2nd ed. (Cambridge, 1967), pp. 124-126.

4. V. R. d'A. Desborough, *The Last Mycenaeans and their Successors, an Archaeological Survey, ca. 1200-1100 B.C.* (Oxford, 1964), pp. 40-47.

5. P. Ålin, *Das Ende der mykenischen Fundstätten auf dem griechischen Festland* (Lund, 1962), pp. 148-50 ; Desborough, op. cit., pp. 220-5 ; *Antiquity* xxxviii (1964), 258-62 ; N. K. Sandars, *Prehistoric Art in Europe* (Harmondsworth, 1968), pp. 192-3 ; *Atti e Memorie del 1° Congresso Internazionale di Micenologia* (Rome, 1968), Vol. iii, pp. 1073-93.

6. In *Discontinuity in Greek Civilization* (Cambridge, 1966, J. H. Gray Lectures), Rhys Carpenter argues for famine resulting from drought as the main cause for this depopulation and minimizes Greek participation with the 'Sea Peoples'. Might it not, in any case, be easier to view the barbarian incursion as immediately following, rather than preceding, the point at which the mainland Greeks were seriously weakened, whether from over-reaching themselves in oriental ventures or from other causes?

7. Desborough, op. cit., pp. 237-41 ; cf. Carpenter, op. cit. pp. 43-6.

8. Desborough, op. cit., pp. 230-7.

9. i 12.

10. Desborough, op. cit., pp. 246-54 ; C.-G. Styrenius, *Submycenaean Studies* (Lund, 1967), p. 163.

11. E.g. *Ergon* 1962, 115, fig. 139 ; *AD* xviii (1963), Part ii.1, 100, pl. 120.

12. Desborough, op. cit., p. 166.

13. A. Furumark, *The Chronology of Mycenaean Pottery* (Stockholm, 1941), pp. 86-9 ; R. A. Higgins, *Greek Terracottas* (London, 1967), pp. 13-14, 139, pl. 4.

14. Cf. *ASAA* xli-xlii (1963-4, new series xxv-xxvi), 7-18 ; Πεπρογμένα τοῦ Β΄ Διεθνοῦς Κρητολογικοῦ Συνεδρίου, Vol. i (Athens, 1968), pp. 374-82 (note Mycenaean imports in Crete). The origins and development of these statuettes are the subject of a much more detailed study by Mrs E. B. French, to be published shortly.

15. Nilsson accepted their votive function, but denied that they represented deities (*Geschichte,* Vol. i, p. 266 ; *MMR²,* pp. 303-8). Alexiou, who takes a more reasonable standpoint, has usefully summarized the conflicting views, with special reference to the 'ψ-idols', in *KCh* xii (1958), 209-14.

16. *AJA* xl (1936), 419-31, fig. 10 ; G. E. Mylonas, *Eleusis and the Eleusinian Mysteries* (London, 1941), pp. 33-49 ; Desborough, op. cit., p. 43.

17. R. Demangel, *Fouilles de Delphes*, Vol. ii, Part v (Paris, 1926), pp. 13-28, figs. 16-33 ; *BCH* lxxxi (1957), 708-10 ; Desborough, op. cit., pp. 43-4. Always provided that this emerges as a single uncontaminated find in the light of more detailed study, such as that by Mrs French.

18. Higgins, op. cit., pp. 14-15, 139.

19. Ibid., pl. 4 *d, e.*

20. *Illustrated London News* 4th Jan. 1969, 25-7, figs. 1, 4-6, 9-12. Associated statuettes of coiled snakes (figs. 7-8) might be appropriate to the 'house-' or 'palace-goddess' (commonly equated with Athena) or to a hero cult associated with the royal tombs. See now also *Antiquity* xliii (1969), 9-7, pls. 9-13, and Addenda, p. 37.

21. See p. 18.

22. E.g. *AE* 1888, 150, pl. 9.15 ; Higgins, op. cit., pp. 15-16, fig. 9 ; others in Athens National Museum (from Mycenae) and Acropolis Museum (from Athens). Variant arm position: *Ergon* 1962, 95-7, figs. 116-7. With poloi: Aegina Museum 936 ; cf. also the head, A. Furtwängler and others, *Aegina, das Heiligtum der Aphaia* (Munich, 1906), p. 374 no. 7, pls. 108.6, 109.6, which belongs either here or with the wheelmade 'ψ-idols' (p. 7).

23. Nilsson, *Geschichte*, Vol. i, pp. 263-272 ; idem, *MMR²*, pp. 309-340 ; *KCh* xii (1958), 243-275. Cf. also n. 15 above and F. Matz, 'Göttererscheinung und Kultbild im minoischen Kreta', *Ak. der Wissenschaften und Literatur, Mainz, Abh. der Geistes und Sozialwissenschaftlichen Klasse* 1958, 385-448. Contrary view that they represent mortals refuted by internal evidence of statuettes and later scenes showing such types as cult images (pp. 21-2) ; but cf. H. Müller-Karpe, *Vom Anfang Roms* (Heidelberg, 1959, *MDAI(R)* Erg. v), pp. 79-82 ; *PP* xiv (1959), 377-391.

24. S. Alexiou, ''Η Μινωϊκή Θεὰ μεθ'ὑψωμένων χειρῶν', *KCh* xii (1958), 179-299 ; on the Cretan handmade statuettes, ibid., 204-8, pl. 9.

25. Uncatalogued life-size snake-entwined hand from such a figure in Heraklion Museum.

26. Visual pun on these in certain Cretan head-vases of *c.* 13th-12th centuries B.C. using pierced ears as spouts, e.g. from Phaistos and Patsos cave-sanctuary: *Museo Italiano di Antichità Classica* ii (1888), 916 no. 4, pl. 14.1 ; M. I. Maximova, *Les Vases Plastiques dans l'Antiquité* (Paris, 1927), pl. 8.31 ; L. Pernier, L. Banti, *Il Palazzo Minoico di Festòs*, Vol. ii (Rome, 1951), pp. 507-512, fig. 288 and colour pl. ; Chr. Zervos, *L'Art de la Crète* (Paris, 1956), figs. 750, 792 ; S. Marinatos, M. Hirmer, *Crete and*

Mycenae (London, 1960), pl. 133, top. Vestigial traces on later Janiform head-mastos from Piskokephalo: J. Boardman, *The Cretan Collection in Oxford, the Dictaean Cave and Iron Age Crete* (Oxford, 1961), pp. 101-103, 106 no. 472, pls. 35-36.

27. Nilsson, *Geschichte*, Vol. i, pp. 244-9 ; idem, *MMR²*, pp. 77-116 ; *ASAA* xix-xxi (1941-3, new ser. iii-v), 40-50.

28. Nilsson, *Geschichte*, Vol. i, pp. 267-8, pls. 1, 2.1 ; idem, *MMR²*, pp. 316-321, fig. 28 ; Zervos, op. cit., figs. 790-1.

29. Nilsson associates the snakes with his 'house-' or 'palace-goddess', denies the birds are attributes so much as concomitants of the divine epiphany.

30. *KCh* xii (1958), 220-43.

31. Date disputed between the Greek and Italian excavators of Mitropolis (Kannia): *PAAH* 1957, 148-9 ; *ASAA* xxxv-xxxvi (1957-8, new ser. xix-xx), 392-3, fig. 4 ; *KCh* xii (1958), 195-202, pls. 6-8 ; *BA* xliv (1959), 237-268, figs. 14-15, 23, 34-6 ; *PP* xiv (1959), 377-80, figs. 1-2 ; Πεπραγμένα τοῦ Β΄ Κρητολογικοῦ Συνεδρίου, Vol. i, pp. 108-10, pl. 6. Cf. also nn. 105, 111 and p. 11.

32. *ABSA* lxii (1967), 203-5, pls. 41-3. The odd proportions may simply be due to loss of skirt cylinder at point of junction with chest cylinder.

33. *ABSA* vi (1899-1900), 106, fig. 3 ; G. Maraghiannis, *Antiquités Crétoises*, Vol. i (Vienne, no date), pl. 29.32 ; Maximova, op. cit., pl. 8.32 ; Zervos, op. cit., fig. 749. Apparently from statuette, not head-vase.

34. *KCh* xii (1958), 215-7, pl. 10.1-2.

35. *AD* xv (1933-5), Suppl., 55, fig. 12 ; *AA* 1933, 297-8, figs. 6-8 ; *KCh* xii (1958), 187-8, pl. 5.2.

36. H. Boyd Hawes, *Gournia, Vasiliki and other Prehistoric Sites of the Isthmus of Hierapetra, Crete* (Philadelphia, 1908), pp. 47-8, pl. 11 ; Nilsson, *Geschichte*, Vol. i, pp. 246, 267-8, pl. 1 ; idem, *MMR²*, pp. 80-82, fig. 14 ; *KCh* xii (1958), 185-7, pl. 5.1 ; Desborough, op. cit., pp. 169, 189.

37. Evans, *PM*, Vol. ii, pp. 335-44, figs. 189, 193 ; Zervos, op. cit., fig. 767 ; *KCh* xii (1958), 202-4, pl. 9.1 ; Marinatos and Hirmer, op. cit., pl. 132, bottom ; P. Demargne, *Aegean Art, the Origins of Greek Art* (London, 1964), figs. 315-6 ; Desborough, op. cit., pp. 169, 189 ; N. Platon, *Crete* (London, 1966, Archaeologia Mundi), pl. 117.

38. *AE* 1937, Part i, 278-91, figs. 1, 4, 8, pls. 1-2 ; Nilsson, *Geschichte*, Vol. i, pp. 246-7, 267, 269, pl. 14.4-5 ; Zervos, op. cit., figs. 771-5 ; *KCh* xii (1958), 188-92, pl. 5.3 ; Marinatos and Hirmer, op. cit., pls. 128-31 ; Desborough, op. cit., p. 189 ; Platon, op. cit., pls. 108-9 ; Higgins, op. cit., p. 11, pl. 5 *d*.

39. *MDAI(A)* xxvi (1901), 247-57, figs. 1-3, pl. 12 ; *KCh* xii (1958), 181-5 (where further bibliography), pl. 5.1 ; Desborough, op. cit., pp. 182, 189-90.
40. *CVA* Oxford ii (1931), 54, pl. 2.1-3 ; Boardman, op. cit., pp. 89, 92 no. 382, pl. 30 ; rightly reassessed by Alexiou: *KCh* xii (1958), 276-7. Sealed base, skewer vents as smaller Prinias idols ; so-called 'baldric' possibly part of snake ; head type much as Patsos cave head-vase (n. 26 above), which may also suggest form of missing head-dress.
41. *ABSA* xxxviii (1937-8), 75-6, pl. 31 ; lv (1960), 29, pl. 14 ; J. D. S. Pendlebury, *The Archaeology of Crete* (London, 1939, 1963), pp. 306, 312, pl. 41.1-2 ; Zervos, op. cit., figs. 803-7 ; *KCh* xii (1958), 192-5, pl. 6.1 ; Marinatos and Hirmer, op. cit., pls. 135-7 ; Demargne, op. cit., figs. 392-5 ; Desborough, op. cit., pp. 172-7.
42. Pendlebury, op. cit., p. 312, pl. 41.3 ; *KCh* v (1951), 98 ; xii (1958), 214, pl. 10.3 ; Desborough, op. cit., p. 190.
43. *ASAA* xxxxix-xl (1961-2, new ser. xxiii-xxiv), 407, fig. 52, 501, fig. 193. Cf. n. 197 and pp. 16-17.
44. Cf. incidence of mainland megaron-type buildings, even at mountain refuges such as Karphi, and scant evidence of late survival of this goddess-type among Minoan Eteocretans, as opposed to Achaean and Dorian elements (p. 12).
45. O. Frödin, W. Persson, *Asine, Results of the Swedish Excavations 1922-1930* (Stockholm, 1938), pp. 74-6, 308 no. 1, figs. 206, 211 ; Nilsson, *Geschichte*, Vol. i, pp. 320-22, pl. 24.2 ; idem, *MMR²* pp. 110-14, fig. 32 ; *JDAI* lxxix (1964), 1-2, fig. 4. So-called 'Lord of Asine', probably rightly identified as female by Evans: *PM*, Vol. iv, p. 756. Form, technique and angle of slender neck seem to counter claimed identification as from sphinx: *Atti e Memorie del 1° Congresso Internazionale di Micenologia* (Rome, 1968), Vol. i, pp. 87-90, pls. 1-3.
46. P. 4. Ear-holes cleaned out by author in 1953.
47. *KCh* xii (1958), 216 n. 127.
48. H. Gallet de Santerre, *Délos Primitive et Archaïque* (Paris, 1958), passim ; Desborough, op. cit., pp. 44-6.
49. K. F. Kinch, *Vroulia* (Berlin, 1914), p. 11, pl. 1 ; A. Plassart, *Exploration Archéologique de Délos*, Vol. xi (Paris, 1928), pp. 145-84, figs. 102-4 ; Nilsson, *MMR²*, pp. 453-4. Free-standing internal offering tables commoner still.
50. *AE* 1902, 1-10, pls. 1-2 ; H. T. Bossert, *Art of Ancient Crete* (London, 1937), fig. 87 ; Demargne, op. cit., fig. 343.
51. Nauplia Museum 8460.
52. Dated by decoration of head-dress: A. Furumark, *The Mycenaean Pottery, Analysis and Classification* (Stockholm, 1941), pp. 316-8, motif no. 27. 13th-century date also likely historically, as Tiryns destroyed in *c.* 1200 B.C., although there was isolated

reoccupation in 12th century: Ålin, op. cit., pp. 25-36; *AD* xviii (1963), Part ii.1, 73.
53. P. 22.
54. *Hesperia* xxxi (1962), 278-83; xxxiii (1964), 326-35; xxxv (1966), 367-71.
55. *Hesperia* xxxiii (1964), 330-31, 333, pls. 60 *e-g,* 61.
56. Pp. 3-4. Their arms easily broken, so that some examples could be of either type.
57. *ABSA* xvi (1909-10), 11, pl. 2 *k.* Context before *c.* 1200 B.C.: Ålin, op. cit., p. 92; Desborough, op. cit., pp. 88, 137.
58. Furtwängler, *Aegina,* pp. 373-4 nos. 6, 8-10, pls. 108.13,15,22, 109. Cf. also n. 22.
59. T. D. Atkinson, R. C. Bosanquet, C. C. Edgar, A. J. Evans, D. G. Hogarth, D. MacKenzie, C. Smith, F. B. Welch, *Excavations at Phylakopi in Melos* (London, 1904, *JHS* Suppl. Paper iv), pp. 202-3, pl. 39.11.
60. J. Boardman, *Excavations in Chios, 1952-55, Greek Emporio* (London, 1967, *ABSA* Suppl. Paper vi), pp. 189, 196 no. 48, pl. 74.
61. E.g. Munich 7607, from Rhodes: J. Schneider-Lengyel, *Griechische Terrakotten* (Munich, 1936), p. 14, pl. 2.
62. Pp. 3, 4.
63. *AJA* lxx (1966), 43-50, pls. 15-16.
64. Pp. 17-18, 21-2.
65. Nilsson, *MMR²,* pp. 77-116. Probably several different goddesses represented; Nilsson, who ignored mainland equivalents of Cretan idols, linked snake-associated 'house-goddess' with Athena: ibid., pp. 485-501; idem, *Geschichte,* Vol. i, pp. 322-6.
66. Nilsson, *MMR²,* pp. 53-76; *BCH* xci (1967), 114-50, xciii (1969), 174-213.
67. *Prähistorische Zeitschrift* xix (1929), 314-39; *JDAI* lviii (1943), 183-98; Higgins, op. cit., pp. 12-13, 16, 139.
68. K. Tuchelt, *Tiergefässe in Kopf- und Protomengestalt* (Berlin, 1962), pp. 26-35.
69. E.g. L. Vanden Berghe, *Archéologie de l'Iran Ancien* (Leiden, 1959, 1966), pp. 6, 83, 120, 123, 125, pls. 3 *a-b,* 107 *c,* 150 *b,* 155 *c,* 159 *e.*
70. *JDAI* lviii (1943), 189-93. There are also early examples from Cyclades and Attica, but no clear evidence of continuing tradition there.
71. Suggested that few of most sophisticated examples of 16th-15th centuries B.C. possibly mouldmade; cf. Higgins, op. cit., p. 12. But this awaits technical verification; remainder seem certainly wheelmade and this technique persists to end.
72. *JDAI* xxvi (1911), 249-70; Tuchelt, op. cit., pp. 36-9, 43-5.
73. Tuchelt, op. cit., pp. 40-43.

74. Atkinson, Bosanquet, etc., *Phylakopi*, pp. 158, 204, fig. 176; cf. also ibid., pp. 203-4, pl. 40.
75. Ibid., p. 205, fig. 177. Hole possibly to take handle of tiny metal double axe? Similar hole also in top of head from Argive Heraeum: n. 98.
76. Matz rightly rejects idea of Minoan bull-god: *KCh* xv-xvi (1961-2), 215-23.
77. *ASAA* vi-vii (1923-4), 135, fig. 57, 171, fig. 98, 197, fig. 120; xiii-xiv (1930-31), 293-4, figs. 35, 39, pl. 22; Higgins, op. cit., p. 6, pl. 5 *b*. On date: Furumark, *Chronology*, p. 74.
78. J. du Plat Taylor and others, *Myrtou-Pigadhes* (Oxford, 1957), pp. 18-23, 80-81 no. 284, pl. 6 *b*; Gjerstad and others, *SCE* Vol. ii, pp. 642-824. Period II at Ayia Irini, assigned by excavators to early Iron Age, yielded items from early 12th-century sanctuary (Period I), such as bull, ibid., pl. 224.3; but, because of later character of some of other Period II votives, ibid., pls. 224.4-5. 225.1-2, 227.1,4, one hesitates to follow Miss Taylor (*PEQ*, 1956, 29, 37) in conflating Periods I and II.
79. On chronology: *PEQ* 1956, 22-37; Desborough, op. cit., pp. 196-205.
80. Gjerstad and others, *SCE*, Vol. ii, pp. 544-5 (nos. 445, 455, 463), 586, 593, 600, 624, 626, pl. 182.2-3. Animals from succeeding Levels II-III allow development to be traced on through late 12th and 11th centuries B.C., but are not illustrated: ibid., pp. 533-61 (nos. 51, 489, 734, 959, 968, 1162), 600-603.
81. Ayia Irini: ibid., pp. 774 (no. 2770), 783, 817, 820-21, pl. 224.1-2. Idalion: ibid., pp. 544-5 (nos. 452, 477), pl. 182.1. Cf. also Taylor, *Myrtou-Pigadhes*, p. 80 no. 389.
82. P. Perdrizet, *Fouilles de Delphes*, Vol. v (Paris, 1908), p. 15 no. 8, fig. 61.
83. Furumark, *Classification*, pp. 322-5, fig. 54.5.
84. Evans, *PM*, Vol. ii, pp. 259-60, Vol. iii, pp. 205-6; *JDAI* lviii (1943), 189-93, figs. 7-9.
85. F. R. Grace, *Archaic Sculpture in Boeotia* (Cambridge, Mass., 1939), p. 77, n. 4. Doubtless associated with re-occupation of 13th-12th centuries B.C., not destruction of late 14th century B.C.: Desborough, op. cit., pp. 121, 220, 226.
86. The author is indebted to Professor Oscar Broneer and to the American Excavations in the Athenian Agora for permission to cite unpublished material.
87. Only partly assembled from fragments; the two figures as distinguished by Mrs Mary Eliot: (1) AF 531 + AP 808 *c, d, f, j*; (2) AP 808 *a, b, e, g, h, i*.
88. North Slope Excavations AP 3002 *b* (*Hesperia* viii (1939), 401, fig. 83 *l*; ibid., fig. 83 *k* does not belong). On context, Ålin, op.

cit., p. 103 ; S. E. Iakovidhes, Ἡ Μυκηναϊκὴ Ἀκρόπολις τῶν Ἀθηνῶν (Athens, 1962), pp. 206-7.

89. North Slope Excavations AP 802 ; Agora Excavations P 17305 from Well U 26:4. Berlin bull: *Prähistorische Zeitschift* xix (1928), 307, 311-14, pls. 34-5 ; *JDAI* lviii (1943), 195-6, fig. 14.

90. From Dörpfeld's excavations in Theatre of Dionysos ; *JDAI* lviii (1943), 183-9, figs. 1-4.

91. Observed by author washed out by rain in cavea of Theatre of Dionysos ; now in Acropolis Museum.

92. P. 13.

93. *AE* 1892, 1-26 ; *MDAI(A)* lii (1927), 1-64.

94. *AE* 1892, 14, pl. 3.1,3,4 ; *MDAI*(A) lii (1927), 38-9, Beil. 6.8,10-13.

95. *MDAI(A)* lii (1927), 38, Beil. 6.14-15 ; Chr. Zervos, *L'Art en Grèce* (Paris, 1934), pls. 43-4.

96. *MDAI(A)* lii (1927), 38-9, Beil. 6.5.

97. Mainly unpublished ; stored in National Museum, Athens. H. Schliemann, *Mycenae ; a Narrative of Researches and Discoveries at Mycenae and Tiryns* (London, 1878), pp. 106-7, figs. 159-60, colour pl. D *n, o*.

98. C. Waldstein, *The Argive Heraeum,* Vol. ii (Boston, 1905), p. 23 no. 72, fig. 28. Shows same kind of vestigial orifice as Melos example, n. 75.

99. Nauplia Museum 3338.

100. *AD* xviii (1963), Part ii.1, 73, pl. 86 γ.

101. *PAAH* 1950, 199, figs. 5, 7.

102. P. 18.

103. Desborough, op. cit., pp. 7-8, 170-79. Cf. *1° Congresso di Micenologia,* Vol. iii, pp. 1078-9.

104. *ABSA* vi (1899-1900), 104, fig. 33 ; *Monumenti Antichi (Ak. dei Lincei)* xix (1909), 18, fig. 4 ; Maraghiannis, op. cit., Vol. i, pl. 29.34.

105. *PAAH* 1957, 148, pl. 75 γ ; *BCH* lxxxiii (1958), 792, fig. 28.

106. *Monumenti Antichi* xii (1902), 118, 122-6, figs. 47, 54 ; Maraghiannis, op. cit., Vol. i, pl. 15 ; Zervos, *L'Art de la Crète,* figs. 795-6 ; Marinatos and Hirmer, op. cit., pl. 134 ; Demargne, op. cit., fig. 326 ; Platon, *Crete,* pls. 70, 120-22 ; Higgins, op. cit., pp. 12-13, 16, pl. 5 *c.*

107. L. Banti, 'I Culti Minoici e Greci di Haghia Triada', *ASAA* xix-xxi (1941-3, New Ser. iii-v), 9-74 ; M. Borda, *Arte Cretese-Micenea nel Museo Pigorini di Roma* (Rome, 1946), pp. 55-63.

108. The idols: Banti, op. cit., 40, 52, fig. 30 ; *KCh* xii (1958), 217.

109. Banti, op. cit., 52-4, figs. 31-6.

110. Ibid., 56-7, figs. 47-55, but some of smaller handmade figures may be later.

111. Ibid., 57, fig. 53 (poor photograph). Still larger sandalled foot from similar figure from Dictaean Cave: Heraklion 2180. Cf. also warrior from Mitropolis (Kannia): *BA xliv* (1959), 248, fig. 16 *b*.

112. Bossert, *Art of Ancient Crete*, figs. 133-5 ; H. L. Lorimer, *Homer and the Monuments* (London, 1950), pp. 200-201, pl. 3.1 ; Marinatos and Hirmer, op. cit., pls. 232-3 ; Demargne, op. cit., figs. 331, 336. On greaves: *MDAI(A)* lxxv (1960), 42-67.

113. Banti, op. cit., 54-6, figs. 43-6 ; Borda, op. cit., pp. 55-6 no. 1, pl. 43.2.

114. Pp. 4, 6. E.g. Heraklion Museum 1812 (from Phaistos?).

115. Cf. however, p. 13 and p. 18 and the sphinx-plaque from Mitropolis (Kannia), Πεπραγμένα τοῦ Β΄ Κρητολογικοῦ Συνεδρίου, Vol. i, pp. 108-9, pl. 2. It seems rather that hollow wheelmade figures of centaurs and bull-men (p. 13) may have developed as a later parallel form from these wheelmade sphinx figures, beginning in about the 10th or earlier 9th centuries B.C. A splendid wheelmade centaur apparently of about this date has, it seems, just been discovered in a tomb at Lefkandi in Euboea, along with a barrel-bodied animal-vase. Cf. also the centaur askos of similar date from Kos, n. 191. See also Frontispiece and Addenda, p. 37.

116. *BCH* lxxxvii (1963), 370-73, fig. 68 *a* ; Χαριστήριον εἰς ’Α. Κ. ’Ορλάνδον, Vol. ii (Athens, 1966), pp. 161-3, pl. 21 *a* ; *AOF* xxi (1966), 62, fig. 6 ; Πεπραγμένα τοῦ Β΄ Κρητολογικοῦ Συνεδρίου, Vol. i, p. 182, pl. 34.

117. Cf. Desborough, *Last Mycenaeans*, pp. 235-7 ; *1° Congresso di Micenologia*, Vol. iii, pp. 1086-7.

118. Evans, *PM*, Vol. ii, pp. 128-39, fig. 69 *k, l* ; Desborough, *Protogeometric Pottery* (Oxford, 1957), pp. 236-7 ; idem, *Last Mycenaeans*, p. 180.

119. Banti, op. cit., 58-62, figs. 58-63 ; Borda, op. cit., pp. 61-3, pls. 48-9.

120. Banti, op. cit., 54, 57, figs. 37, 56.

121. Pp. 13-14.

122. *Museo Italiano* ii (1888), 913-6, pl. 14. Also others in Heraklion Museum.

123. Heraklion Museum 7293 and uncatalogued fragments.

124. Heraklion Museum 1715.

125. *ABSA* xxxviii (1937-8), 92, pl. 32.1.

126. Maraghiannis, op. cit., Vol. i, pl. 29.36 ; Boardman, *Cretan Collection*, pp. 61-2 nos. 260-61, pl. 21.

127. *AJA* v (1901), 149-50, pl. 5.

128. E. H. Hall, *Excavations in Eastern Crete, Vrokastro* (Philadelphia, 1914), pp. 101-2, 108-9, fig. 56. Also further examples, uncatalogued, in Heraklion Museum.

Plate 3

a

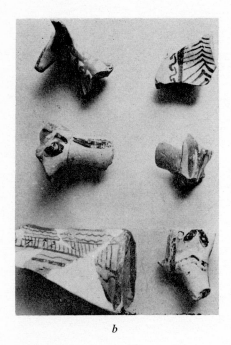

c

b   *d*

a Delphi Museum, from Delphi (p. 9); *b* Athens, Stoa of Attalos Museum, North Slope Excavations AF 531, Agora Excavations P 17305, North Slope Excavations AP 3002 *b*, AP 808 *b*, AP 808 *a*, AP 802 (pp. 9-10); *c* Athens, Acropolis Museum, from Theatre of Dionysos (p. 10); *d* Athens, National Museum, from Acropolis (pp. 13-14)

Plate 4

a Cambridge, Fitzwilliam Museum GR.22.1963 (p. 18); b London, British Museum 1930.6-17.2, from Crete (p. 18); c Athens, Stoa of Attalos Museum T 175, from Agora Excavations (p. 17); d Athens, National Museum, from Lemnos (p. 17)

129. *RA* Series iv, xxi (1913), 278-300 ; BCH liii (1929), 382-429.
130. *ASAA* xxxiii-xxxiv (1955-6, New Ser. xvii-xviii), 233, fig. 26.
131. Pp. 5-6.
132. Hall, op. cit., p. 101 no. 1, fig. 55 *b*.
133. Ibid., pp. 108 no. 1, 111-12 no. 3, figs. 55 *a, 63* ; Pendlebury, op. cit., p. 322, pl. 41.4 ; *JDAI* lxix (1964), 15, fig. 14.
134. Arms missing, but apparently not prominent ; predecessors of 7th-century wheelmade votive figures. Schiering's identification as the dead, dubious: *JDAI* lxxix (1964), 15.
135. Meagre material from another shrine at Kavousi seems to span period from Late Bronze Age to historical times: *KCh* x (1956), 8-19.
136. N. 127 above.
137. *AJA* v (1901), 375-92 ; *ABSA* viii (1901-2), 254-9, 271-81 ; *BCH* xxvi (1902), 571-80.
138. Pp. 9, 11.
139. Gjerstad and others, *SCE,* Vol. ii, pp. 777-92, 810-14, 820-24, pls. 224-8 (bulls and bull-men), 189-223, 229-38 (human figures, chariots, etc.).
140. Gjerstad, *SCE,* Vol. iv, Part ii, pp. 421-7 ; *AJA* lxvii (1963), 15-42 ; J. N. Coldstream, *Greek Geometric Pottery* (London, 1968), pp. 318-20 ; cf. also ibid., pp. 305-10.
141. Gjerstad and others, *SCE,* Vol. ii, pp. 586-7, 616-7, 624-8, pl. 182.
142. Taylor and others, *Myrtou-Pigadhes,* pp. 81-2, pl. 6.
143. J. H. Young and S. H. Young, *Terracotta Figurines from Kourion in Cyprus* (Philadelphia, 1955), pp. 41-3, pl. 12.
144. N. 116 and p. 11.
145. E.g. from Iron Age sanctuary at Ayios Iakovos: Gjerstad and others, *SCE,* Vol. i, pp. 361-70, pl. 68.
146. Πεπραγμένα τοῦ Β΄ Κρητολογικοῦ Συνεδρίου, Vol. i, pp. 180-85, pls. 31-33.
147. Higgins, op. cit., pp. 17, 18, 20-21.
148. Desborough, *Last Mycenaeans,* pp. 246-8, 254.
149. Pp. 9-10.
150. K. Kübler, *Kerameikos, Ergebnisse der Ausgrabungen,* Vol. iv (Berlin, 1943), pp. 20, 40, pl. 26 ; Demargne, op. cit., fig. 373 ; Higgins, op. cit., pp. 21, 140, pl. 7 *d*.
151. Kübler, op. cit., Vol. iv, p. 20 ; Higgins, op. cit., p. 21.
152. Athens, National Museum, uncatalogued ; stored with Acropolis sherds.
153. Agora Excavations, T 3711.
154. Agora Excavations, MC 677 and MC 678, from Well L 11:1.
155. Agora Excavations, MC 860, from Well K 12:1.

156. *Hesperia* iv (1935), 192-3, fig. 2 *d.* Cf. also elaborate wheeled chariot model of 13th century B.C. from Mega Monasterion, Thessaly: *AR* 1964-5, 20, cover-picture.
157. North Slope Excavations, AF 904, from Well A, but clearly much earlier ; cf. *Hesperia* ix (1940), 141-3.
158. 10th century B.C.: *AD* xxii (1967), Part ii.l, 49, pl. 70 α, γ (from the grave of a child and so, in this case at least, presumably a toy). End of 10th or early 9th centuries B.C. (on decoration): Agora Excavations, T 963.
159. Kübler, *Kerameikos,* Vol. v, Part i (Berlin, 1954), pp. 69, 121, pl. 142 (where dated to end of 10th century B.C., apparently on false analogy with painted horses on vase).
160. *ABSA* lii (1957), 15, pl. 3 (from Eretria, but apparently Attic) ; G. M. A. Richter, *Handbook of Greek Art* (London, 1959), p. p. 219, fig. 323 *a ;* Kübler, *Kerameikos,* Vol. v, Part i, p. 245, pl. 144 ; Higgins, op. cit., pp. 23, 140, pl. 8 *a ;* Agora Excavations, T 1725, MC 385, MC 685.
161. Athens, National Museum, 14936 (+ 14979 ?), from Sounion, 19165 and 19190, from Vari ; Agora Excavations, T 2408, from Well A 17:1.
162. Pp. 9, 11.
163. E. T. H. Brann, *The Athenian Agora,* Vol. viii, *Late Geometric and Protoattic Pottery* (Princeton, 1962), p. 68 no. 331, pl. 19 ; *Hesperia Suppl.* ii (1939), 65 no. XII.24, fig. 42 ; D. B. Thompson, *Miniature Sculpture from the Athenian Agora* (Princeton, 1959), fig. 9 ; Higgins, op. cit., p. 22, pl. 8 *b.* Also example in British Museum from Elgin Collection, assembled by Professor C. M. Robertson.
164. *Hesperia* ii (1933), 617-9, figs. 83-5.
165. *Hesperia Suppl.* ii (1939), 63-4, 67, nos. XII.18, 19, 21, 25, fig. 40. Now assembled together with additional fragments.
166. Desborough, *Last Mycenaeans,* pp. 158-9, 228, 233 ; Boardman, *Greek Emporio,* pp. 5-31.
167. P. 7, n. 60.
168. Boardman, op. cit., pp. 188, 195 no. 25, pl. 73.
169. Ibid., pp. 188-9, 195 no. 26, pl. 73 ; cf. also ibid., p. 196 nos. 27-8, pl. 73.
170. Ibid., pp. 189-93, 196-9, fig. 131, pls. 73-9.
171. *MDAI(A)* lv (1930), 1-20 ; lviii (1933), 146-73.
172. D. Ohly, 'Frühe Tonfiguren aus dem Heraion von Samos', I, *MDAI(A)* lxv (1940), 57-102.
173. E.g. Boardman, op. cit., p. 188 ; Higgins, op. cit., p. 18.
174. *AA* 1964, 493-502 ; Boardman, op. cit., p. 187 ; Coldstream, op. cit., pp. 288-93.

175. Now largely met: H. Walter, *Samos*, Vol. v, *Frühe samische Gefässe* (Bonn, 1968), pp. 11-23, 85-6, pls. 1-10. But chronology probably still requires a little revision.
176. *MDAI(A)* lxxii (1957), 36-8, pls. 49-50 ; *AA* 1964, 220-31, fig. 10 ; B. Freyer-Schauenburg, *Elfenbeine aus dem samischen Heraion* (Hamburg, 1966), p. 117.
177. Ohly, op. cit., 95, 99-100, pl. 52. Cf. p. 10, nn. 90, 95.
178. Ohly, op. cit., pl. 47, no. 1178.
179. Ibid., pl. 54, no. 426.
180. Ibid., pl. 53, no. 424. Cf. p. 13, n. 150.
181. E.g. Ohly, op. cit., pls. 49-50, no. 1239.
182. Ibid., 88, pl. 62. Also Samos 1222 (unpublished leg of wheeled animal). Cf. pp. 13-14.
183. *MDAI(A)* lxvi (1941), 1-46. Also additional material, most of it rather later: *MDAI(A)* lxxiv (1959), 10-34 ; lxxvi (1961), 25-59 ; *AA* 1964, 503-34.
184. *AJA* xxxiv (1930), 455-79 ; *Hesperia Suppl.* vii (1943), 114-8.
185. Higgins, op. cit., pp. 19-21, 23, 140-41, pls. 6 *e*, 7 *c*, 9 *c-e*.
186. Despite time-gap, have been linked with vases and statuettes from northern Balkans: *AA* 1948-9, 26, 33-4, fig. 4 ; Desborough, *Last Mycenaeans*, p. 260 ; *Proceedings of Prehistoric Society* xxxi (1965), 219-20, pl. 32 ; *Acta Universitatis Carolinae, Philosophica et Historica* v (1966), 65-71. Cf. also Sandars, *Prehistoric Art*, pp. 172-5, fig. 66, pls. 167-8.
187. *ABSA* xlii (1947), 55, fig. 24 ; *PAAH* 1955, 94-6, pl. 25 β, γ ; Marinatos and Hirmer, op. cit., p. 177, pl. 236.
188. *Hesperia* xviii (1949), 282, 287-8, 296-7 nos. 22, 23, fig. 12, pls. 67, 70. On context: Desborough, *Protogeometric Pottery*, pp. 54, 125, pl. 15 ; Coldstream, *Geometric Pottery*, pp. 10-13.
189. *AE* 1898, 103-4, pl. 4.4 ; *Hesperia* xviii (1949), 287, pl. 71. On context: Coldstream, op. cit., pp. 16-21.
190. Same technique used for latest of Attic wheeled donkeys carrying jars (n. 161) and for large statuettes of birds, e.g. fowls from Kerameikos: Kübler, *Kerameikos*, Vol. v, Part i, p. 245, pl. 144 ; Coldstream, op. cit., p. 46 (on context).
191. Higgins, op. cit., pp. 20, 140, pl. 6 *a-b*.
192. *AJA* lxiv (1960), 11-12 nos. 43-6, pl. 4 ; Desborough, *Last Mycenaeans*, pp. 14, 98-100, pl. 10 *f*.
193. Currently being studied by Desborough. In Athens by *c.* 1050 B.C.: *MDAI(A)* lxxviii (1963), 149-53, Beil. 54.
194. H. Payne and others, *Perachora, the Sanctuaries of Hera Akraia and Limenia*, Vol. i (Oxford, 1940), pp. 34-51, pls. 8-9, 117-20 ; *ABSA* xliii (1948), 101-2 no. 600, pl. 45 (only the roof fragments belong). Already of 7th century, but possibly still reflecting Dark Age building-types: *AE* 1931, 1-53 ; *MDAI(A)* lv (1930), 16-17, fig. 6, Beil. 4 (in limestone). In general, see now

also B. Schweitzer, *Die geometrische Kunst Griechenlands* (Cologne, 1969), pp. 233-5, figs. 129-30, pl. 239.

195. *Hesperia* xxxvii (1968), 92-7 nos. 22-3, pls. 23-7 (publishes early examples and gives bibliography of remainder) ; *Record of Art Museum, Princeton* xxviii, No. 2 (1969), 3-14, figs. 1-4, 7.

196. Amnisos: *BCH* xci (1967), 777-8, fig. 2. Palaikastro: *ABSA* lx (1965), 279, 286 no. 20, fig. 14, pl. 75 *f.* Phaistos: *Monumenti Antichi* xii (1902), 127-9, fig. 55 ; Evans, *PM,* Vol. ii, pp. 130, 133, figs. 55 and unnumbered, *b* ; M. Ebert, *Reallexikon der Vorgeschichte,* Vol. v (Berlin, 1926), p. 224, pl. 73 *a-c.* Karphi: *ABSA* lv (1960), 27-8, pl. 10 *a.* Knossos: Evans, *PM,* Vol. ii, pp. 128-30, figs. 63-4 ; *KCh* xii (1958), 205-6, pl. 9.1, left.

197. *KCh* iv (1950), 441-62, fig. 9, pls. 29-30, 32 ; xii (1958), 277-81, pl. 13.2 ; Marinatos and Hirmer, op. cit., p. 154, pls. 138-9 ; Demargne, op. cit., fig. 411 ; *ABSA* lxii (1967), 66, fig. 2 ; Schweitzer, op. cit., p. 234, pl. 238.

198. E.g. group of eight round granaries excavated at Mallia, originally misinterpreted as cisterns: F. Charpouthier, P. Demargne, A. Dessene, *Fouilles Exécutées à Mallia, Quatrième Rapport* (Paris, 1962), pp. 17-19, pls. 21-2. Cf. also *AJA* v (1901), 150-54, fig. 12.

199. Müller-Karpe, *Vom Anfang Roms,* pp. 87-8 ; *ABSA* lxii (1967), 66.

200. *ABSA* xlix (1954), 220-21, fig. 5, pl. 20.1 ; lxii (1967), 64-6, fig. 3.

201. E.g. *ASAA* i (1914), 18-111, pls. 4-6. Chimney and hearth also quite appropriate to early Cretan temple. Cf. also Müller-Karpe, op. cit., pp. 50, 88.

202. *MDAI(A)* lv (1930), 155-6, Beil. 42-3 ; R. Hampe, *Frühe griechische Sagenbilder in Böotien* (Athens, 1936), pp. 32-8 ; Grace, *Archaic Sculpture in Boeotia,* pp. 77-82 ; Higgins, op. cit., pp. 24, 141, pl. 9 *a-b.*

203. G. Karo, *Führer durch Tiryns* (Athens, 1934), pp. 47-8, fig. 17 ; Hampe, op. cit., p. 63, pl. 42.

204. N. 146 and p. 13.

205. *KCh* xii (1958), 275-92.

206. *MDAI(A)* lxvi (1941), 9-10, pls. 1-2 (8th century B.C. or earlier ; later examples listed, ibid., 5-6).

207. C. Blinkenberg, *Lindos, Fouilles et Recherches 1902-1914,* Vol. i (Berlin, 1931), p. 466 no. 1879, pl. 83.

208. *Festschrift für James Loeb* (Munich, 1930), pp. 70-72, fig. 2, pl. 8 ; *Hesperia* ix (1940), 424-5 no. 6, fig. 77.

209. *AE* 1937, Part ii, 651-3, pl. 3.

210. *Hesperia* ii (1933), 604-9 no. 277, figs. 72-3 ; Thompson, *Miniature Sculpture,* fig. 10.

211. F. Winter, *Die antiken Terrakotten,* Vol. iii, *Die Typen der figürlichen Terrakotten,* Part i (Berlin and Stuttgart, 1903), p. 24, fig. 4.

212. Pp. 21-2.

213. Pp. 4-6, 10-12. See in general: W. Lamb, *Greek and Roman Bronzes* (London, 1929), pp. 19-28, 35 ; Schweitzer, op. cit., pp. 126-32, pls. 105-114.

214. Bossert, op. cit., figs. 311-12 ; Borda, op. cit., pp. 80-83, pls. 59-60 ; Zervos, *L'Art de la Crète,* figs. 452, 472-3, 475-7, 500, 504-5, 508, 757-60, 762, 783 ; Platon, *Crete,* pls. 32, 37, 63-6, 107.

215. *ABSA* vi (1899-1900), 107-8, fig. 39, pl. 10 ; Maraghiannis, op. cit., Vol. i, pl. 29.1-25 ; Zervos, op. cit., figs. 453-4, 479, 485, 506-7, 761 ; Boardman, *Cretan Collection,* pp. 6-13, pls. 1-8.

216. *Museo Italiano* ii (1888), 913-5, pl. 14.5-10 ; Boardman, op. cit., pp. 76-8, pls. 25-6.

217. *AA* 1937, 222-3, figs. 3-4.

218. P. 3.

219. E.g. Hall, *Vrokastro,* p. 121, fig. 71 ; D. G. Mitten, S. F. Doeringer, *Master Bronzes from the Classical World* (Exhibition Catalogue, Cambridge, Mass., St Louis and Los Angeles, 1967-8), p. 31 no. 7, with fig.

220. Ayia Triadha sanctuary material helpful for dating, in so far as it is pure. Also certain of most elaborate bronze animals, e.g. from Dictaean Cave, show possible resemblances in leg, hoof and head treatment to some of more ambitious wheelmade terracotta creatures of 12th-11th centuries B.C.

221. *Museo Italiano* ii (1888), 913, pl. 14.8 ; *British Museum Quarterly* v (1930-31), 51-2, pl. 23.3.

222. *AR* 1965-6, 49, fig. 9, right.

223. Lamb, op. cit., p. 35 ; Boardman, op. cit., pp. 118-9. The Kavousi shrine shows much wider time-range than Boardman allows (cf. n. 135) ; thus all contexts seem ambiguous.

224. H. W. Catling, *Cypriot Bronzework in the Mycenaean World* (Oxford, 1964), pp. 248-58, pls. 43-6. Cf. also *AOF* xxi (1966), 64-5, fig. 7 ; *BCH* xci (1967), 309, fig. 75 ; *Mycenaean Art from Cyprus* (Nicosia, 1968, Cyprus Dept. of Antiquities Picture Book No. 3), pp. 26-8, pls. 19-21.

225. Catling, op. cit., pp. 190-223, pls. 27-39 ; *Mycenaean Art from Cyprus,* pp. 28-31, pls. 22-3, 25.

226. *AA* 1962, 1-39, figs. 18-22 ; Catling, op. cit., pp. 255-6 no. 6, pl. 46. *BCH* lxxxviii (1964), 353-4, pl. 16 ; *AOF* xxi (1965), 59-69, fig. 1 ; *Mycenaean Art from Cyprus,* p. 26, pl. 19.

227. Cf. *BCH* lxxi-ii (1947-9), 221-30 ; Boardman, op. cit., pp. 76-7 ; *Hesperia* xxxviii (1969), 141-9, pls. 38-41.

228. Schliemann, *Mycenae,* pp. 111-2, fig. 120.
229. *BCH* lxxx (1956), 361 ; Desborough, *Last Mycenaeans,* pp. 54, 72, 84 ; *Proceedings of Prehistoric Society* xxxi (1965), 224.
230. Zervos, op. cit., fig. 616.
231. *ABSA* vi (1899-1900), 108, fig. 39 ; Maraghiannis, op. cit., Vol. i, pl. 29.20. Cypriot wheels rather different: Catling, op. cit., pls. 35-6.
232. E.g. G. Kaulen, *Die Stilphasen der geometrischen Kunst in Keramik und Plastik* (Cologne, 1962), passim.
233. Coldstream, op. cit., pp. 345-6.
234. Boardman, *Cretan Collection,* pp. 135-9 ; *ABSA* lxii (1967), 63 ; Coldstream, op. cit., pp. 347-8, 356-9, 382-3.
235. *BCH* lx (1936), 257-85, 485-7, pl. 63 ; P. Demargne, *La Crète Dédalique* (Paris, 1947), pp. 259-60, pl. 15 ; idem, *Aegean Art,* figs. 452-5.
236. Boardman, op. cit., p. 137 ; *ABSA* lxii (1967), 61.
237. See in general: Lamb, op. cit., pp. 36-52 ; Schweitzer, op. cit., pp. 133-73, pls. 117-203.
238. In many instances doubtful if these northern bronzes are actually earlier in date ; in some cases they are influenced by Greek work: Sandars, *Prehistoric Art,* pp. 211-15.
239. E.g. *MDAI(A)* lxix-lxx (1954-5), 12-32.
240. Pp. 12, 13, 14, 15.
241. Lamb, op. cit., p. 43 ; *JDAI* lxxix (1964), 17-71.
242. A. Furtwängler, *Olympia,* Vol. iv, *Die Bronzen* (Berlin, 1890), pp. 38-9 nos. 240-41, pl. 16 ; K. A. Neugebauer, *Staatliche Museen zu Berlin, Katalog der statuarischen Bronzen in Antiquarium,* Vol. i (Berlin, 1931), pp. 20-21 no. 29, pl. 5 ; *Olympiabericht* iv (Berlin, 1944), pp. 105-6, pl. 32 ; *A&A* ii (1946), 98-101, figs. 2-4 ; *AA* 1962, 627-9, figs. 25-6 ; Schweitzer, op. cit., pp. 133-5, fig. 92, pls. 117-23. Cf. also n. 219 and p. 18.
243. *ABSA* xxxv (1938), 74-130 ; F. Willemsen, *Dreifusskessel von Olympia* (Berlin, 1957, Olympische Forschungen iii), passim ; Schweitzer, op. cit., pp. 178-98, pls. 208-221. On oriental influences that transformed them at end of Dark Age: H. V. Hermann, *Die Kessel der orientalisierenden Zeit* (Berlin, 1966, Olympische Forschungen vi), passim.
244. *CVA* Athens i, pl. 1.9. The stratified fragments of moulds for tripod legs of ornate type from Lefkandi in Euboea might indirectly imply a distinctly earlier date for tripod-cauldrons of the kind carrying statuettes, but here there seems the possibility of ambiguity in the context: *AR* 1966-7, 13, fig. 19.
245. E. Bielefeld, 'Götterstatuen auf attischen Vasenbildern', *Wissenschaftliche Zeitschrift der Ernst Moritz Arndt-Universität, Greifswald,* iv (1954-5), 379-403, especially figs. 1-2. Cf. also E. Lang-

lotz, 'Aphrodite in den Gärten', *SHAW* 1953-4, Abh. ii, 29-32, figs. 1, 5, pls. 1.1, 6.3-5, 7.1.

246. E.g. i 18.5, i 23.7, i 26.6, i 27.1, i 36.2, i 42.5, ii 17.5, ii 19.3, ii 30.4, iii 14.7, iii 15.10-11, iii 19.2 (wood with bronze sheathing ?), iii 19.7-8, iii 23.3-4, vii 4.4-7, vii 25.13, viii 17.2, viii 53.8, ix 3.1-6, ix 16.3-4, ix 40.3-4.

ADDENDA

The recently uncovered Mycenaean sanctuaries at Mycenae (pp. 3-4 and n. 20). A further season's excavations by Lord William Taylour is reported as helping to confirm that the earliest of the large human idols may date back to the fourteenth century B.C., but as suggesting that they may also span much of the thirteenth century B.C. It has also revealed that there are in fact two separate adjacent sanctuaries, that with the storeroom of idols and that with the frescoes, and in each a wheelmade terracotta idol was found in position on a low bench or platform as at the time of destruction, one of them being apparently of the type of the goddess with raised arms.

The newly discovered terracotta centaur from Lefkandi in Euboea (see frontispiece and n. 115). The most remarkable work of art yet known from the height of the Greek Dark Age, this figure is to be published in *ABSA* lxv, to appear in 1971, and a short interim account of it is given here by the kindness of Mr M. R. Popham and of the Committee of the British School of Archaeology in Athens. It was found headless in a grave of about the later tenth century B.C., along with a battered wheelmade animal vase, possibly representing a donkey. The centaur's head was found in another grave nearby, seemingly of slightly later date, suggesting that it may have been retained for a time as a keepsake by one of the relatives after the figure had been ritually broken at the earlier burial. The centaur is about 14 inches high, richly painted with stripes and lattice, lozenge and dogs'-teeth triangle patterns and seems originally to have had its eyes inlaid. Its animal body is a hollow wheelmade cylinder with two vents, but its legs and human chest, arms and head are solid. Its ears show vestigial piercing, suggesting a link with certain of the earlier sphinx figures, e.g. with the head from one of these possibly found at Phaistos, Heraklion Museum 1812 (cf. pp. 11-12).

THE FALL OF THEMISTOCLES

G. L. Cawkwell

My introduction to Book VIII of Herodotus, and so to Themistocles, was due to the scholar whom we honour in this volume, and an essay on Themistocles may therefore seem not inappropriate from one who has a large debt of gratitude from those early days. The part played by Professor Blaiklock in maintaining the study of ancient civilization in a new country is a large achievement indeed, and all of us join in wishing him a long retirement and long enjoyment of ancient literature.

The fall of Themistocles from favour with the δῆμος, his ostracism and exile, remains something of a mystery. In 480 he had been at the height of his power. It was he who had urged the Athenians to 'trust to the wooden walls' of the fleet which he had created, who had taken a leading part in the councils and actions of the Greeks. He had gone as far north as Tempe to try and make a stand and had refused to leave Artemisium while the defenders of Thermopylae still stood. Above all, he had played, or was thought to have played, a decisive part in the battle of Salamis. At the end of the year he was honoured as ἀνὴρ πολλὸν Ἑλλήνων σοφώτατος throughout Greece, not least at Sparta, where praise was not lightly given (Hdt. viii 124). After 480 he continued to hold power. He played a leading part in the rebuilding of the walls of Athens, and Thucydides (i 93.4) remarked without further explanation that Themistocles τὴν ἀρχὴν εὐθὺς συγκατεσκεύαζεν. After winter 479/8 the evidence grows slight. Such anecdotes as concern Themistocles in the 470s are not necessarily reliable. Yet that he was ostracized shows that he continued to be important; ostracism was a device for getting rid of political opponents, not political nonentities. Nowhere however is there a satisfactory explanation of why

Themistocles fell. Plutarch, in his life of Themistocles (22.1), speaks of Themistocles becoming λυπηρός in his speeches of self-defence, but he does not explain what the διαβολαί against him were, and his ostracism follows mysteriously. Similarly with his exile. Thucydides (i 135.2) is brief on the cause. Τοῦ δὲ μηδισμοῦ τοῦ Παυσανίου οἱ Λακεδαιμόνιοι πρέσβεις πέμψαντες παρὰ τοὺς Ἀθηναίους ξυνεπητιῶντο καὶ τὸν Θεμιστοκλέα, ὡς ηὕρισκον ἐκ τῶν περὶ Παυσανίαν ἐλέγχων, ἠξίουν τε τοῖς αὐτοῖς κολάζεσθαι αὐτόν. οἱ δὲ πεισθέντες . . . . No word of explanation is given of what the two were alleged to be jointly contriving with the Persians, nor of why the Athenians were persuaded, nor does Thucydides explicitly say what he himself thought of the whole affair.

Herodotus however made clear enough what he thought by the tone of his account of Themistocles in 480 and 479. Although he does not neglect Themistocles' part or omit to record the high honour in which he was held throughout Greece at the end of the Salamis campaign (viii 124), he constantly denigrates him, both his motives and his reputation, and Themistocles emerges as a cunning, corrupt, self-seeking schemer, the master of doing 'the right thing for the wrong reason'. The very words that introduce him (vii 143) cast a slur on his origins. ῍Ην δὲ τῶν τις Ἀθηναίων ἀνὴρ ἐς πρώτους νεωστὶ παριών, τῷ οὔνομα μὲν ἦν Θεμιστοκλέης, παῖς δὲ Νεοκλέος ἐκαλέετο. It was notorious in Athens that Themistocles' mother had been foreign; some said Carian, some Thracian, nationalities common enough among Athenians' slaves. Παῖς δὲ Νεοκλέος ἐκαλέετο adds the suggestion that Themistocles' real father was not necessarily given by the patronymic. At any rate, no other Athenian is introduced in this fashion, least of all Aristides (viii 79).[1] Next, Herodotus, having recorded Themistocles' famous interpretation of the 'wooden walls' oracle, recorded (vii 144) the advice, which ἐς καιρὸν ἠρίστευσε, to use the surplus money suddenly accruing from Laurium on building 200 ships ἐς τὸν πόλεμον, the fleet which largely saved Greece: but this is not to be set to Themistocles' credit. The war he meant was the war against Aegina. Οὗτος γὰρ ὁ πόλεμος συστὰς ἔσωσε τότε τὴν Ἑλλάδα, ἀναγκάσας θαλασσίους γενέσθαι Ἀθηναίους. The large number of ships proposed proclaims that Themistocles had more in mind than the war against Aegina. The truth must rather be with Thucydides (i 14)—Ἀθηναίους Θεμιστοκλῆς ἔπεισεν Αἰγινήταις πολεμοῦντας, καὶ ἅμα τοῦ βαρβάρου προσδοκίμου ὄντος, τὰς ναῦς ποιήσασθαι. When the ships were built, the Persian invasion was already expected, as Herodotus himself elsewhere shows (vii

20, 138), but he will concede no more merit to Themistocles than he has to. So too elsewhere. The battle of Artemisium was fought as part of a combined attempt on land and sea to stop the Persians in the Thermopylae area. If the Greek navy had deserted its post at Artemisium, the forces under Leonidas would have been left in the lurch and Persian troops easily landed in the rear, and when Themistocles used his influence with Eurybiades, the Spartan nauarch, to stay and fight the battle, he was clearly advocating what was both honourable and strategically right. But according to Herodotus (viii 4, 5), Themistocles acted because he had received an enormous bribe of 30 talents from the Euboeans, which he proceeded to distribute in a thoroughly Themistoclean way—5 for Eurybiades (ὡς παρ'ἑαυτοῦ δῆθεν διδούς), 3 for Adimantus of Corinth, 22 for Themistocles. Πλεονεξία indeed, of the masterly sort which he was to display during the siege of Andros later in the year (viii 112). Themistocles, οὐ γὰρ ἐπαύετο πλεονεκτέων, demanded with menaces, and obtained, money from other islands, λάθρῃ τῶν ἄλλων στρατηγῶν. The truth is left to conjecture. Fleets cost money. The Corinthians with 40 ships at Artemisium (viii 1) were perhaps feeling the pinch. What more natural than that money should be collected from those not actively engaged in the defence of Greece to pay for the costs of naval campaigns? Out of these tentative efforts of 480 came the tribute of the Delian League. But Herodotus will not see other than Themistoclean cunning and greed. His Themistocles is master of taking what does not belong to him. In the account of the debate of the Greek generals whether to fight at Salamis or not (viii 56-64), Themistocles is represented as returning to the Athenian fleet with the news of the decision to move to the Isthmus, and then receiving a strong warning from Mnesiphilus (57) that such a move would ruin the Greek cause; οὐδὲν πρὸς ταῦτα ἀμειψάμενος, Themistocles, who, if there is anything in Thucydides' judgment of him as ἄριστος εἰκαστής (i 138.3), might be supposed to be well aware of what the move would mean and indeed to have already said as much to the council, returns to Eurybiades as bidden by Mnesiphilus and καταλέγει ἐκεῖνά τε πάντα τὰ ἤκουσε Μνησιφίλου, ἑωυτοῦ ποιεύμενος, καὶ ἄλλα πολλὰ προστιθείς (58). That is, Themistocles got the credit which did not fully belong to him.[2] Perhaps it is not to go too far in conjecture to suppose that the real point of Themistocles' return to Eurybiades, and of his successfully demanding a recall of the council of generals, lay in those ἄλλα πολλά, which contained the declaration that, if the Greeks moved to the Isthmus, the Athenians would not join them (62.2). But for Herodotus Themistocles is a cheat.

So much for Herodotus' general attitude; but in one passage (viii 108 f.) he goes so far as to attribute to Themistocles a motive which suggests that Themistocles was not above treasonable communications with the Persians. Unable to persuade the Greeks to sail to the Hellespont and cut the Persian line of communications, he then dissuaded his own countrymen from doing so themselves, partly with the aid of the argument Eurybiades had used to counter him.[3] Ταῦτα ἔλεγε ἀποθήκην μέλλων ποιήσεσθαι ἐς τὸν Πέρσην, ἵνα ἤν ἄρα τί μιν καταλαμβάνῃ πρὸς 'Αθηναίων πάθος, ἔχῃ ἀποστροφήν: τά περ ὦν καὶ ἐγένετο (109.5). If such had been Themistocles' motive, presumably he did not divulge it, and it was by no means necessary for Herodotus to explain his conduct in such terms: if all the Greeks would not sail to the Hellespont, it would have been dangerous folly for the Athenians to go on their own.

The reason for Herodotus' antipathy is not far to seek. He plainly drew much of his information about Athens from Alcmeonid sources, which repeat themselves in his account of the murder of Cylon (v 71) and in his laboured defence of the family against the charge of showing the shield at Marathon (vi 121-131); and, since it was an Alcmeonid, Leobotas son of Alcmeon, who accused Themistocles of medism on the occasion of his exile (Plut. *Them.* 23.1) and was named, it would appear, in the inscription recording the εἰσαγγελία (Craterus F11), it seems likely enough that Herodotus' view of Themistocles is coloured with Alcmeonid prejudice. The second mission of Sicinnus, in particular, seems more appropriate to an Athenian prosecution than to sober history. The first mission, recently rejected as plain invention,[4] will nonetheless continue to find a place in the history of the Persian Wars. If Aeschylus (*Pers.* 361 f.) could within eight years of the battle ascribe so important a part to the δόλος "Ελληνος ἀνδρός, whether or not the Athenians were deceived in thinking that it brought on the battle, it must have happened. Presumably, too, Sicinnus later received the citizenship of Thespiae (Hdt. viii 75) for more than merely being the slave of Themistocles. So the mission of Sicinnus the night before Salamis must be accepted even if it is devalued. But the case of the second mission, that from Andros, is quite different. On this occasion Herodotus declares that Sicinnus was not sent by himself, but in the company of those who shortly afterwards delivered the threatening demands for money in the islands (viii 110, 112.1). It is hard to believe that a mission, so pointless from a Greek point of view, would be made known to more than the messenger himself, or that that messenger would risk a second encounter with the King whom he had earlier helped to mislead. Slipping across the bay by night was one thing, taking ship from Andros to find the King somewhere on his way north was another. Nor was the tradition firm. In one version (Plut. *Them.* 16.5) it was a captive eunuch of the King's, Arnaces, who was sent. So it does seem as if this second mission is a fanciful embroidery of what happened at Salamis. Although Thucydides accepted the account (i 137.4), as he accepted much else about Themistocles and Pausanias, it is more credible that it is the invention of enemies who secured for it a place in the tradition and in the pages of Herodotus.

Herodotus, then, is ready to suspect the worst of Themistocles. Yet it is notable that nothing that he records of 480 or 479 could be labelled medism. The worst, and it is a bad worst, is that he represents Themistocles envisaging in 480 that he will later need a bolt-hole in the very part of the world where he could least expect in 480 ever to want or find one. If therefore we are to find what is behind the charges of medism at the time of exile, charges which somehow linked him and Pausanias, we must look to the period after the Persian Wars.

There too it is hard to imagine that there was anything solid in the Alcmeonid charge of medism. Until Themistocles was ostracized, he had no occasion to seek the friendship of the Great King; afterwards, he had very little to offer. He could do nothing with the one city in which he had real influence, and, although in Argos he may have been popular, Argos was already an ally of the Great King and the services of a mediser were not required (Hdt. vii 151). Nor is it likely that the sort of influence that he had acquired elsewhere in the Peloponnese[5] was such as to render him more attractive to Persia, or Persia more attractive to the Peloponnese. Nor did his behaviour on first reaching Asia argue the guilt of medizing. Far from proceeding directly to the King, confident that he would be well received, he did not dare approach until Xerxes had died— a considerable lapse of time (even on the hypotheses of those most concerned to diminish it). But perhaps Themistocles in ostracism, like Alcibiades in exile, was seeking return by hook or by crook? Is it so improbable that a Greek statesman excluded from his own city should turn to its enemies? Thucydides forbids such a notion in the case of Themistocles. For in glossing the phrase, εὐεργεσία ὀφείλεται, in the letter of Themistocles to Artaxerxes (i 137.4), he

refers only to events of 480 and makes no mention of recent acts
of medism. So he evidently thought that there was nothing in the
Spartan charges, and the Ephoran version (Diod. xi 54 f.) supports
his view.[6] The only charge made against Themistocles by the Spartans was that he had not made public what Pausanias had revealed
to him of his treasonable designs (54.4, 55.8). So too Plutarch
(*Them.* 22). Neither probability nor evidence convicts Themistocles
of active medism.

Why then was he accused of medism? And why were the Athenians persuaded by the Spartans? What was there about him or
his political record that made such charges credible? A certain
answer is not possible. The evidence for the 470s is too slight. But
the probable answer must be that Themistocles had been advocating policies which aimed more at the establishment of Athenian
power in Greece than at taking vengeance on the Persians and pre-
venting their return.[7] The humiliating failure of Xerxes' attempt to
incorporate Greece in his realm must have made it seem very unlikely to many that the Persians would invade Greece by land again.
In so far as they needed to be opposed, they would be opposed on
the sea. For this reason, in Thucydides' opinion (i 93.7), Themistocles concentrated on the navy, and Ephorus may well have been
right to record his law providing for the building of twenty new
ships a year in close connection with the building of walls (Diod.
xi 43.3), which followed immediately on the Persian withdrawal in
479/8 (Thuc. i 89.3).[8] But in maintaining and strengthening the
navy, Themistocles had more in mind than defence against Persia.
Τόν τε Πειραιᾶ ὠφελιμώτερον ἐνόμιζε τῆς ἄνω πόλεως, καὶ
πολλάκις τοῖς 'Αθηναίοις παρῄνει, ἦν ἄρα ποτὲ κατὰ γῆν
βιασθῶσι, καταβάντας ἐς αὐτὸν ταῖς ναυσὶ πρὸς ἅπαντας ἀνθίστασθαι (Thuc. i 93.7). Clearly he had in mind, to some degree,
the Spartans. Not only did he entertain no sympathy with their
request to Athens not to refortify the city, but at the meeting of the
Delphic Amphictyony shortly after the Persian withdrawal[9] he was
sufficiently suspicious of Sparta to oppose the plan to exclude the
states which had medized: whereupon he came into direct opposition to the Spartans, who gave their support to Cimon, his princi-
pal opponent in Athens (Plut. *Them.* 20). Cimon's policy was the
Panhellenist ideal of the shared hegemony, and received its clearest
expression in the debate over the Spartan appeal for help in 465.
Ephialtes opposed help and called on the Athenians 'to let the
pride of Sparta be laid low and trampled in the dust', while Cimon,
according to Critias, considered the increase of his country's power

less important than the interests of the Spartans and persuaded the people to march out to their aid with a large force of hoplites; and Ion recorded the actual remark Cimon made in getting the Athenians to move, calling on them μήτε τὴν 'Ελλάδα χωλήν μήτε τὴν πόλιν ἑτερόζυγα περιϊδεῖν γεγενημένην (Plut. *Cim.* 16). Such was Themistocles' opponent, friend of Sparta, friend of the allies (*op. cit.* 11), and it seems clear enough that he, who τὴν ἀρχὴν εὐθὺς συγκατεσκεύαζεν,[10] and who envisaged opposition πρὸς ἅπαντας, was, from 478 on, the firm opponent of Sparta. His ambitions in Greece are presumably the truth behind the story of his proposing to burn the rest of the Hellenic fleet at Pagasae (Plut. *Them.* 20). With that clarity of vision that Thucydides commended (i 138.3), Themistocles saw Sparta as Athens' real enemy, and this must inevitably have muted his zeal for the war against Persia. There is, it must be conceded, no direct evidence that he had ceased to fear a Persian return. That he should choose to go in ostracism to Persia's ally in Greece argues little; Argos was a convenient base for meddling in Peloponnesian affairs (Thuc. i 135.3). But, as many have seen, the very fact that accusations of medism were credited at Athens shows that Themistocles had been less than zealous for the Μηδικὸς πόλεμος.

To infer the policies of Themistocles from the charges laid against him after his ostracism may seem to some a curious method, but such a method is frequently enough necessary in Greek history. The charges, for instance, against Demosthenes in the 330s of taking money from the Persians, or those made by Demosthenes in 343 against Aeschines of being in Macedonian pay, or those made against Timagoras in 366 of selling Athens' interests to the Thebans, are not to be taken literally.[11] Such allegations were frequently unverifiable when they were made and in Athens one was not obliged by exacting rules of evidence. The important question is always what in the policies of statesmen could make such an interpretation of their acts remotely credible, and the right answer seems to be again and again that behind such 'medizing', or 'Philippizing', or 'Boeotianizing', were policies of avoiding hostilities with Persia, or Macedon, or Thebes. So Themistocles' medizing is a common enough sort of occurrence in Athenian politics. Indeed, there is a very similar case a few years earlier. At Marathon someone made, or was thought to have made, a shield signal to the Persians. No one at the time was shown to be responsible; if he had been, he would have been dealt with. But rumour fastened on the Alcmeonids for whom Herodotus engaged in his long defence (vi 115, 121-

131), and we are left to inquire why they in particular could be suspected of such treasonable traffic. The probable answer is that they had been lukewarm about the Ionian Revolt, regarding it as the hopeless venture that Herodotus was to represent it, presumably in part under Alcmeonid influence.[12] From a policy of leaving Asia to itself came suspicions of medism in the case as later in that of Themistocles.

This picture of Themistocles in the 470s, as primarily concerned to challenge Sparta for the hegemony of the Greeks and confident that the Persians would not come again, is, as already remarked, far from novel. What is to be considered here is the circumstances in which Themistocles' policy was discredited. In late 479, the Athenians, Θεμιστοκλέους γνώμη (Thuc. i 90.3), refortified Athens despite Spartan wishes and Themistocles began to counsel them to be prepared πρὸς ἅπαντας ἀνθίστασθαι (*op. cit.* 93.7). Early in 478, presumably,[13] he clashed with Sparta at the meeting of the Delphic Amphictyony (Plut. *Them.* 20), and Sparta rewarded his hostile suspicions by turning to his political opponents. In the course of 478, the conduct of Pausanias alienated the allies who turned to Athens, and the Spartans were confronted with the important decision, whether to retire gracefully or to dispute Athens' assumption of the hegemony (Thuc. i 95). In Thucydides, the Spartan retirement is presented in words which conceal debate: they retired, 'fearing lest those who went abroad from Sparta should be corrupted, as they observed in the case of Pausanias, and wanting in fact to be rid of the Persian War, καὶ τοὺς 'Αθηναίους νομίζοντες ἱκανοὺς ἐξηγεῖσθαι καὶ σφίσιν ἐν τῷ τότε παρόντι ἐπιτηδείους'. Fortunately the debate recorded by Ephorus (Diod. xi 50), which presumably belongs to this occasion,[14] makes clear that there was a serious crisis and there was very nearly war against Athens ὑπὲρ τῆς κατὰ θάλατταν ἡγεμονίας. The decision left Athens free to organize the Delian League (Thuc. i 97) in late 478 (*Ath. Pol.* 23.5). It was carried out not by Themistocles, but by his rival Aristides.[15] The first blow was delivered. Themistocles had expected a struggle for the hegemony. Within a year he was proved wrong.

Later came more alarming news, but before considering it, we must first deal briefly with chronology. Fortunately, this paper does not depend on any particular date for the battle of Eurymedon. No matter here whether or not one sympathizes with recent attempts to establish the lower date.[16] But two points are relevant; first, that it was the siege of Naxos which Themistocles encountered on his flight across the Aegean, and, secondly, that the revolt and siege of Naxos

belong to the campaigning year prior to that of the battle of Eurymedon. There can be no doubt that Thucydides wrote Νάξον at
i 137.2. As often observed, the following ἀφικνεῖται ἐς "Εφεσον
almost demands it, and in any case Nepos appears to have followed
Thucydides, and he wrote of Naxos (*Them*. 8.6, 9.1). But was
Thucydides mistaken? Did Themistocles flee by way of Thasos and
Cyme, as the reading of one manuscript of Plutarch's *Themistocles*
(at 25.2) has suggested to many?[17] There is no point in refighting
here this battle. We all have our positions, and I have no new
forces to deploy. I must simply profess that for me the authority of
Thucydides is decisive. He may not have had precise information
about what became of Themistocles once he was inside the Persian
Empire, but for the Greek details of the story he is far the most
credible source.[18] So in this paper it is presumed that Themistocles
fled in the year of the siege of Naxos. The other point is less clear
and less important. The common presumption that Eurymedon fell
in the year of Naxos has no firm argument to support it. If it is
right that the battle was in 469, the range of possibility for the siege
of Naxos is small. Eion was captured in 476/5 (Schol. Aesch. 2.31).
We must allow for the capture of Skyros and the war against
Carystus (Thuc. i 98.3). That would appear to confine the revolt
of Naxos to the late 470s, and only those who are determined to
exile Themistocles in 465 have great difficulty in accepting that the
year 471/0, which is commonly agreed to be either the date of his
ostracism or his exile,[19] is the year of the latter. For better or for
worse, the author of this paper believes that Themistocles fled in
471/0 and that Eurymedon was fought in 469.[20] But for the paper
itself no more is necessary than that the siege of Naxos, which
nearly saw the capture of Themistocles, fell very shortly before the
battle of Eurymedon. It is a presumption.

So much for chronology. As I have already argued, Themistocles
was quickly proved wrong, or so it appeared, about Sparta. Later
he was proved wrong, or so it appeared, about Persia. The Persian
Empire was a very slow moving affair. For whatever reasons, expe-
ditions took a long time to prepare. The most notable instance is,
of course, the expedition of 480. According to Herodotus, the
Greeks knew about the coming invasion πρὸ πολλοῦ (vii 138), and
indeed the Persian preparations took four years (vii 20.1). The
Greeks had ample forewarning, and when in 483/2 the mines of
Laurium gave Themistocles the chance to build a large fleet (*Ath.
Pol.* 22.7), the Persians were known to be preparing (Thuc. i 14).
So for Xerxes' invasion they had at least two years warning, possibly

a good deal more. Nor did it need a Demaratus for more than the very early warning he was able to give (Hdt. vii 239). Preparations could not be concealed. The news of the naval preparations which led up to the battle of Cnidus in August 394 came in winter 397/6 (Xen. *Hell.* iii 4.1). The preparations for the invasion of Egypt in 351/0 occasioned a debate in Athens about Persian intentions in 354/3.[21] It is a paradox, especially to those imbued with Greek notions of Persian power, that an empire of such great resources should labour so obviously in mounting an expedition, but labour it did, and Phoenicia could not contain the news.[22] So when the King decided on the great expedition that came to disaster on the Eurymedon, he in all probability decided a good two years in advance and the news of his preparations must have reached Greece well before the revolt of Naxos. Indeed that revolt, and its suppression, should be seen as preliminaries to the coming struggle: Naxos was preparing, or must have seemed to be preparing, to default at the moment when unity was essential; the Persians had once already shown themselves ready to exploit Naxian *stasis* in order to extend their power in the Aegean (Hdt. v 28 f.); now the Hellenes must have feared a repetition. Not that the fears were necessarily very realistic. The first aim of the combined land and sea force that was stopped at the Eurymedon would have been to subject Ionia, and, given the Persian taste for combined operations, it was unlikely that the Persian fleet would be cruising freely in the Aegean. But the danger of a resurgence of Persian naval power was there and the Greeks were right to fear. It was this fear, I suggest, that undid Themistocles. He had in no way trafficked with the Persians, but, having been less resolute than Cimon about the national crusade, he was vulnerable. Sparta saw her opportunity. Themistocles, whose residence in Argos had enabled him to frequent the parts of the Peloponnese where Spartan control was weakening, and who may indeed have had some influence in the synoecisms of Elis and Mantinea, had become more than a nuisance,[23] and charges of complicity in the medism of Pausanias offered a means of ruining Themistocles as well. Documents, not for the only time in Spartan history,[24] were found. In great fear of the coming conflict with Persia, the Athenian people were persuaded. Themistocles fled.

Time would show that Themistocles was indeed τῶν μελλόντων ἐπὶ πλεῖστον τοῦ γενησομένου ἄριστος εἰκαστής (Thuc. i 138.3). Ultimately the conflict with Sparta had to be resolved, and the conflict with Persia reach stalemate and compromise. But the 470s

belonged to Cimon, amity with Sparta, and exaggerated fears of a
new 480. His opponent fled and made what he could of his new
bad name. Κράτιστος δὴ οὗτος αὐτοσχεδιάζειν τὰ δέοντα, he
fared not too ill.

It would be easy to stop here, but one cannot dissociate Themistocles and Pausanias. What of the medism of Pausanias? What did
he propose to Xerxes, or what was he alleged to have proposed?
And what of the friendship of Themistocles and Pausanias, on
which stories of complicity in treason could draw credit? These
awkward questions must be put.

For two reasons the questions are awkward. First, as ever with
Sparta, there is τῆς πολιτείας τὸ κρυπτόν, and answers may prove
impossible. Secondly, Thucydides' account of Pausanias and
Themistocles is peculiarly open to question. Evidence of what became of Themistocles after he landed at Ephesus must have been
very hard to test, and one reads with astonishment what purports
to be the message of Themistocles to Artaxerxes (i 137.4). By no
stretch of the imagination is it probable that a copy of such a letter
ever reached Greece. It is much more likely that the text is a free
composition, and indeed a free composition not uninfluenced by
slander.[25] For can one seriously entertain the idea of the King of
Kings being told by a suppliant Greekling that he could do him
great benefits but wanted to wait a year before saying what they
were? He would not seem from Thucydides' account to have been
in hiding. Μετὰ τῶν κάτω Περσῶν τινὸς πορευθεὶς ἄνω ἐσπέμπει
γράμματα . . . . (i 137.3). That is, he was in Susa. If he expected
a reply, he must have made his presence public. Yet, although the
King wondered, ὡς λέγεται, at what Themistocles had in mind, he
did not satisfy his curiosity, but accepted a year's delay. In that
year Themistocles learnt as much Old Persian as he could, and,
armed with Persian manners as impeccable as possible, he promised
to subject Greece, and did well for himself (i 138). No one can
prove that all this did not happen exactly so, nor that the account
did not come from Themistocles himself in his last years in Magnesia. But good sense suggests that someone's imagination had been
at work, and someone, at that, who imagined perhaps that Themistocles' conversation with the King was so blackly treacherous that
no intermediary, no interpreter could be trusted to hear the dark
secrets. Thucydides has accepted, if not all he was told, at any
rate a great deal more than was consistent with his careful method.

Not that the romantic last days of Themistocles are of great historical importance, but, when one turns to Pausanias, doubts cannot be stifled and much is at stake in our understanding of Sparta. Thucydides was far from uninformed about Sparta. He had been there (i 10). He had studied the inscription concerning Pausanias' burial (i 134.4), and the precision of patronymics and of social rank in the history shows that he had access to much exact information about the state, which presumably he did not omit to visit in the freedom of his exile (v 26). His knowledge of the mysterious disappearance of the helots who thought too much of themselves (iv 80) argues something of that intimacy which enabled Xenophon to recount the conspiracy of Cinadon (*Hell.* iii 3.4 f.). So, without going further into the matter here, it is clear that, when Thucydides talks about Sparta, he knows what he is talking about and his account of the end of Pausanias is not to be lightly discounted. None the less, there are disquieting features.

First, the exchange of letters with Xerxes. Each letter is introduced by τάδε. So we are invited to believe that we are reading the authentic texts. But where could such texts have come from? Did Pausanias keep copies of his correspondence? And, if he kept the letter from Susa, is it likely that he kept a copy of his proposal to marry the Great King's daughter, and to subject Sparta and the rest of Greece to Persia? Proof is not possible, but prudence prompts scepticism, of the sort which Herodotus showed on the subject of Pausanias' marriage (v 32). It looks as if Thucydides has been less than usually critical of the Spartan version.[26] Secondly, there is the story of the Argilian man (i 131).[27] We are invited to believe that this man observed a succession of messengers departing never to return, and, discovering that his own message carried a postscript requesting the death of the bearer, confronted Pausanias with some of the Ephors in hiding and reproached him in terms that made clear to his listeners that there had been a number of services to Pausanias in connection with the Great King; Pausanias admitted the truth of his reproaches, would not allow him to be angry περὶ τοῦ παρόντος, but begged him to be on his way as quickly as possible καὶ μὴ τὰ πραττόμενα διακωλύειν (i 133), which was uncommonly cool. Now there are Thucydidean neo-fundamentalists to whom this story may seem credible. But how did it reach Thucydides? Not from Pausanias, just conceivably from the Argilian, but more probably from Spartiates, and we know enough of governments which are concerned to foster τῆς πολιτείας τὸ κρυπτὸν to suspend belief when they bolster charges of deviation with confirmatory details. It is true that it is all ὡς λέγεται (i 132.5). Thucydides may himself have meant it to be treated as the Apocrypha. But elsewhere he eschews λόγοι and personal anecdotes, and one suspects that in this part of the first book we have a sample of the early Thucydides whose rigorous standards have yet fully to form themselves. His defenders may counter that the mature Thucydides let the story stand; if it is as vulnerable to criticism as is here suggested, he might be expected to see so for himself. That is true, and that is why we are left in no more than doubt about his account of Pausanias. But doubt there is.

Of one thing we may be sure. If Pausanias really was negotiating with the helots as Thucydides so confidently asserts (i 32.4 καὶ ἦν δὲ οὕτως), any conceivable act of medism was far less serious in Spartan eyes. Greece would take care of Persia. The defence of the Spartan social order was the overriding concern of Sparta. Pausanias, the medizer with un-Spartan ways (Thuc. i 94.5, 130.1), could be tolerated, as it would appear, for no little time,[28] Pausanias, the helotizer, not for an instant. Given this priority of evils at Sparta, one cannot avoid the suspicion that the whole story of the medism of Pausanias was a Spartan fabrication which gained credit from his well-known excesses in command of the Greeks, but which was primarily aimed at involving Themistocles in his ruin. If this suspicion were correct, Thucydides' account would be almost entirely misleading, an uncomfortable consequence that few will seriously entertain. So we are turned back to speculate what sort of plans Pausanias could have been engaged on (τὰ πρασσό-μενα of Thuc. i 133), which could interest or involve the Great King.

It has recently been proposed[29] that the death of Pausanias preceded the exile of Themistocles by a considerable lapse of time, but neither does the account of Thucydides (i 135.2) give any support to this nor, if I have argued correctly about the fall of Themistocles, is there any need to explain why Pausanias was accused of medizing so long after his two excursions to the Hellespont. The report of Persian preparations for renewed offensive, which excited the fears exploited by the accusers of Themistocles, gave Pausanias reason to seek Persian help in his plans, or at any rate he could be credibly represented as seeking help. Xerxes was thought to be preparing to come again. Pausanias had large un-Spartiate ambitions (Thuc. i 132).[30] His enemies could have suspected that he had much to hope for from the Persians. The Messenian revolt of 490 had coincided with the Persian campaign to Marathon:[31]

presumably they had expected the Persians to win, and at the least Sparta to be unaided in dealing with the revolt. So Sparta had much to fear from the return of the Persians, as was shown when they preferred to have 35,000 helots with them at Plataea (Hdt. ix 10.1). Not that Pausanias is likely to have planned the liberation of the helots of Messenia. Messenian nationalism sought independence, not social reform. But he may have entertained plans for liberating helots of Laconia ἵνα μοναρχῇ (Ar. *Pol.* 1307A3), and for their attainment he may have been prepared to seek Persian support. Or so it could be said. *Non liquet.*

There is no end to speculation about Pausanias and perhaps little point in it, but whoever has read as far as this will perhaps tolerate one more straw. In the crisis for Spartan strategy produced by the disaster of Pylos, the limitation on the range of Spartan military operations was overcome by the revolutionary measure of Brasidas whereby helots were used for foreign service (Thuc. iv 80). Within a few years the institution of *neodamodeis* had come into being and begun to play an important part in the Spartan Empire.[32] In what sense they were in the δᾶμος we cannot even guess, but presumably the name means that they were. They got perhaps what Thucydides (i 132.4) asserted Pausanias offered in his dealings ἐς τοὺς Εἵλωτας, to wit ἐλευθέρωσιν καὶ πολιτείαν, but this was when the number of Spartiates had disastrously declined. Earlier 2000 helots had been deceived by Spartan offers of freedom into professing their aspirations and they paid with their lives (Thuc. iv 80). Such was earlier the Spartan fear of what they later had to accept. But the man who originated the idea of freeing helots had been Pausanias. He may have dreamed of the total overthrow of the Spartan system, a freak of the Agiad line. He may, on the other hand, have intended much less, viz. the first *neodamodeis*. Shocked appalled, those who later murdered the 2000 contrived Pausanias' ruin, in which was involved Themistocles whose presence in the Peloponnese gave comfort to the opponents of aristocracy outside the Spartan state. Is it inconceivable that so much was made by his opponents of so little, that Pausanias was a sensible man, not a monster? Thucydides does not enlarge on τὰ πρασσόμενα (i 133), does not discuss in what way exactly Pausanias was learnt ἐς τοὺς Εἵλωτας πράσσειν (i 132.4). He talks as if the helots were an organized, if clandestine, trade union, which from all we know they certainly were not.

There is ample room for speculation. The only hypothesis which I wish to press here is that it was the news of the Persian decision

to renew the struggle which set the scene both for the exiling of
Themistocles and for the ruin of Pausanias, whether for his hopes
or merely for Spartan fears. One question remains. Why was it believed that Pausanias might have communicated to Themistocles
treasonable plans? If the burden of the first part of this paper is
correct, their policies had much in common. When Pausanias sailed
out ἰδίᾳ after his first recall and trial, he professed that he went
ἐπὶ τὸν 'Ελληνικὸν πόλεμον (Thuc. i 128.3) which by Thucydidean
usage should mean 'the war against the Hellenes'.[33] That is, when
after the advice of Hetoimaridas (Diod. xi 50) Sparta left Athens
to the hegemony of the Greeks, Pausanias went out, not to fight
Persia (for he was shortly alleged to be medizing again), but to
fight for 'Ελληνικὴ ἀρχή. So he is the Spartan counterpart of
Themistocles. But their policies should have made them opponents.
How could they be thought to be in league? Of course, the events
of 480 and 479 may have made them not only partners but friends.
Presumably they had encountered each other at the meetings at the
Isthmus, even if they do not meet in the pages of Herodotus. But
one would expect there to be more to it than that. By 478 Sparta
had turned against Themistocles (Plut. *Them.* 20). The friendships
of 480, like its signal honours (Hdt. viii 124), would have been for-
gotten. Why were they thought in the late 470s to be likely to be in
communication? Perhaps the right answer, lame though it may
appear, is simply that both had lacked zeal for the war against
Persia, both were in eclipse in their own states, the one ostracized,
the other discredited, and there was one remedy that both could
share, or both be made to share, if the Persians ever came again.

So the two great leaders of the Persian Wars fell, under the
coming shadow of the Eurymedon campaign, but their accusers will
always be less successful with posterity than they were with their
contemporaries.

NOTES

A draft of this article was read to the Classical Society of Worcester
College, Oxford in May 1960, and I am grateful to Professor A. E.
Raubitschek and Mr W. G. Forrest for their criticisms of that draft.

1. The only other case of such an introduction in the whole work is
   at vi 88—καὶ ἦν γὰρ Νικόδρομος Κνοίθου καλεόμενος ἐν τῇ
   Αἰγίνῃ ἀνὴρ δόκιμος—but we have no idea of Herodotus' attitude towards him. For his introduction of other notable Athen-

ians of the period, cf. vi 131.2 and 136 (Xanthippus), viii 17 (Clinias), viii 21 (Abronichus). Ed. Meyer, *Forschungen* II p. 223 noted the oddity of ἐς πρώτους νεωστὶ παριών about a man who had been archon as early as 493/2 (the right date, cf. R. J. Lenardon, *Historia* V, 1956, p. 401 f.). Probably Herodotus meant that the family of Themistocles had been obscure.

2. H. Bischoff, *Der Warner bei Herodot* (Marburg, 1932), p. 8f. collected and discussed the instances of 'das Beraten in schwierige Lagen.' What is remarkable about the advice of Mnesiphilus (on whom Themistocles was said to have modelled himself—Plut. *Them.* 2.6) is that Themistocles took it without acknowledgement. Cp. Macan ad loc.

3. Compare viii 108.3 with 109.2.

4. C. Hignett, *Xerxes' Invasion of Greece,* p. 403f.

5. Thuc. i 135.3 (ἐπιφοιτῶν δὲ καὶ ἐς τὴν ἄλλην Πελοπόννησον) is tantalizingly brief, but, as all have agreed in seeing 471/0 as the year in which he either went to the Peloponnese in ostracism or fled into exile, and as that is the year in which the synoecism of Elis was set by Diodorus' chronological source (Diod. xi 54), it is probably right to suppose Themistocles not uninterested in such important social changes. Cf. A. Andrewes, *Phoenix* VI 1952, p. 4.

6. Ephorus may have been reasonably informed about the charge against Themistocles. At any rate, Plutarch, who had Stesimbrotus to guide him, accepted the same version (*Them.* 23). Nor is the Ephoran account to be rejected because it speaks of the Spartans demanding that Themistocles be tried in the κοινὸν συνέδριον (Diod. xi 55.4 f.). There probably was such a synedrion, to judge by the case of Timocreon (Plut. *Them.* 21.7 συγκαταψηφισαμένου τοῦ Θεμιστοκλέους). The exile decreed by the Athenians and recorded by Craterus (F11) may have followed Themistocles' flight. The only suspect element in the Diodorus version is his account of an earlier trial in which Themistocles was acquitted (Diod. xi 54.5-55.7). Τὲ πρότεραι κατηγορίαι of Plutarch's account (*Them.* 23.4) appear to have been answered by letter, and not in person, which suggests that Themistocles was already in ostracism. So there is nothing in Plutarch to support Diodorus, and, while it is probable enough that Themistocles was on trial before his ostracism, the charge of medism seems unlikely. For, if the Spartans had been accusing Themistocles before his ostracism of receiving treacherous letters from Pausanias, they would at least have had the φανερὸν σημεῖον of Pausanias' medism Thucydides says they lacked (i 132.1). Either Diodorus has misrepresented Ephorus' account, or Ephorus was himself confused.

7. Cf. Ed. Meyer, *G.d.A.* III, p. 511, and C. Hignett, *Hist. Ath. Const.,* p. 190.

8. The Hetoimaridas debate (Diod. xi 50), which belongs to late 478 (v.i.), is followed by a comment on its effect on Athenian policy: it released the Athenians from the fear which had led them to be building more triremes. This confirms the dating of Themistocles' naval law to 479/8.

9. Cf. R. Flacelière, *R.E.A.* LV., 1953, p. 19f.

10. For the meaning of ἀρχή here, cf. J. de Romilly, *Thucydides and Athenian Imperialism* (English translation, 1963) pp. 59 and 119 n. 6.

11. For these cases cf. *C.Q.* N.S. XIII, 1963, p. 204, and XI, 1961, p. 83f; and Aesch. III 238, etc. and *C.Q.* XIX, 1969, p. 176f.

12. Various explanations have been advanced for Herodotus' antipathy to the Ionian Revolt, and no doubt there were various influences. But what is notable is that, having conceived the war of East and West as having its origins in the remotest past (cp. i 4.1, 5.1 and 3), he speaks of the ships sent by Athens at the start of the revolt as the ἀρχὴ κακῶν "Ελλησί τε καὶ βαρβαροίσι v 97.3 and cf. viii 142.2), when the 'evils' of Ionia had on his own account begun long before. His viewpoint is thus in large measure Athenian isolationist.

13. Cf. art. cit. in note 9.

14. The years under which Diodorus disposes his narrative are not significant. What does matter is whether the notice about the Hetoimaridas debate (xi 50) is separated from the narrative of Hellenic affairs of 478 (in ch. 47) by material that probably belonged to the same narrative in Ephorus and that could not have happened in 478. No such matter does so intervene; there are only Sicelica and chronographic notices in chs. 48 and 49. Ch. 50 can follow closely on ch. 47.

15. Cf. Hdt. viii 79.3, Plut. *Them.* 2.1-3.4, 9.5, 22.2-4, 24.6, 25.10 ; all of which passages, no matter how dubitable in detail, are based on the fact of a constant antipathy.

16. See in particular M. E. White, *J.H.S.* LXXXIV, 1964, p. 140, who argues that, if Pausanias had died as early as the dating of Themistocles' exile to 471/0 requires, he would probably not have had time to sire his three sons, the eldest of whom Pleistoanax was, she claims, under twenty at the battle of Tanagra. This argument is not cogent. On the one hand, there is no proof that, in describing Pleistoanax as νέος in 458, Thucydides necessarily meant that he was a minor ; Alcibiades in 420 is described as ἔτι τότε ὢν νέος ὡς ἐν ἄλλῃ πόλει (v 43.2, and cf. vi 18.6 with 2.8 and 21.2), and it is by no means clear that the Spartans would cheerfully entrust the command of their army to a man as soon as he became of military age, even if on occasion Polemarchs could be very young (Hdt. viii 85.1) ; he might still be too young

to command at 25. On the other hand, there is plenty of time biologically speaking. Pausanias could have sired his youngest son the day before he made his fatal visit to meet the Argilian man and his eldest in 477. Nor is Professor White's argument helped by the statement in Plutarch (*Per.* 22.2) that Kleandridas accompanied Pleistoanax in 446 as his 'warden and adviser' διὰ τὴν ἡλικίαν; Kleandridas went as ephor (cf. Suidas s.v. "Εφορος), and ephors always accompanied kings on campaign, let Plutarch adorn the fact as he will.

17. Recently and most notably to W. G. Forrest, *C.Q.* N.S.X., 1960, p. 221f., who argues that the reason why Themistocles fled into exile from Argos was that there had been a change at Argos and he could no longer count on those in power to shelter him. This presumed change is in any case a movable feast, but the explanation of his flight may well be that Argos, which could harbour without scruple or fear an Athenian *ostracisé,* might well hesitate to refuse a demand of the Hellenes (cf. n. 6) ; the city's medizing might no longer be tolerated, if it sheltered an (allegedly) active collaborator.

18. The Thasos-Cyme version of Themistocles' route into exile probably derived, as often surmised, from the local patriotism of Ephorus (cf. *F.G.H.* 70 F1, F 97, F 100, F 236), a poor prop for chronology. Of course Themistocles may well have been said to have been in Cyme during the interval between his arrival in Asia and the accession of Artaxerxes.

19. Cf. Gomme's *Commentary,* Book I, p. 401.

20. Accepting the brilliant conjecture of *A.T.L.* III, p. 160, that the reason why in spring 468 all the generals were installed as judges in the theatre (Plut. *Cim.* 8.7-9) was that this was the first occasion after the Eurymedon when Cimon and his colleagues were all together in public in Athens. It is true that, whereas the other instances, in that chapter, of exceptional honours for Cimon are explained, Plutarch gives no explanation of this honour and it might be that the whole affair sprang from the φιλονικία καὶ παράταξις τῶν θεατῶν. But such a departure from custom suggests that the board of generals were especially popular at that moment, and some success which had involved them all (which would not presumably have been the case with the capture of Scyrus or the siege of Naxos) seems to be required. If the battle of Eurymedon was in 469 and the siege of Naxos 470, it is no surprise that the year 471/70 is that under which Diodorus puts the Themistocles story, and apparently the year according to Cicero for the flight (*de Amic.* 12.42). This is just one more matter in which the discovery of a full Craterus (cf. F11) would silence debate: the sources of Cicero were less constricted than ours.

21. The date of the invasion of Egypt is derived from the date in

Dionysius of Halicarnassus (*Letter to Ammaeus,* p. 726) which happens to be the date under which it is put in Diodorus (xvi 40). That Dem. 14 (of 354/3 acc. to Dion. Hal. l.c.), was part of the debate excited by news of Persian preparations is asserted by the Hypothesis to the speech, but that the preparations were for the expedition against Egypt is a guess, albeit a reasonable one.

22. The preparations for the invasion of Egypt in 373 took 'several years' (Diod. xv 41.2) and began certainly by mid 375 (Diod. xv 38.1). *Hell. Oxy.* 19.2 implies that preparations regularly took a longish time ; the King was κατ' ἀρχάς niggardly. The three years for the war against Egypt of Isoc. 4.140 probably covers two years of preparation and one of invasion: the strategic problem was to get into Egypt while the Nile was low ; if the Persians had not won in the vital months, they had to retire to Phoenicia and begin again. For the lengthy preparations of the invasion of 342, cf. *C.Q.* N.S. XIII, 1963, p. 122 f. Perhaps the recall of Cimon from ostracism in 452/1 was occasioned by news of new Persian preparations, against which he sailed in 450. Since trade between Greeks and Phoenicia went on, it was inevitable that the sort of news brought to Athens by a Syracusan in 397/6 (Xen. *Hell.* iii 4.1) always reached Greece.

23. Cf. Forrest, art. cit., p. 229, and v.s. n. 5.

24. Cf. Diod. xiv 13.8.

25. Cf. M. A. Levi, *Parola del Passato,* VII, 1952, p. 109. No great literary skill was needed to compose in Greek a letter from Xerxes. The formulae were not unfamiliar. Cf. Hdt. viii 85.3, iii 140.1, and Tod *G.H.I.*² no. 12. Disbelief in the authenticity of the letter is widespread. Cf. A. Lippold, *Rh. Mus.* N.F. CVIII, 1965, p. 334f, and C. W. Fornara, *Historia* XV, 1966, p. 262f.

26. There is not a formal clash. (Cf. Gomme, ad. i 128.7.) In Thucydides Pausanias has the effrontery to propose himself for the hand of the King's daughter and Xerxes omits reply. It is conceivable that Pausanias then married the daughter of the King's cousin, or was rumoured to have done so, Herodotus being sceptical about the matter. But it seems more likely that Thucydides and Herodotus are reporting varying versions of the same affair, Thucydides accepting where Herodotus doubted (pace H. Schaefer, *P.W.* XVIII 4 col. 2577 who thinks that Thucydides was better informed).

27. When there is so much that is odd in the Pausanias story, it is pointless to seek to purge any of the oddities. What was Pausanias doing abroad ἄνευ Λακεδαιμονίων (Thuc. i 128.3) when Spartiates were not allowed such independence (Isoc. 11. 18, Ar. *Frag.* 500), and what was he doing away from Sparta when he was still regent (Thuc. i 132.1), and how did he come to have a

σκυτάλη when he was there ἰδίᾳ (Thuc. i 128.3 and 131.2), and
was an eminent Spartiate able to send off messengers on private
business in this carefully controlled state (Thuc. i 132.5)? So it is
probably idle to ask what an Argilian was doing in Sparta, and for
some time at that, having been Pausanias' boy-friend. According
to Gomme ad loc. the Argilian 'was a slave, as can be seen from
Pausanias' promise not to punish him', but in that case why did
he run off to Taenarum risking the wrath to come and not quietly
make his way to Argilos? If we amended 'Αργίλιος to Αἰγίλιος,
some sense would enter the story, for there was a locality of
Laconia called Αἴγιλα (Paus. iv 17.1). However, Nepos *Paus.*
4.1 has 'Argilius', and evidently drew his account from Thucydides
(who presumably would not have been as precise about the
origins of a perioec or a slave).

28. Some have taken refuge in the statement of Justin ix 1.3 (that
Pausanias occupied Byzantium *per septem annos*) to bridge the
gap between his return to the Hellespont in 477 and the fall of
Themistocles. But, as J. Wolski, *EOS,* 49, 1954, p. 78f. pointed
out, the Ephorus papyrus (*F.G.H.* 70, F191) suggests that Pausanias was no longer in control of Byzantium when Cimon sailed
out to the siege of Eion. (*Pace* Lippold, art. cit. and Fornara,
art. cit.) One may add that, if Pausanias had been so long in
Byzantium, he would in all likelihood have used its strategic position to some purpose, and there is nothing to suggest that he
did. Either Justin was misled or the text is corrupt.

29. Forrest, art. cit., p. 237, who thinks that Pausanias probably died
about 474/3. But what, on this hypothesis, was he doing between
477 and then? If Thucydides' narrative conceals that gap, there
is no great difficulty in supposing that the gap was a bit longer
and that Pausanias died in 471. Cf. Lippold, art. cit., p. 328, n. 33.

30. Cf. Ar. *Pol.* 1307 A3f.

31. Plato *Laws* 692 D and 698 E provide the date for this revolt. There
is no reason for placing it in 491.

32. References are collected by R. F. Willetts, *C.P.* XLIX, 1954, p. 27.

33. According to J. Wolski, art. cit., p. 88 f., Pausanias went with
official support, barely ἰδίᾳ. But, despite the σκυτάλη (Thuc.
i 130) which might argue public business (but which Pausanias
may have carried as regent), this does too great violence to
Thucydides. Gomme is not, however, convincing in arguing (ad
i 128.3) that the 'Ελληνικὸς πόλεμος was the war against Persia.

ΔΙΚΗ IN ARISTOPHANES' CLOUDS[1]

W. F. Richardson

The theme[2] of *Clouds* is the conflict between science and religion. The play portrays vividly this conflict in the experience of one Strepsiades, a man of conventional piety who for the first time in his life encounters scientific views of the universe. His story, as he moves through temptation, sin and repentance, is the plot of the play. We must first trace this plot in some detail, after which we can proceed to examine the position of the moral law (δίκη) in the play.

I. *Plot*

The character of Strepsiades as presented in the opening scenes of the play affords a fairly obvious portrait of conventional piety. He has a certain belief in the gods, with Zeus at their head. When his belief in Zeus is challenged, he will make some sort of a fight for it (367 ff.). The gods are useful to swear by (1, 246), and before embarking on a new project he will pray to them for success (127). But apart from this his religion has no influence whatever on his way of life.

Temptation and Sin

To this man of conventional piety comes temptation through money. He is plagued with debts which his son has incurred, and his creditors are becoming urgent for payment (13 ff.). As the play opens he has been pondering in the night on his position. A man of stronger piety than Strepsiades might have been pondering on ways of paying his debts; Strepsiades has been pondering on how to avoid paying them, and has concocted a fraudulent scheme that will achieve this end.

His scheme is thoroughly dishonest and amounts to simple theft (the verb ἀποστερεῖν will be applied to it at 1305 and 1464, cf. 487). Yet throughout most of the play he feels no qualm of conscience about it, even when, faced with Pheidippides' refusal of co-operation, he himself sets it in motion by presenting himself for instruction at Socrates' Thought-Factory. Near the end of the play (1463-4) he will discover that his action in conceiving this scheme and setting it in motion is the basic sin from which all his troubles are derived.

As a direct result of his attendance at the Thought-Factory he is assailed by a further temptation and falls into a further sin. This time the temptation comes to him through the person of Socrates, who commences his education by introducing him to scientific views of the universe. The result is that Strepsiades is tempted to abandon even such slender religious beliefs as he has. The process is made quite explicit as the play unfolds.

Strepsiades broaches the subject quite accidentally when he swears 'by the gods' to pay Socrates any fee he may ask (245-6). Socrates pounces immediately on this (247-8): 'This is your first lesson (πρῶτον): the traditional gods are no longer current coin with us.' He then introduces the clouds as the only gods[3] whom the scientists now recognize.

'The Greeks did not worship them [i.e. the clouds] as deities, but regarded them simply as part of the mechanism by which Zeus sends rain' (K. J. Dover, *Aristophanes: Clouds*, p. lxviii). Their symbolic value here is thus obvious: they symbolize the replacement of the traditional gods with Zeus at their head by the natural phenomena studied by science. The old religion has been done away with; science now reigns in its stead.

In the lengthy passage which follows (365-426), Socrates is concerned with one thing: to break down Strepsiades' belief in Zeus.[4] He attacks this belief by giving scientific explanations, based on the agency of the clouds, for phenomena which Strepsiades had been accustomed to ascribe to the action of Zeus. Strepsiades puts up a fight for his religious belief in Zeus (368, 374, 379, 397); but the temptation to abandon it is overwhelming and he eventually falls. In 423-6, at Socrates' prompting, he vows that in future he will have nothing to do with the traditional gods. This rejection of the traditional religion with Zeus at its head is the climax to which the whole first section of the play has been leading up.

The next stage in Strepsiades' career begins when Socrates discovers that he is unteachable and expels him from the Thought-

Factory. Turning to the clouds, Strepsiades asks them what he should do, and they advise him to send his son to be taught in his place (794-6). The fact that this advice comes from the clouds will be picked up at a key passage later in the play (1452-61). In the scene that follows Strepsiades takes over Socrates' position as tempter: having been led astray himself he proceeds to lead others astray. In the dialogue that follows, as he tries to persuade Pheidippides to take his place, his new-found scientific beliefs are stated firmly and unequivocally, though not without humour (e.g. 825-8). But it is only by dint of a strongly emotional appeal (861-4) that Strepsiades finally persuades his son to go to the school and hence, by implication, to reject Zeus in favour of science (for he well knows that this is the first lesson his son will have to learn, cf. 247). At this point Aristophanes puts a significant comment into Pheidippides' mouth (865): 'You'll regret this some day.' This is strictly accurate. By his conversion[5] of Pheidippides Strepsiades has set in train the events which will lead to his own punishment.

The culminating sin in this catalogue of evil is ὕβρις, which is the keynote of Strepsiades' two scenes with his creditors.[6] The point of these scenes is the high-handed arrogance with which Strepsiades, freed from the restraint of a belief in Zeus and relying on his son's new-found skill to get him unscathed out of any resultant lawsuit,[7] sees fit to conduct himself (1239-41):

> Πα. οὔ τοι μὰ τὸν Δία τὸν μέγαν καὶ τοὺς θεοὺς
> ἐμοῦ καταπροίξει. Στ. Θαυμασίως ἥσθην θεοῖς,
> καὶ Ζεὺς γέλοιος ὀμνύμενος τοῖς εἰδόσιν.

No tragic hero ever made a more hybristic remark than that; and there can be little doubt that, when Aristophanes makes Amynias use the very word ὕβρις at 1299, he intends it to be understood, not merely as 'assault', but also in the technical sense of tragedy. The vengeance of heaven follows immediately and inevitably.

Punishment

Strepsiades' punishment is achieved through the indirect agency of Pheidippides. This is the reason why it had to be he and not Strepsiades who succeeded in learning all Socrates' lessons at the Thought-Factory.[8] Had Strepsiades succeeded in learning them he would have become invulnerable to punishment, capable of arguing his way unscathed out of any situation. As it is he finds himself, as a result of his sins, at the mercy of a son who not only proceeds to

beat his father but proves that he is right to do so. All this is foreshadowed in the short chorus which precedes this scene (1303-20):
the chorus are beginning to come out in their true colours, which
will be so tellingly revealed later in the play (1458 ff.).
The punishment for Strepsiades' ὕβρις is a belabouring about
the head and jaw (1324), for this is comedy, not tragedy, and it
would be out of place for the vengeance of heaven to take any
severer form. Yet those hard knocks are sufficient to clear Strepsiades' head, and at the end of his *agon* with Pheidippides (1351
ff.) he is beginning to see things in their proper light again. As
Pheidippides offers to prove that he is entitled to beat, not only his
father, but also his mother, Strepsiades realizes for the first time
since the play began that this sort of attitude, which might have
been his own if he had gone on with Socrates' course, is evil
(κακόν: 1444). Only a few lines ago he was still prepared to
acquiesce and to admit that Pheidippides was right to beat him
(1437-9); now he sees that to beat one's father is evil and to
beat one's mother an even worse evil (1444), which can only lead
its perpetrator to complete and utter ruin (1447-51). He has, in
other words, turned his back on the teachings which Pheidippides
now embodies; and his repentance begins at this point.

Repentance

Strepsiades' repentance involves reaching the realization that he
is himself responsible for his present position and that the blame
for it lies squarely on his own shoulders. The stages by which his
arrogance in the creditor scenes is broken down to this humble
acceptance of blame are clearly portrayed. At first he blames the
clouds (1452-3), but they, with great emphasis, put him right
1454-5):
　　Χο.　αὐτὸς μὲν οὖν σαυτῷ σὺ τούτων αἴτιος . . .
This reply puzzles him. He had looked upon the clouds as his
friends and mentors; why, then, did they keep egging him on to his
doom (1456-7)? The explanation is rapidly forthcoming (1458-61):

　　Χο.　ἡμεῖς ποιοῦμεν ταῦθ' ἑκάστοθ' ὅταν τινὰ
　　　　　γνῶμεν πονηρῶν ὄντ' ἐραστὴν πραγμάτων,
　　　　　ἕως ἂν αὐτὸν ἐμβάλωμεν ἐς κακόν,
　　　　　ὅπως ἂν εἰδῇ τοὺς θεοὺς δεδοικέναι.

One can hardly overestimate the effect of this speech on Strepsiades at this time. He had put his whole trust in the clouds. At
their behest he had solemnly forsworn, and later mocked at, the

traditional gods. The phenomena of science were his new gods. With science on his side Zeus and the other gods were quite unnecessary. Yet already, as a result of Pheidippides' treatment of him, he had begun to wonder, even to doubt. The consequences in the ethical sphere of these anti-Zeus views seemed all wrong (1444, 1447-51). What had happened? Now of a sudden the veil is viciously ripped aside and the true situation revealed. All along he has been deluded.[9] Science, the erstwhile god, is shown to be nothing but a servant of the gods, a servant whose function is to test the faith of men on earth.

In a flash Strepsiades' ideas are reorientated. He had been puzzled that things seemed to be going wrong; now, from his new viewpoint, everything appears in correct perspective. His punishment may be severe, but he has deserved it (1462). The fault is entirely his own; he has no-one but himself to blame. The whole sorry process has its origin in his totally immoral desire to cheat his creditors out of their money, and for this desire and the plan which he evolved in pursuit of it he himself bears the sole responsibility (1463-4):

> Στ. οὐ γάρ μ' ἐχρῆν τὰ χρήμαθ' ἁδανεισάμην
> ἀποστερεῖν.

At this point his repentance is complete.

Atonement

The desire to make what amends one can for one's sin is an essential concomitant to repentance. The basic responsibility for what happened must lie with Strepsiades himself, as he has now recognized. But Socrates and his school have treacherously played upon his weakness; instead of helping him back to moral sanity they led him on with their pernicious doctrines (223-456) until he found himself floundering in his present morass. But for them he might have seen the danger in time and avoided all this trouble. They are a positive danger to society! Here, then, is one way in which he can seek to make amends. In 1464-6 he invites Pheidippides to join him in destroying Socrates and his chief henchman. The idea is frustrated by Pheidippides' refusal to co-operate; but in the dialogue which follows the invitation the depth of Strepsiades' penitence is made very clear (1464-77).

The final scene of the play shows the final vindication of the gods. Strepsiades, who had previously been prepared to assert dogmatically that there were no gods, now bends humbly to the statue of

Hermes, asks for pardon (1479-80), and seeks the god's advice. How is he to make atonement? The god's answer is soon forthcoming. He is to strike at the root of the trouble by burning down the Thought-Factory (1484). And so Socrates and Chaerephon are punished for their ὕβρις (1506), just as Strepsiades was before. We thus observe a double (chiastic) parallelism in the plot, whereby Strepsiades is tempted by Socrates, then Pheidippides by Strepsiades, and at the end Strepsiades is punished by Pheidippides and Socrates by Strepsiades. Of the three, only Strepsiades repents; and his repentance results in the removal from society of the taint represented by the Thought-Factory. And thus for Zeus, the clouds and the Athenian state as a whole all ends happily.

II. Δίκη

In presenting in this play the conflict between science and religion Aristophanes is concerned, not with the problem in general, but with one particular aspect of it. If the scientists are allowed to do away with Zeus and the other gods altogether, what will be the effect on human life in the field of morality? In answering this question Aristophanes starts from a view of the moral law which is firmly Aeschylean. The following quotation from Denniston and Page's edition of *Agamemnon* (note on 184 ff.) puts the matter in a nutshell (my italics): 'Aeschylus tells us that Justice is not man-made: *it is a rule for life on earth imposed by Zeus.* If you break his law, he will teach you to mend your ways by inflicting punishment; you will learn perforce not to ignore the divine origin and sanction of the rules of conduct which govern civilised society.'

This is precisely the background which Aristophanes assumes for *Clouds*. Its connection with the plot as set out above, and especially with 1458-61, is obvious.

The rule for life on earth imposed by Zeus is δίκη; and δίκη is the key idea in the understanding of *Clouds*. That Aristophanes is accepting the Aeschylean view of the transcendence of δίκη is seen from the following lines (902-3):

Αδ.   οὐδὲ γὰρ εἶναι πάνυ φημὶ δίκην.
Δι.   οὐκ εἶναι φῇς; Αδ. φέρε γὰρ ποῦ 'στιν;
Δι.   παρὰ τοῖσι θεοῖς.

Hence δίκη in *Clouds* is the transcendent standard, or set of rules, by which any man's conduct can be judged as moral or immoral. Conduct which obeys the rules is moral (δίκαιος = in accordance with δίκη) and conduct which disobeys them is immoral (ἄδικος = not in accordance with δίκη). It is the gods, and Zeus in particular, who impose these rules: morality depends on the traditional religion. Reject Zeus, as the natural scientists are trying to do, and this morality must automatically go as well, for then the absolute standard is gone. Then the sole rule for life on earth will be the expediency of the individual: 'every man for himself'. The danger inherent in this situation is the main point which Aristophanes is endeavouring to make in this play. We proceed to examine his development of this idea by following through the occurrences of δίκη and its cognates in the light of the plot.

Setting the Stage

The first occurrence of the root is at 25. Though this is merely an aside thrown out by the dreaming Pheidippides, it illustrates exactly the view of δίκη set out above. Pheidippides is dreaming that he is taking part in a chariot race, the rules of which require that each competitor keep in his own lane. But one of his rivals has left his own lane and is trying to crowd Pheidippides off the course. And so Pheidippides shouts ἀδικεῖς: 'You're breaking the rules!' This use of ἀδικεῖν recurs at 497, 1080 and 1175.

The first important passage comes when Strepsiades, having conceived his brilliantly clever scheme (76) for getting rid of the burden of his debts, wakes Pheidippides up to tell him about it. He shows Pheidippides the Thought-Factory and tells him about the men in it (98-9):

> Στ. οὗτοι διδάσκουσ', ἀργύριον ἤν τις διδῷ,
> λέγοντα νικᾶν καὶ δίκαια κἄδικα.

A few lines further on he amplifies their claims (112-5):

> Στ. εἶναι παρ' αὐτοῖς φασιν ἄμφω τὼ λόγω,
> τὸν κρείττον', ὅστις ἐστί, καὶ τὸν ἥττονα.
> τούτοιν τὸν ἕτερον τοῖν λόγοιν, τὸν ἥττονα,
> νικᾶν λέγοντά φασι τἀδικώτερα.

These two passages must claim our attention at greater length, for much that follows is dependent on them.

It has long been realized that the background to exegesis here is the dictum of Protagoras τὸν ἥττω λόγον κρείττω ποιεῖν. Protagoras taught that on any matter two opposing statements (λόγοι) could be made, representing two opposite points of view. To a normal person under normal circumstances one of these would appear self-evidently correct: this is the stronger (κρείττων). The other, which a normal person considering the two would reject as obviously false, is the weaker (ἥττων). But, said Protagoras, a skilled arguer could take the weaker position and, by manipulating his arguments, convince his hearers of its rightness, i.e. could cause it to become the stronger position (τὸν ἥττω λόγον κρείττω ποιεῖν). Now, it is these two statements of two opposite points of view which, as personified by Aristophanes, are said (112-3) to dwell in the Thought-Factory. Individually each is nothing more than a neutral statement of an attitude; but if they are brought together there is an immediate conflict between them and they dwell in a constant state of bickering (as Aristophanes will illustrate later in the play). Each of them will then strive to prove superior to the other and to convince hearers of the rightness of his own viewpoint; and so the λόγοι become, not mere statements, but statements with a persuasive purpose, i.e. arguments.[10] Likewise λέγειν means 'to state (neutrally) one's point of view'; but in a context of debate, where the purpose of this activity is to induce others to accept one's point of view (νικᾶν or πείθειν), it means 'to state one's point of view with a persuasive purpose', i.e. 'to argue'.

Aristophanes has complicated this situation by making a moral judgment upon it. For him, a way of arguing (λόγος) which shows the superiority of the stronger position is δίκαιος (= in accordance with δίκη), and one which shows the weaker position as superior is ἄδικος (= not in accordance with δίκη). Thus victory in debate is Right or Wrong according as the type of arguing used is δίκαιος or ἄδικος; and this is the meaning of 99, in which the words δίκαια κἄδικα should be taken ἀπὸ κοινοῦ with both λέγοντα and νικᾶν.

In debate, the κρείττων λόγος becomes a δίκαιος λόγος, and the ἥττων λόγος an ἄδικος λόγος. For, if the rules are obeyed (if Right be done) the stronger position will by definition be victorious in debate, so that naturally he will argue in accordance with Right (δίκαια λέγειν). The only chance of the weaker position is to dis-obey the rules and become an ἄδικος λόγος. Apparently the stron-ger position has no come-back if the weaker position adopts these tactics; as far as this play is concerned, arguing in a way contrary to Right always wins the victory. Granted that this is so,[11] the threat to δίκη is obvious; and it is with this that Aristophanes is concerned.

We must now return to the specific case of Strepsiades. In the two passages under discussion he is simply repeating what others have told him: he is not concerned to make on his own account moral judgments on the types of arguing involved. As a man of very little religion he has very little sense of δίκη either. It is immaterial to him whether these ways of arguing are in accordance with δίκη or not; he is concerned purely with his debts.

Now, concerning justly and legally incurred debts two opposing statements might be made: (a) that they should be paid back, and (b) that they should not. Of these the first is the κρείττων and the second the ἥττων λόγος. But according to Protagoras a skilful arguer could take position (b) and argue for it in such a way as to convince hearers of its rightness. This is the essence of Strepsiades' brilliantly clever scheme; for if the rightness of position (b) can be convincingly established, he will not have to pay his debts. Somewhere he has heard this type of arguing described as 'immoral' (cf. 115), but this has no influence on him. On the contrary, his whole scheme depends on learning this system, and he has no interest whatever in the other, 'moral', type (116-8, cf. 245, 657, 885).[12] Hence from the outset his whole enterprise is branded as morally wrong. Not to pay back one's debts is 'immoral'; and to learn a type of arguing which will enable one to achieve this end is 'immoral' as well. This, as we have already seen, is Strepsiades' basic sin to which he ultimately owes his punishment.

In the opening scene, then, Aristophanes has laid his foundations for the lesson he wishes to draw. The audience are assumed to be familiar with Protagoras' systems of arguing. Aristophanes sets before them a man who, though not a villain in the deep-dyed sense, is proposing to use one of these systems for a purpose which they would recognize as wholly immoral. The plot is thus nicely launched. Will Strepsiades be successful? Or will δίκη triumph?

The Interview with Socrates

Pheidippides having refused to have any part in the scheme, Strepsiades himself goes to the Thought-Factory and explains his wants to Socrates. He is not interested in arguing in accordance with the rules; it is τὸν ἕτερον λόγον, the 'immoral' type of arguing, that he is after (244-5). When he swears by the gods to give Socrates any fee he may exact, Socrates replies with a most important line and a half (247-8) which must again engage our attention (cf. p. 60).

The word πρῶτον (247) is important. The sentence which it introduces is Strepsiades' first lesson, and a moment's thought shows why this is so. It is basic to the whole position ascribed to Socrates in this play. So long as the traditional gods, with Zeus at their head, remain, the δίκη administered by Zeus will also remain and there will be a moral stigma against the type of arguing which Strepsiades wishes to learn which will inhibit its use: a person with moral scruples will not only never be able to use it but will not even be able to learn it properly. But if one can get rid of Zeus, then this transcendent moral law will cease to exist, the moral stigma on sophistic argument will be gone, and one will be left with two ways of arguing and nothing more. Each individual will then have a simple choice, uninhibited by any moral considerations, between the two in any given situation, and can freely choose whichever is most beneficial to himself at the time. Later in the play Aristophanes will demonstrate the type of situation this could lead to.

Aristophanes sees the natural science which has, to its own satisfaction, got rid of Zeus, as the source of this amorality. From their own point of view the sophists are not immoral but amoral: there is no δίκη, just as there is no Zeus, and hence they can feel free to argue in any way they like. But a man in whom any vestige of belief in Zeus remains will not be so free; and hence the non-existence of Zeus is the first lesson that must be learned in the sophistic training. Only when this moral freedom is obtained can the other studies follow. This is the reason why the non-existence of Zeus[13] is laboured at such length through the scientific arguing that takes place before and after the arrival of the clouds.[14] It is the reason why 423-6, where Strepsiades finally renounces entirely his belief in Zeus and the traditional gods,[15] are to be viewed as the climax of this early portion of the play: they make the rest of the play possible, and the action after the *parabasis* depends on them. And lastly it is the reason why the clouds, after Strepsiades has made this affirmation (and not before), are able to promise him that he will get what he wants (431).

Up to the point where the *parabasis* begins, then, δίκη is definitely coming off second best. Strepsiades' scheme, on the other hand, is proceeding smoothly.

The Contest between the two Λόγοι

After the *parabasis* Strepsiades' scheme strikes an unexpected snag (we have already seen why the exigencies of the plot made this necessary: p. 61): although the required basis (rejection of Zeus) has been laid, he simply is not sufficiently intelligent to learn the lessons required of him. He therefore persuades Pheidippides to go in his stead. At this point the two λόγοι are brought on to fight it out between themselves, ostensibly so that Pheidippides can choose between them, but really to give Aristophanes an opportunity of expanding on his idea of δίκη and his attitude to it in this play.

The two λόγοι are statements of two opposing views on life. One of them accepts a transcendent standard of morality: this is the κρείττων λόγος. The other rejects it (ἥττων λόγος).[16] In this scene they are brought together, and tension and bickering immediately results. The bickering is channelled by the chorus into a set debate.

Once the debate begins, the λόγοι become λόγοι in the other sense, as each seeks to put his viewpoint forward in a persuasive manner. The rules of the debate are set out in 935-8. The κρείττων λόγος, as always, will abide by the rules, and in debate becomes a δίκαιος λόγος; but the ἥττων λόγος, eager as always for victory, must become an ἄδικος λόγος. Hence he does not abide by the rules of the debate, but indulges his talent for making the worse appear the better cause and, inevitably, wins.

The two outlooks on the world embodied in the two λόγοι are the result of training and education in childhood. That is why the basic topic of debate in this contest is the difference between two systems of education: the old (producing δίκαιοι, people who recognize the existence of δίκη) and the new (producing ἄδικοι, who do not recognize the existence of δίκη). The basic question to be set before Pheidippides (and the audience) is: 'Here are two systems of education, producing two different sets of results. Which do you prefer?'

The κρείττων λόγος speaks first, and gives an idea of the sort of training he used to make his pupils undergo when there was no competition from other systems. It is a training which has as its end the instilling of σωφροσύνη (962), 'self-control'. The children were taught about the moral law (τὰ δίκαια λέγων: 962) and, knowing its demands, trained themselves to control their desires and passions so as to keep within it; i.e. they were taught to obey the rules, and that not only in moral matters but also in others such as music (969-71). This system achieved results: the men who fought at Marathon were its products (985-6). If Pheidippides would like to be fit and healthy in every respect, as they were, then let him, too, choose this system! So, in outline, runs the argument (961-1023).

It is then the turn of the ἥττων λόγος (1036-1104). He makes it

very clear from the outset that he is not going to obey the rules in
this debate. Not for him a systematic account of the type of training he represents; instead he intends simply, by clever conceits, to
score points off his rival's argument and so throw it into confusion.
Already before the debate he had given notice of his intention to do
this (942-4), and at the beginning of his speech-in-reply he states
the same intention (1036-7). His whole speech, he goes on to point
out, will be an illustration of the benefits which his type of training
will bring, and which are worth so much to him (1038-43).

After a preliminary skirmish about hot baths (1045-54) he comes
to the real core of the system advocated by the κρείττων λόγος, the
self-control (τὸ σωφρονεῖν: 1060) which it inculcates as its prin-
cipal virtue. Lines 1061-2 are the key to his approach:

Αδ.   ἐπεὶ σὺ διὰ τὸ σωφρονεῖν τῷ πώποτ' εἶδες ἤδη
         ἀγαθόν τι γενόμενον, φράσον, καί μ' ἐξέλεγξον εἰπών.

He goes on to show that self-control (a) never did anybody any
good, and (b) is actually disadvantageous, because it forces people
to miss pleasures to which they are by nature entitled. Furthermore,
he says, self-control is in any case pointless. Nothing that you do
can conflict with the moral law (δίκη) for (as he has already insisted: 902) there is no such law. Hence, if you indulge your
desires so freely as to break the civil law and get hauled before the
court as a result, you can defend yourself on the grounds that you
have not broken any moral rules (ὡς οὐδὲν ἠδίκηκας: 1080); for
your actions have been in acordance with personal expediency, and
that is the only moral law you recognize. And (this with much
irony) you can prove your point by observing that Zeus himself[17]
acts likewise (1080-2; cf. 904-6). In brief, then, his offer to Pheidippides is freedom to break the moral law with a clear conscience
(because there is no moral law) and to break the civil law with
impunity (because he will invariably be able to argue his way out
of any trouble). The result is moral anarchy; and this is precisely
the point which Aristophanes is driving at. The next scenes of the
play will show this moral anarchy in action.

In the last lines of the contest we see foreshadowed another point
which Aristophanes will be making later in the play. The menace
of this approach to the moral law is not static, but presents an
urgent and ever-increasing problem. Leave it alone for too long and
the old values will all have been irretrievably swallowed up in this
anarchy, just as the κρείττων λόγος here expresses himself convinced by the arguments of the ἥττων λόγος and ends by joining
him.

Moral Anarchy in Action

The two scenes with Strepsiades' creditors are a fairly obvious illustration of this moral anarchy in action. Δίκη here reaches its lowest point as Strepsiades' personal expediency reigns supreme. He goes to the ultimate length of breaking an oath sworn to the gods (1227) and, not content with that, mocks at the gods as well. It is a picture of a man acting with a complete lack of moral principle. It is a perfect example of ὕβρις.

Yet the audience might well be expected to feel a certain sympathy with Strepsiades at this point. He has succeeded in sending his creditors away with a flea in their ear; would that they could do the same! Perhaps there is something in this sophistic education after all! The possibility of this attitude must be firmly suppressed if the play is to have the effect its author intends; and the suppression is carried out (a) by the punishment of Strepsiades which immediately follows, and (b) by the far more terrible activities of Pheidippides, which are intended to produce an immediate revulsion of feeling.

The scene in which Strepsiades is beaten up by Pheidippides introduces a sort of second *agon*. The key lines here are 1331-3:

> Στ. τὸν πατέρα τύπτεις; Φε. κἀποφανῶ γε νὴ Δία
> ὡς ἐν δίκῃ σ᾽ ἔτυπτον. Στ. ὦ μιαρώτατε,
> καὶ πῶς γένοιτ᾽ ἂν πατέρα τύπτειν ἐν δίκῃ;

Δίκη here is used in two different senses, and the answer to Strepsiades' question depends entirely on which sort of δίκη is meant. Strepsiades uses it in the sense of a transcendent moral law; at long last he is beginning to realize (if only momentarily) that such a thing does exist. He is helped to this conclusion by simple ideas of self-preservation: for one of the transcendent moral laws requires reverence and respect for one's parents. For Pheidippides, on the other hand, such δίκη does not exist. His moral standard now is simply that of personal expediency, and he thinks of justice in the weakened sense of what we would describe as 'only fair'. He will proceed to prove in the *agon* that follows that it is 'only fair' that he should beat Strepsiades (1338-43); no amount of logic could ever prove that father-beating was just in the transcendental sense.

Just before the *agon* begins, Strepsiades confesses to a certain gloomy curiosity (1344):

> Στ. καὶ μὴν ὅ τι καὶ λέξεις ἀκοῦσαι βούλομαι.

But more than just gloomy curiosity is involved; for in fact a great deal hinges on what Pheidippides says. If he does not manage to give a convincing proof of his thesis, then that is the end of the matter; but if he does manage it the consequences for Strepsiades and for Athens in general will be very far-reaching. It will mean that Strepsiades can look forward to many years of punishment at his son's hand whenever he does something of which his son disapproves. It will mean that morality in the best sense of Athens' past years must go by the board and must be replaced by a debased type of justice founded on the principle of 'every man for himself'. This is, in fact, a test case; and if Pheidippides wins it then something will have to be done, or the outlook is bleak indeed.

In the *agon* Strepsiades has the stronger position, arguing that children should reverence and respect their parents. He puts his case as strongly as he can, pointing out the basis of gratitude for services rendered on which this respect should rest (1380-5). Pheidippides, in his defence, argues the weaker position. His main point, as we now expect, is 'fairness'. Strepsiades beat him when he was a boy; it is therefore 'only fair' that he should now beat Strepsiades. He uses δίκαιον in this sense of 'only fair' at 1405 and 1411; and he so succeeds in persuading Strepsiades of the rightness of his viewpoint that Strepsiades uses it in the same sense at 1437 and 1439. Strepsiades has lost that momentary vision which he had of that transcendental δίκη which would not allow all this to happen. Pheidippides has won.

His victory means that nothing in the moral sphere is now outlawed. Theft, murder, adultery, all can be justified quite as readily as Pheidippides has justified his treatment of his father. An audience which could look with an indulgent and sympathetic eye on a man who rid himself of his debts in this way cannot but be appalled when they consider the result of taking this type of approach to its logical conclusion. Yet the position seems hopeless. How has all this come about? What can be done to repair the damage? Strepsiades' repentance provides the answer. The old religion, with Zeus and a transcendent δίκη, takes care of all such matters. Hence in this moral crisis the claims of the old religion must be reasserted.

The Final Scene

The claims of the old religion are dramatically reasserted in the final scene of the play. Three things combine to drive the point home: the clouds' revelation of their true identity and function,

Strepsiades' repentance, and the burning of the Thought-Factory. There are moral ills in the state, and they are on the increase; but this is how to cure them. Man's safest rule for life lies with the old gods.

III. *Conclusion*

Hence Aristophanes' treatment of the conflict between science and religion is very much on a practical level. The criticism of science is not that it is atheistic, but that it is replacing the traditional gods with unsatisfactory substitutes. The unsatisfactory nature of these substitutes is most clearly to be seen in the field of the moral law; for, unlike Zeus, they impose no δίκη upon the world, and therefore leave man in a state of moral chaos. In such a case man's only moral standard would be his own individual expediency; and if at first sight that might seem to be not such a bad idea, on second thoughts the utter uselessness of such a debased standard of justice and morality becomes apparent. The solution is a reassertion of the claims of the traditional gods, and in particular of the Aeschylean δίκη administered by Zeus.

NOTES

1. Professor Blaiklock, whom we honour in this volume, is widely known for his religious, as well as his classical, writings. In this article, which pursues a religious theme through a famous work of classical antiquity, I seek to pay tribute to both these aspects of his achievement, to which I, in common with many others, am profoundly indebted.
2. I am assuming that our version of the play, which is the author's revision of an earlier version now lost, is sufficiently coherent to have a theme. C. H. Whitman (*Aristophanes and the Comic Hero,* (Harvard, 1964) ch. 4) writes: 'Interpretation of the *Clouds* is seriously hampered by the fact that our version is not the original one', and later: 'The parabasis alone . . . suffices to show that it [i.e. the surviving version] is an ill-adjusted mingling of earlier and later passages . . . . All these facts prompt the serious question of how far it is justifiable to attempt an interpretation of a play which may not, as it was left, represent the poet's wishes in any very clear way.' The interpretation in this article is offered as its own justification.

3. They are δαίμονες at 253, but θεοί at a key passage (423-4).

4. This is the consistency which, *pace* Dover (op. cit. p. xxxv), lies behind Socrates' brand of atheism: the whole point of his gods and divinities is that none of them is Zeus. See also n. 13 below.

5. The main task of conversion will, of course, fall on Socrates (cf. L. Strauss: *Socrates and Aristophanes* (New York, 1966), p. 50). But Strepsiades alone is responsible for getting Pheidippides to the Thought-Factory; and his reason is still the basic one from which all his sins stem, that of wanting to defraud his creditors: 882-5.

6. 'Many commentators have fancied that, in these scenes, we have illustrations of the sophistic art, which Strepsiades had wished— but in vain—to acquire, in order to escape the clutches of his creditors' (W. J. M. Starkie, *The Clouds of Aristophanes* (Macmillan, 1911), p. xx). Starkie goes on to point out, rightly, that 'there could be no greater misconception than this' (loc. cit.). In fact, Strepsiades' pseudo-sophistic language here is quite as ridiculous as it has been earlier; and at the end of the scenes he is quite as much in debt as before, and faces the prospect of legal action, not only for recovery of money, but probably for assault as well.

7. He has said precisely this at 1142-3, cf. 1211, 1228-9.

8. It also provides the explanation of the curious song addressed by the chorus to Socrates at 804-13. Strepsiades has been dismissed from the Thought-Factory; there must be no chance of Pheidippides suffering a similar exclusion, or the clouds' carefully laid scheme (as hinted in 813, they are deceiving Socrates as well as Strepsiades) would fall to the ground. Hence they play upon Socrates' mercenary instincts (as portrayed in this play) by urging him to make as much as possible out of Strepsiades by giving Pheidippides the full treatment.

9. The first hints of this surprise ending were given as far back as 813 (see n. 8 above) and 865.

10. In several places 'ways of arguing' is a closer equivalent. The extension of meaning is very slight.

11. Certainly Aristophanes has taken this for granted; and perhaps we are dealing here with one of those exaggerations which are an integral part of comic technique. It is necessary for the plot and does not affect the theme.

12. This, of course, makes him an unfair representative of Protagoras' teachings, but not of the type of use to which an unscrupulous person might put them.

13. For, if Zeus can be got rid of, it matters not what gods are set up in his place, for they have no δίκη involved with them. See also n. 4 above.

14. The passage dealing with lightning (395-406) is specially import-
    ant. Strepsiades had previously viewed this as Zeus' way of pun-
    ishing those who transgress a certain part of the transcendent
    moral law (τοὺς ἐπιόρκους: 397). By doing away with Zeus in
    his explanation, Socrates does away with such punishments as
    well. Hence the fact that Strepsiades *is* later punished helps to
    make him see things in their true light.
15. The presence of Chaos in the trinity which he vows to recognize
    is noteworthy. Chaos is a state in which, by definition, there are no
    rules of any sort, moral or other.
16. Cf. Dover's edition (op. cit.), in which the designations of the
    two characters are changed from the traditional δίκαιος and
    ἄδικος λόγος to κρείττων and ἥττων λόγος. This is strictly
    accurate.
17. We must distinguish here between Zeus the object of genuine wor-
    ship, who administers δίκη, and Zeus the god of mythology, who
    acts as if he had never heard of it. The ἥττων λόγος makes his
    point here and at 904-6 by implying (presumably from convic-
    tion) that the latter is the only Zeus. But it is with the former
    Zeus that Aristophanes is concerned in this play, and on a return
    to whom the moral welfare of the state depends.

ΓΡΑΦΗ ΣΥΚΟΦΑΝΤΙΑΣ

L. W. A. Crawley

When the Thirty had established themselves in control of Athens, one of their first acts was to rid the city of the sycophants. According to Lysias, they professed to be cleansing the city of criminals (τῶν ἀδίκων καθαρὰν ποιῆσαι τὴν πόλιν[1]). Xenophon records the action in this way: 'after making their arbitrary appointments to the Council and executive offices, they set about arresting and prosecuting on capital charges the men who were generally known as making a profession of sycophancy in the democracy and as being a thorn in the side of gentlemen of good standing. The Council was only too glad to condemn them, and no offence was given to anyone else whose conscience on that score was clear.'[2] In recording the same occasion Aristotle speaks of the Thirty as eliminating 'sycophants, and demagogues who were criminals and men of evil character'.[3] This was a welcome measure. Xenophon might be expected to approve: but even Lysias, though admittedly in a speech for a client who was anything but democratic, and admittedly in reference rather to sycophancy in politics, goes as far as to say: 'if the Thirty had confined themselves to punishing these, even you [i.e., the restored democrats] would have looked on them as good men.'[4]

This raises the question as to what a sycophant was, in the eyes of the law, and whether there was a specific crime which went by the name of sycophancy. If sycophancy was a crime, it could be punished in the courts; if it was not a crime, there could have been no such thing as a γραφὴ συκοφαντίας. Authorities are not as explicit on this point as when Kennedy confidently wrote: 'There was a γραφὴ συκοφαντίας tried before the Thesmothetae. Any person who brought a false charge against another, or extorted money by threat of legal proceedings, or suborned false witnesses, or engaged in a conspiracy to ruin the character of an innocent man, was liable to this γραφή. He might be proceeded against by φάσις, ἔνδειξις, ἀπαγωγή, προβολή or εἰσαγγελία:' and so on. This is in fact a tissue of imagination, hindsight and false deduction from the sources. R. J. Bonner says 'Among the direct measures taken against sycophancy were γραφὴ συκοφαντίας, εἰσαγγελία, and προβολή.'⁵ The requirements for compression in a short article have made this a more categorical pronouncement than is altogether consistent with the more cautious and argued treatment in Bonner and Smith.⁶ But even here the conclusion is that the γραφὴ συκοφαντίας did exist. J. O. Lofberg, *Sycophancy in Athens*,⁷ provides the material for Bonner and Smith, who in their turn are quoted as authorities on the point. The latest instance I have noticed is D. Macdowell in his edition of Andocides, *On the Mysteries*:⁸ 'A γραφὴ συκοφαντίας could be brought against a prosecutor who failed to obtain one-fifth of the votes' (ad § 7); 'The introduction of . . . the γραφὴ συκοφαντίας does not seem to have been very effective in checking the practice' (ad § 86). The second of these notes is true; on the first, though there is evidence for the punishment incurred by a prosecutor who failed to secure one-fifth of the votes, there is no evidence that the punishment arose from a γραφὴ συκοφαντίας. Rather it is taken for granted that this punishment was incurred automatically. Demosthenes LVIII.12 cites a law by which the penalty was prescribed.

The chief evidence for the existence of a γραφὴ συκοφαντίας is as follows:

(1) Isocrates XV.313-314: Σόλωνα μὲν γάρ, τὸν πρῶτον τῶν πολιτῶν λαβόντα τὴν ἐπωνυμίαν ταύτην [sc. σοφιστήν], προστάτην ἠξίωσαν τῆς πόλεως εἶναι, περὶ δὲ τῶν συκοφαντῶν χαλεπωτέρους ἢ περὶ τῶν ἄλλων κακουργιῶν τοὺς νόμους ἔθεσαν. τοῖς μὲν γὰρ μεγίστοις τῶν ἀδικημάτων ἐν ἑνὶ τῶν δικαστηρίων τὴν κρίσιν ἐποίησαν, κατὰ δὲ τούτων γραφὰς μὲν πρὸς τοὺς θεσμοθέτας, εἰσαγγελίας δ' εἰς τὴν βουλήν, προβολὰς δ' ἐν τῷ δήμῳ, νομίζοντες τοὺς ταύτῃ τῇ τέχνῃ χρωμένους ἁπάσας ὑπερβάλλειν τὰς πονηρίας.

Whether the anachronisms in this passage invalidate it as evidence at all is a question which for the moment can be left unanswered. The existence of three methods of proceeding against sycophancy, namely, γραφή, εἰσαγγελία, and προβολή, is ascribed by Isocrates to the fact that sycophants exceed all criminals in villainy: so that Athens allows three ways of attacking them. Isocrates' fifteenth oration is ostensibly directed against a sycophant. The suggestion that there are three methods of dealing with sycophancy could in fact be taken as indicating that there was no one single effective way: that sycophancy was less susceptible to identification and definition than, say, murder: that it was not a crime in itself, which could be dealt with by the appropriate court, but a practice which might be associated with a number of specific crimes for which there were recognized courts. Sycophants might be, and frequently were, charged with crime for which their prosecutors proceeded by γραφή, εἰσαγγελία, or προβολή. The establishment of sycophantic motives in the accused was a regular and expected element in the prosecution's case, and so sycophancy was a familiar charge in council, ecclesia and dicastery. But it is not proved to have been an indictable offence. It certainly was, however, what Isocrates calls it, a τέχνη.

(2) Aristotle, *Ath. Pol.* XLIII.5: ἐπὶ δὲ τῆς ἕκτης πρυτανείας πρὸς τοῖς εἰρημένοις καὶ περὶ τῆς ὀστρακοφορίας ἐπιχειροτονίαν διδόασιν [sc. οἱ πρυτανεύοντες] εἰ δοκεῖ ποιεῖν ἢ μή, καὶ συκοφαντῶν προβολὰς τῶν Ἀθηναίων καὶ τῶν μετοίκων μέχρι τριῶν ἑκατέρων, κἄν τις ὑποσχόμενός τι μὴ ποιήσῃ τῷ δήμῳ.

This passage mentions, not a γραφὴ συκοφαντίας but a προβολή, and is included here for its relevance to the connexion between a γραφή and a προβολή, which is discussed below. But it introduces a further point which may have some significance. Metics are included among the sycophants, and there is a third group of people who stood in danger of being subject to προβολή, namely, κἄν τις ὑποσχόμενός τι μὴ ποιήσῃ τῷ δήμῳ. The fact that the latter are clearly distinguished from sycophants (otherwise we should require κἄν τις ἄλλος . . .) weakens Bonner and Smith's suggestion that sycophants might have been held liable under 'the ancient law cited by Demosthenes (XX.100): ἔστι δὲ δήπου νόμος ὑμῖν, ἐάν τις ὑποσχόμενός τι τὸν δῆμον ἢ βουλὴν ἢ δικαστήριον ἐξαπατήσῃ, τὰ ἔσχατα πάσχειν'.[6] But Bonner and Smith do not regard this law as originally aimed at the sycophant, since 'at the time of the drafting of the law the sycophant was not as yet a problem.'[9] In any case, certain areas of the sycophant's activity, e.g., blackmail and intimidation, need never have reached demos, council or law-court. This provision could never have touched such practitioners.

The questions associated in this passage with sycophancy, namely, ostracism and deception of the people, are political in the broadest sense. This suggests that the sycophancy here in mind is also of a political nature, as indeed one would expect with a προβολή. The presence of metics in the list of those against whom proceedings are taken on a political question becomes intriguing. The metics, as far as we know, by their exclusion from full citizenship, were also excluded from personally bringing cases before the dicasteries. They could therefore not be classed as sycophants in the popular sense of the word. The sycophants who were *Athenians*, against whom Aristotle mentions προβολαί being brought, are not the petty characters who subsist on mischief-making, so familiar from Aristophanes and the orators. They were men prominent in public life. No others would be candidates for ostracism or liable to embarrassment for failing to fulfil promises made to the people. Nonentities would not make promises, or would not be taken seriously if allowed to do so. Who then were the *metic* sycophants? In order to be grouped with the citizen sycophants as potential targets of προβολή, they would presumably also be prominent characters, in social, if not in political, life. Such people were normally the victims of sycophancy, not its practitioners. It follows that in this passage συκοφαντῶν must have the significance which it frequently has in Isocrates and not infrequently elsewhere, that of political intriguers. The prominent metics, though debarred from holding office and exercising direct political power, were none the less so much a force to be reckoned with that provisions were made to deal with them officially in the sixth prytany: but their influence operated not through sycophancy in any of the commonly accepted senses. It was their commercial power, operating through their trading and banking activities, which emphasized not only their importance to the community but also the threat they posed if allied with the enemies of democracy. The wealthy metics, except a few like the family of Lysias whose wealth derived from munitions (and perhaps even these), stood to lose if trade were disrupted by war. The citizen-Athenian enemies of democracy, predominantly property owners or aristocrats or both, were likewise averse from war. A combination of the two groups in a time of crisis could be embarrassing for the democracy. It looks as if the sixth prytany provided yet another opportunity for guarding against oligarchy. Sycophancy, or, in more euphemistic terms, the right of whoever wished to institute proceedings against the wrongdoer, was one of the cornerstones of democracy. That a provision of a democratic nature, such as that cited by Aristotle, allows for proceeding against sycophants indicates that sycophancy here is to be regarded in a special sense, and that a γραφὴ συκοφαντίας, if one is to be inferred from this passage, is not the sort of thing that would have a broadly deterrent effect on sycophancy as a whole, which it is claimed was the aim of the γραφή.

(3) Pollux VIII.46: προβολαὶ δὲ ἦσαν καὶ αἱ τῆς συκοφαντίας γραφαί.

This is not an equation of the A = B type: nor is it to describe a γραφὴ συκοφαντίας as merely one of the things which are προβολαί. The spheres in which the two processes are concerned are different. A προβολή is heard in the ecclesia, a γραφή in a dicastery: and though the ecclesia might on rare occasions in its sovereign role assume the functions of the dicastery which it normally allowed to represent it, there is no qualification to say that such was the case here. Προβολή denotes the practice of 'presenting' to the ecclesia the names of those against whom one might subsequently bring a formal prosecution, presumably with a general indication of the proposed charge, and asking for something in the nature of a vote of no confidence in the people so 'presented'. It was not a trial, and the vote of the ecclesia had no penal validity. If the vote favoured the potential prosecutor, he had a stronger case to bring to court, and presumably a jury to some extent prejudiced in his favour. The προβολή was non-technical, almost unofficial. In such a proceeding a man might be presented as guilty of sycophancy, not as a specific crime, but as a dishonest and self-interested way of achieving a particular end which might itself be criminal. If the ecclesia supported the contentions of the προβάλλων, he might institute a prosecution, not, however, for sycophancy, but for the specific crime involved. Pollux' statement should be interpreted: 'Likewise the (so-called) prosecutions for sycophancy (i.e., those which the tradition has recorded as γραφαί) were (in reality) προβολαί', i.e., Pollux is denying that the term γραφὴ συκοφαντίας is accurate, and maintaining that the actions against sycophancy, which the tradition has assumed were γραφαί, are wrongly so named, since they were nothing more than προβολαί.

(4) Aeschines II.145: τῶν δὲ συκοφαντῶν ὡς κακούργων δημοσίᾳ προβολὰς ποιούμεθα.

This sentence can reasonably be regarded as supporting the interpretation of Pollux' statement above. In the context Aeschines is developing a rhetorical and forced contrast between φήμη and συκοφαντία, saying all the good he can of φήμη and all the bad of συκοφαντία. Of φήμη he says, finally, that to her, as to a goddess, the Athenians officially make sacrifice. To balance this, as the severest condemnation of συκοφαντία, he says that the Athenians allow themselves προβολαί against sycophants as against malefactors. Either, then, a προβολή is to be regarded as a harsher procedure than a γραφή, which is at least unlikely, since it carried no sentence; or there was no provision for a γραφὴ συκοφαντίας; otherwise Aeschines would have cited γραφή as the culminating mark of disapproval against the sycophants.

(5) Lysias XIII.65 (establishing the destructive character of Agoratos): περὶ δὲ συκοφαντίας, ὅσας οὗτος ἢ δίκας ἰδίας συκοφαντῶν ἐδικάζετο ἢ γραφὰς ὅσας ἐγράφετο ἢ ἀπογραφὰς ἀπέγραφεν, οὐδέν με δεῖ καθ᾽ ἕκαστον λέγειν· συλλήβδην γὰρ ὑμεῖς ἅπαντες καὶ ἐν τῷ δήμῳ καὶ ἐν τῷ δικαστηρίῳ συκοφαντίας αὐτοῦ κατέγνωτε . . .

For his purpose of the moment Lysias does not restrict himself to technical accuracy, and his expression is loose. The phrase συκοφαντίας αὐτοῦ κατέγνωτε indicates a verdict which would be reached ἐν τῷ δικαστηρίῳ, not ἐν τῷ δήμῳ. Admittedly, as pointed out above, the sovereign ecclesia had the power to take over the function of the jury which acted as its committee in judicial matters, but its doing so would make the occasion a *cause célèbre*, and Lysias would hardly have missed the opportunity here of underlining the gravity of an offence for whose punishment the ecclesia had assumed responsibility instead of following the usual practice of entrusting it to a dicastery. For whatever Agoratos was condemned, he was not condemned ἐν τῷ δήμῳ. The presence of the phrase ἐν τῷ δήμῳ suggests that here we have an instance of a προβολή in the ecclesia preceding a γραφή in the dicastery. If Lysias' audience is prepared to accept this trifling inaccuracy, or rather condensation (συλλήβδην), it would also go as far as to understand that, when Lysias names sycophancy as the charge upon which Agoratos was condemned, he means that the charge was something more specific, like παρανομία for instance, that sycophancy was a prominent factor accompanying παρανομία, and that sycophancy rather than παρανομία is cited in this passage because it is sycophancy which Lysias is trying to demonstrate in his description of the character and career of Agoratos.

(6) Demosthenes XXV.19: τί γὰρ ἂν γένοιτο συκοφαντίας καὶ παρανομίας δεινότερον, ἐφ᾽ οἷς ἀμφοτέροις οὗτος ὤφληκεν;

We might interpret συκοφαντίας καὶ παρανομίας as 'sycophantic illegality', but we are prevented from taking the phrase as a hendiadys by ἀμφοτέροις in the relative clause. "Ἀμφοτέροις,, however, rather than ἑκατέροις, does suggest that the two concepts, συκοφαντία and παρανομία, form a pair, each member of which would be expected to accompany the other. That is, in the case of Aristogiton, παρανομία is inevitably accompanied by συκοφαντία, so that when he is prosecuted for παρανομία, the judgment also involves condemnation for the attendant συκοφαντία, as in the Lysias passage above. The context does not, however, necessarily mean that Aristogiton has in fact appeared in a dicastery and been condemned for συκοφαντία and παρανομία. Certainly ὀφλισκάνω may mean to be the actual loser in a legal action, and so to be liable for the penalty resulting from the defeat: but it can equally well mean to lay oneself open to certain charges, without implying that the charges have actually been brought or that any sentence has been imposed. There is no need to imagine a γραφὴ συκοφαντίας on the strength of the question Demosthenes here puts.

(7) Demosthenes LVIII.12: ἀκούετε τῶν νόμων, ἃ κελεύουσι πάσχειν ὦ ἄνδρες δικασταὶ τὸν συκοφάντην.

This sentence immediately follows the citation of a law in the prosecution of Theocrines, which apparently prescribes the punishment to be inflicted on a sycophant, but whose terms have not been preserved. The word συκοφάντην is, however, not to be interpreted as the perpetrator of an illegal action, namely, συκοφαντία. It is a derogatory word replacing the person referred to in the previous context by a participle, τὸν συκοφαντοῦντα τοὺς ἐμπόρους καὶ τοὺς ναυκλήρους, and in the later context by the plural participle οἱ συκοφαντοῦντες. In other words, it indicates, not in itself a criminal, but a person who has an attitude, or employs a method, in this as in many instances, for committing a crime. He is ταύτῃ τῇ τέχνῃ χρώμενος, in Isocrates' phrase. Demosthenes is dealing at this point with legislation protecting merchants and ships' captains from pettifogging litigation. The 'crime' in this instance, which is accompanied by συκοφαντία, or committed by συκοφαντῶν τις, is that of failing to secure one-fifth of the votes of the jury. The penalty for this failure was a fine of 1,000 drachmas and the deprivation of certain citizen privileges. That this failure was the 'crime' in question here is proved by the twice-repeated mention of αἱ χίλιαι in the context, on each occasion the presence of the definite article indicating the established, recognized, penalty, not for sycophancy, but for failure to secure one-fifth of the votes. Unless sycophancy is this failure (and there is no evidence of such a specific and restricted definition), this passage in Demosthenes should put us on our guard if an orator mentions a penalty and says it was for sycophancy.

The peculiar feature about the law cited here by Demosthenes was that, in an effort to make it more difficult for mischief-makers to cripple trade, legislation made the unsuccessful prosecutor of merchants and captains, if he failed to secure one-fifth of the votes, not only liable to the fine of 1,000 drachmas, but faced with arrest, either summarily (ἀπαγωγή) or as a result of information laid (ἔνδειξις). Since the fine rested, not on συκοφαντία, but on dismal failure in the prosecution, it is reasonable to suppose that in this law specially framed for the merchants an additional penalty was prescribed for the same 'offence', namely, failure to secure one-fifth of the votes, not for an additional offence, namely, sycophancy. If sycophancy had officially been regarded as a crime, to be pursued by a γραφὴ συκοφαντίας, there would have been no need for this special legislation safeguarding the merchants. In the following context (§ 23) Demosthenes writes: 'εἰ μὲν ἑώρων ἐν τοῖς ἀνεγνωσμένοις νόμοις γεγραμμένον "ταῦτα δ' εἶναι κύρια περὶ τῶν συκοφαντούντων, ἂν μὴ . . . "' The use of the participle συκοφαντούντων supports what has been said above. He could equally well have expressed his meaning by τῶν ταύτη τῇ τέχνη χρωμένων.

(8) Aristotle, *Ath. Pol.* LIX.3: εἰσὶ δὲ καὶ γραφαὶ πρὸς αὐτοὺς [sc. τοὺς θεσμοθέτας] ὧν παράστασις τίθεται, ξενίας καὶ δωροξενίας (ἄν τις δῶρα δοὺς ἀποφύγῃ τὴν ξενίαν) καὶ συκοφαντίας καὶ δώρων καὶ ψευδεγγραφῆς καὶ ψευδοκλητείας καὶ ἀγραφίου καὶ μοιχείας.

This is the most unequivocal statement we have of the existence of a γραφὴ συκοφαντίας. But in this list of offences which might be the subject of a γραφή it does look as if συκοφαντία is the odd-man-out. All the other offences are specific and of such a nature that they could be readily proved to a jury if adequate evidence were offered. Athenian juries admittedly placed undue weight on circumstantial evidence and arguments from probability, where modern juries would demand factual evidence. But in a prosecution for ξενία, for example, a demonstration that the defendant's father was undoubtedly a foreigner would leave no doubt in the mind of a jury about the correct verdict: and factual evidence of this character was possible in connexion with all the other offences in Aristotle's list; whereas the hypothetical prosecutor for sycophancy could hardly hope to establish such conclusive proof of his contention. The other offences are related to acts committed, whereas sycophancy deals with attitudes, motives and methods. The other offences are susceptible to legal definition. Sycophancy is not. It is curious, and perhaps significant, that this section in which Aristotle is describing the duties of the thesmothetae is immediately preceded by a sentence which indicates the activity of these officials in connexion with προβολαί. The association, and possible confusion, of γραφαί and προβολαί has been noticed above: and there is at least a possibility that what should have been included in the sentence dealing with προβολαί has found its way into the list of γραφαί.

The foregoing provide the more obvious apparently positive evidence for the recognition of sycophancy as a specific crime, to be proceeded against by means of a γραφή. The negative evidence for its non-recognition is very strong. Apart from the dubious cases of Agoratos and Aristogiton which have been discussed above,[10] there is no record of any individual having been condemned, or even prosecuted in a dicastery, on a charge of sycophancy, though it is apparently to be recognized that general charges of sycophantic activity might form the basis of a προβολή. Some instances of occasions when, on the evidence presented, the charge, if legally available, would have been appropriate are discussed below.

The problem which would have faced an Athenian who wished to establish a law under which a γραφὴ συκοφαντίας might be instituted, and the problem which also faces us, is the definition of συκοφαντία. The origin of the term need not concern us, though it might be helpful to know what the original συκοφάντης was. Such knowledge might establish the principle out of which grew the very widespread practice of classical times. But the variety of manifestations of the sycophancy noticed, e.g., in the comic writers and the orators, indicates that the Athenians themselves used the term without any consciousness of its root meaning. Kennedy's definition is well known: a sycophant is a 'happy compound of the common barrator, informer, pettifogger, busybody, rogue, liar, and slanderer'. This of course is not really a definition but an attempt at a comprehensive description of characteristics of the Athenian sycophant at large. Certainly no legislator in his senses would attempt to frame a law under which a person of this description could be charged. Any one of the accusations would be difficult to establish, and in any case some would not involve a crime. An informer might have been a perfectly honest man, and democracy itself was regarded as resting on the activity of men who were in some sense busybodies. Aeschines II.145 has been quoted as supplying a definition: συκοφαντία δ' ἐστίν, ὅταν πρὸς τοὺς πολλοὺς εἷς ἀνὴρ αἰτίαν ἐμβαλών, ἐν τε ταῖς ἐκκλησίαις ἁπάσαις πρός τε τὴν βουλὴν διαβάλλῃ τινά. This, however, is only to give one manifestation of sycophancy, namely, slander, and to say that it is sycophancy. The practice was much wider than this. The levels of sycophantic activity also vary very widely. In the high political sphere a man might attack Demosthenes for his anti-Macedonian policy. If he did this from disinterested motives, he might be a patriot: if his sole motive was the retainer he received from Philip, he qualified for the charge of sycophant. In internal politics Isocrates repeatedly uses the term of people whom he regards as unscrupulous demagogues. His reactionary attitude was unjustified when honesty accompanied a democratic programme. At the other end of the scale the charge of sycophancy might be levelled against an opponent suspected of sophistry in argument, as, for example, Thrasymachos accuses Socrates of being a sycophant.[11] He shortly afterwards describes συκοφαντεῖν as ἐξ ἐπιβουλῆς ἐν τοῖς λόγοις κακουργεῖν.[12] This mild interpretation of sycophancy as sharp practice, or deliberate trickery, either in argument or for the purpose of securing some dishonest advantage, is the one which developed in New Comedy. In Plautus the synonyms of *sycophantia*, are *fallacia, doli, perfidia, mendacia*. But for the ordinary Athenian the term sycophancy, when applied in its full sense, implied activity connected with the dicasteries: and perhaps a definition acceptable to him would have been: 'a sycophant is one who uses legal process, or threatens to use it, not to secure justice, but for his personal advantage.' In terms of this conception a man could be a temporary sycophant for one specific purpose, as we might suspect Callicles was in his efforts to gain possession of the farm of his neighbour:[13] but the real sycophants, οἱ συκοφάνται with the definite article, were those who made a profession of it. Their existence is clearly recognized. Isocrates has a recurring phrase, ὁ προῃρημένος συκοφαντεῖν, one who has deliberately taken up sycophancy as a way of life. In Xenophon Theramenes applauds the action of the Thirty in ridding the city of τοὺς ὁμολογουμένως συκοφάντας, a group previously described as οὓς πάντες ᾔδεσαν ἐν τῇ δημοκρατίᾳ ἀπὸ συκοφαντίας ζῶντας.[14] Isocrates speaks of οἱ συκοφαντικῶς βεβιωκότες,[15] Demosthenes of ζῶντες ἐκ τοῦ συκοφαντεῖν[16] and Aristophanes' sycophant in the *Birds* says παππῷος ὁ βίος συκοφαντεῖν ἐστί μοι.[17] Though Athenians might not have known just what sycophancy was, they would in many cases have agreed on who was a sycophant, i.e., not merely συκοφαντῶν τις, but a member of οἱ συκοφάνται. If then there was a recognized group of such men, and if their activity made life uncomfortable and even intolerable in Athens, it should not have been beyond Athenian wit to devise measures of thwarting or at least curbing them. The threat of a γραφὴ συκοφαντίας might have met the situation. But there were serious obstacles.

Freedom to prosecute was firmly associated with Solonian democracy. In Solon's reorganization Aristotle lists three features which he regards as δημοτικώτατα.[18] Two of these are in point: first, the right of appeal to a dicastery (ἡ εἰς τὸ δικαστήριον ἔφεσις), which Aristotle says is the basic provision maintaining the power of the people, and, secondly, the right of anyone who wished to take up cudgels on behalf of those suffering injury (τὸ ἐξεῖναι τῷ βουλομένῳ τιμωρεῖν ὑπὲρ τῶν ἀδικουμένων). These constitute the platform of the sycophant. He posed as the watchdog of democracy. Theophrastos' φιλοπόνηρος describes him as 'watchdog of the people, for he keeps an eye on criminals; we shan't have people who will help us in toiling for the common welfare if we throw men like him overboard.'[19] Demosthenes refers to the same metaphor, but adds that the sycophant refuses to bite those whom he accuses of being wolves, and devours the sheep he claims to protect.[20] Elsewhere he chides the jury for putting up with people who maintain that ἡ τοῦ δήμου σωτηρία διὰ τῶν γραφομένων καὶ συκοφαντούντων ἐστίν.[21] Lycurgus makes perhaps the strongest plea on their behalf, though he naturally does not call them sycophants: 'it is beneficial for the city to have within it men who prosecute transgressors of the laws . . . ; but the man who risks his personal security and incurs unpopularity on behalf of the general welfare gets a reputation, not for patriotism, but for officiousness . . . ; neither the law nor the verdict of the court has any value in the absence of a man to present transgressors to them.'[22] Antiphon's client illustrates what appears to be an honest application of this principle.[23] On two occasions he has detected misuse of public funds and has instituted proceedings against the officials concerned. The verdict of guilty secured on both occasions and the efforts to block him each time make it appear that he was a public-spirited citizen doing his duty. On the other hand, his opponent Philocrates is charged (§ 43) with dishonestly harrying magistrates at their εὔθυναι. Here, on the face of it, we have two men doing approximately the same thing, but with different motives. It is not the thing they do which constitutes sycophancy, but their reason for doing it. Something of the same situation is indicated in Aeschines I.32: ἐὰν δέ τις... συκοφαντῇ καὶ ἀσελγαίνῃ, καὶ μηκέτι τὸν τοιοῦτον ἄνθρωπον δύνηται φέρειν ἡ πόλις, 'δοκιμασίαν μέν', φησίν [sc. ὁ νομοθέτης] ἐπαγγειλάτω 'Αθηναίων ὁ βουλόμενος, οἷς ἔξεστιν,' ὑμᾶς δ' ἤδη κελεύει περὶ τούτων ἐν τῷ δικαστηρίῳ διαγιγνώσκειν· καὶ νῦν ἐγὼ κατὰ τοῦτον τὸν νόμον ἥκω πρὸς ὑμᾶς. In the opening paragraph of this speech against Timarchos Aeschines claims that he himself is ἰδίᾳ συκοφαντούμενος. Yet he does not make sycophancy the formal basis of his charge, but attacks Timarchos in a δοκιμασία. This of course does not prove that he could not equally well have relied on a γραφὴ συκοφαντίας. Since Aeschines defeated Timarchos, it looks as if the jury at least regarded the allegations made as true. If so, Aeschines had material for bringing a γραφὴ συκοφαντίας, for which the penalty would presumably have been much more severe than the comparatively light disabilities suffered by a man defeated at a δοκιμασία. In the case of Timarchos, who, it appears, would have been the ideal target under a γραφὴ συκοφαντίας, a milder course is pursued. As in so many instances, συκοφαντία is tossed in with other vague general charges, like ἀσέλγεια or πονηρία, to establish the wickedness of the opponent's character.

Perhaps the other two men against whom the most vicious accusations of sycophancy were made, and who were yet prosecuted not for sycophancy but on other charges, were Aristogiton and Theocrines. It is instructive to analyse the activities which the orators labelled as sycophancy in them.

For Aristogiton the evidence comes from Demosthenes and Dinarchus. The charges made by the orators are not of course necessarily true, but they suggest what might be accepted by the jury as involving sycophancy. Taking the Demosthenic speech seriatim: 'Aristogiton is chief of the beasts who are τόλμαν καὶ κραυγὴν καὶ ψευδεῖς αἰτίας καὶ συκοφαντίαν καὶ ἀναισχυντίαν καὶ πάντα τὰ τοιαῦτα συνεσκευασμένοι (§ 9).' Here συκοφαντία is cited in a list on a level with other undesirable activities or qualities. Yet no one suggests that there existed, for example, a γραφὴ ἀναισχυντίας. 'He is anti-democratic and subversive (§ 32).' 'There are no altars established ἀναισχυντίας οὐδὲ συκοφαντίας οὐδ' ἐπιορκίας οὐδ' ἀχαριστίας, all attributes of Aristogiton (§ 35).' Again notice the non-indictable offences of the list in which sycophancy occurs. 'Aristogiton has brought seven γραφαί against the speaker, hiring himself out to Philip's supporters, and has twice accused him at his εὔθυναι. All these attempts have failed—ἀεὶ συκοφαντῶν ἠλέγχου (§ 37).' But there is no threat of prosecuting him for sycophancy. 'Aristogiton speaks in the courts though legally debarred from doing so. He has prosecuted a coppersmith, a tanner, etc., neglecting the politicians whom it was his duty to attack in his capacity of watchdog of the democracy (§§ 38, 40).' 'Unsuccessful in the assembly, in the face of the united Athenians, he attacks them one by one in the courts; but he avoids the recognized speakers and attacks only the inexperienced rank and file, his purpose being to make money (§ 41).' 'He will claim that because he is so useful to the city he should not be condemned (§ 42).' 'He is πονηρὸς ἁπλῶς καὶ πικρὸς καὶ συκοφάντης (§ 45)'—again note the associations which are not technically criminal. Πονηρία is in fact the quality most commonly associated with, and apparently regarded as in the same class as, συκοφαντία. 'Aristogiton is a trafficker in πονηρία, and all but brings scales and weights for the purpose of selling his services to the highest bidder (§ 46).' 'He "sold" the impeachment of Hegemon, abandoned the prosecution of Demades, made all manner of charges against Agathon and then acquiesced in his release, and instigated an impeachment against Democles and then mishandled it (§ 47).' 'Βοῶν, συκοφαντῶν, ἀπειλῶν οὐκ ἐπαύετο (§ 49)'—unpleasant associations again, but not criminal. 'He would have accepted a small sum to desist from his ranting attack on the generals (§ 50).' 'He cannot point to any trade or profession he follows (§ 51),' that is, he is one of οἱ συκοφάνται, one of οἱ ζῶντες ἐκ τοῦ συκοφαντεῖν. 'Is he not a villain? οὐκ ἀσεβής; οὐκ ὠμός; οὐκ ἀκάθαρτος; οὐ συκοφάντης; (§ 63).' 'He is always protesting in the assembly that others are treacherous conspirators, and that he is the only friend of democracy (§ 64).' 'He has been rejected from office, convicted of illegal action (παρανόμων) and fined five talents (§§ 67-8).' The circumstances of this latter offence are given in the hypothesis to the speech and referred to by Dinarchus.[24] Aristogiton brought a lying accusation against the priestess of Artemis Brauronia and her family. At a subsequent trial his accusers made the truth known and Aristogiton was fined. The five talents mentioned above (§ 68) was the sum set down for a γραφὴ παρανόμων. This was therefore presumably the charge, not sycophancy, though Aristogiton's action was a plain instance of sycophancy. 'The misfortunes of others are Aristogiton's bread and butter (§ 82).' 'He nominated death as the penalty for the targets of his sycophancy, even before the vote on guilty or not was

taken: but he did not secure one-fifth of the votes (§ 83).' This
latter failure was regarded as the clearest indication of irresponsible
prosecution. Yet there is no hint that anyone proceeded against
Aristogiton under a γραφὴ συκοφαντίας. 'Aristogiton all but rings
a bell to draw attention to actions which other men try to conceal
(§ 90).' This is a characteristic of the professional sycophant. He
must advertise his activities in order to be more successful in his
blackmail of potential victims.[25]

Dinarchus adds some details to this picture.[26] He says that
'Aristogiton has spent more time in gaol than out, and even when
in gaol had been caught stealing (§§ 2, 12).' 'He went to gaol διὰ
πονηρίαν (§ 9),' obviously not a specific charge, any more than
συκοφαντία is. 'He appears in court relying on προφάσεις and
φενακισμοί (§ 4).'

The picture drawn by the two orators is inevitably too highly
coloured, but we are entitled to conclude that Aristogiton really
was a professional sycophant, ζῶν ἐκ τοῦ συκοφαντεῖν. As such he
could have been proceeded against by a γραφὴ συκοφαντίας, if it
had been available: but he is prosecuted for being an insolvent public debtor and for exercising citizen rights to which he is not
entitled until the debt is paid.

The Theocrines of Demosthenes LVIII, on the showing of the
speaker Epichares, is likewise a professional sycophant who com-
bines political activity with private actions for gain. 'Though under
civil disabilities, he persists illegally in sycophantic proceedings
against many citizens (§ 2).' 'He has persuaded Epichares' supporters to abandon him (§ 4; cf. § 59).' 'He is πολλαῖς ἐνδείξεσιν
ἔνοχος (§ 5),' though sycophancy is not specified as an offence for
which he runs a risk of ἔνδειξις or γραφή. 'He laid an information
on a mercantile matter but did not carry the case through because
he was bribed by the defendant (§ 6).' 'He is supported by others
of his ilk, who have tampered with Epichares' witnesses, using
threats and persuasion (§ 7; cp. §§ 39-40, 44).' 'He makes a practice of prosecuting by a γαρφὴ παρανόμων, though in his admitted
position of debtor to the state he is legally debarred from doing
so (§ 14).' 'He will claim that he is being victimized by those who
wish to avoid his γραφαὶ παρανόμων (§ 22; cp. § 36).' 'After his
brother's murder Theocrines sought out the murderers and came to
terms with them, for a consideration (§ 28).' 'Securing a reputation as a public-spirited man by his prosecution of Epichares'
father in a case concerning an orphan, he proceeded against another
man whom he alleged to have been in collusion with Epichares'

father, but abandoned the charge for a consideration, betraying the orphan for 200 dr. (§ 32).' 'If Epichares' father had been wealthy enough to buy off Theocrines with 1,000 dr., he would have escaped the γραφὴ παρανόμων (§ 33).' 'Theocrines claims to keep an eye on those who propose illegal legislation (cp. § 45), and maintains that when γραφαὶ παρανόμων are defeated the democracy is shaken. In spite of that he has been bought off many times for small sums (§ 34)'; 'for example, he accepted 1½ minae in connexion with a decree about Tenedos (§ 35).' 'The defection of Aenos to Philip is due to his sycophantic activity (§ 37).' 'The sycophants make a public showing of mutual animosity, but they are really hand in glove (§§ 39-40; cf. 44), and Epichares is compelled to contend with τὰς τούτων ἑταιρείας (§ 42).' This again points to a recognized group, οἱ συκοφάνται, though I should not go as far as Lofberg[27] and interpret ἑταιρείας literally, on the assumption that sycophants organized themselves into formal societies for mutual protection and assistance. 'Theocrines had brought an accusation παρανόμων against Demosthenes (§ 43)', but by a fiddle which was apparently technically legal he had allowed the trial to be adjourned and never resumed, presumably because he had been bought off. 'People like Theocrines do not speak in the assembly, but get money by prosecuting politicians (§ 62).' 'Sycophants claim that they get no payment from the state, but that the salvation of the democracy depends on them (§ 63).' 'They claim that their services decrease crime, but in fact they increase it, since criminals have to steal more, in order to pay the sycophants (§ 64).' 'The normal refuges from other criminals (law, fair trial, etc.) are the workshops of the sycophants. They consider the givers their friends, the inoffensive their enemies (§ 65).'

Aristogiton and Theocrines typify sycophancy on a grand scale, conducted in the full glare of publicity, with relatively important issues at stake. They are prosecuted, not for sycophancy, but for exercising certain citizen privileges to which they are not entitled. There were plenty of sycophants in the lower échelons. Athens was notorious throughout Greece for their presence and their prosperity. 'What a curse they are in Athens!' says Aristophanes' Megarian.[28] The orators repeatedly draw attention to their activity and assume that the juries likewise regard them as a scourge. Some men found it impossible to live in Athens because of their persecution. Aeschines speaks generally of οἱ συκοφαντηθέντες ἐκ τῆς πόλεως,[29] and mentions a specific case, that of Leosthenes, who was driven into exile by sycophants.[30] Lysias records the same fate of Nicias' brother Diognetos.³¹ Others found various methods of dealing with their attacks. It was not enough to lead a blameless life, Isocrates says, because the innocent were used as a practice ground upon which the sycophants could sharpen their powers.³² A case in point was the apparently law-abiding Crito, whose story is told by Xenophon.³³ His position may have been typical. His anxiety to avoid the worries of litigation became a weapon in the hands of the sycophants, who levied blackmail by threatening to institute proceedings against him, though they had no grounds for doing so. Callias rejoices in his poverty because he is relieved of the attentions of sycophants who plagued his days of affluence.³⁴ Xenophon's Ischomachos is described as conscientiously practising all the personal and civic virtues which make him a model citizen. Perhaps Socrates would imagine that this would result in his being generally regarded as καλὸς κἀγαθός? 'Not at all,' says Ischomachos; 'the result is that ὑπὸ πολλῶν πάνυ συκοφαντοῦμαι.'³⁵

What was the remedy against all this sycophantic activity? Some, like Callias, took what seemed the easiest way out and merely paid the sycophants, until their funds were exhausted. Some, like Diognetos, took the hard way, and retired from a city which it had become impossible for them to live in. Crito, on Socrates' advice, employed a domestic sycophant to keep the others at bay. Callias, Diognetos and Crito were wealthy men, who presumably would have had the resources to enable them to take legal action, if it had been available to them under a γραφὴ συκοφαντίας. But in fact the courts gave them no protection: they were the 'workshops of the sycophants'. The provision for dealing with men who had 'deceived the people'³⁶ might curb the activity of sycophants in the political sphere, but it would be ineffective in private cases. The only real deterrent was the punishment inflicted on prosecutors who failed to secure one-fifth of the votes. This was a gamble, which sycophants were ready to take and their victims in most cases were not. The victims were in general men worth blackmailing, the wealthy, and in democratic Athens they had doubts about the impartiality of the democratic courts. Terence, translating Apollodorus, says of juries

> qui saepe propter inuidiam adimunt diuiti
> aut propter misericordiam addunt pauperi.³⁷

It may be argued that the γραφὴ συκοφαντίας did exist, but that prosecutors preferred to proceed on other charges because specific crimes were easier to prove, and sycophancy, though it might be a useful adjunct like *maiestas* in the early Roman empire, was such a vague and slippery charge that it could not be substantiated on its own. It is, however, more probable that the Athenians were realistic enough not to legislate against a practice which could not be legally demonstrated. Having no precise conception of what a sycophant legally was, or hesitating to frame a distinction between him and a genuine democratic watchdog, they devised no specific means of proceeding against him, as a sycophant, in the courts.

NOTES

1. Lys. XII. 5.
2. *Hell.* II. iii. 12.
3. *Ath. Pol.* 35.3.
4. XXV. 19.
5. *O.C.D.* s.v. *Sycophants.*
6. *The Administration of Justice from Homer to Aristotle,* II p. 70ff.
7. Chicago, 1917 (private ed.).
8. Oxford, 1962.
9. Op. cit. II p. 62.
10. Pp. 82-3.
11. Plat. *Rep.* 340 D.
12. Ibid. 341 A.
13. Dem. LV.
14. Xen. *Hell.* II. iii. 38 and 12.
15. XV. 164.
16. LVIII. 63.
17. v. 1452.
18. *Ath. Pol.* IX. 1.
19. *Char.* XXIX.
20. XXV. 40.
21. LVIII. 63.
22. *In Leocr.* 3-4.
23. *Or.* VI.
24. II. 12.
25. Cf. Isoc. VIII. 24.
26. *Or.* 2.
27. Op. cit. p. 59ff.
28. *Ach.* 829.
29. III. 236.
30. II. 124.
31. XVIII. 9.

32. VIII. 24.
33. *Mem.* II. ix.
34. Xen. *Symp.* IV. 30.
35. *Oec.* XI. 20.
36. Callixenos in Xen. *Hell.* I. vii. 35 faced a προβολή on this charge which was to be followed up in a dicastery.
37. *Phorm.* 276f.

ARISTOTLE AND THE DEMOCRATIC CONCEPTION OF FREEDOM

R. G. Mulgan

I

Though it is common knowledge that Aristotle, like Plato before him, rejected the ideals of Periclean Athens and especially the democratic principle of personal freedom, both the extent and the grounds of his opposition have often been misunderstood. In the last thirty years, Greek political theory has become one of the battlegrounds in the ideological war between 'liberal democracy' and 'totalitarianism' with Pericles and Socrates on one side drawn up against Plato and Aristotle on the other.[1] But ardour is not always compatible with accuracy and this controversy, though it has certainly revitalized, has frequently confused the study of Greek politics. Aristotle has been more fortunate in this respect than Plato. He is less extreme (some would say more muddled) than his master and has attracted correspondingly fewer and less passionate detractors and partisans. Nevertheless, there are some aspects of his political theory which we are in danger of misunderstanding in our attempt to accommodate them to the preoccupations of the present. In particular, eagerness to divide Greek writers on politics into two 'liberal' and 'authoritarian' camps is likely to obscure the precise nature of Aristotle's own idea of freedom as well as the point of his criticisms of democratic freedom.

The words ἐλευθερία (freedom) and ἐλεύθερος (free) mark one side of the distinction between the free man and the slave and the history of Greek ideas of freedom is the history of this distinction. From its original and basic application to the master-slave relation, it was later extended to the contrast between political autonomy and subjection to the laws of others, first in collective terms, for example, the 'freedom' of the Greek cities from 'slavery' to the

rule of the barbarians, and then in individual terms, the 'freedom'
of the individual citizen from control by the laws of the state.[2]
Thus ἐλευθερία in Greek, like 'freedom' in English, is a complex
notion the content of which varies with the context and viewpoint
of the speaker.

For Aristotle, freedom as a political ideal is especially associated
with democracy. It is the basic principle of democracy in the same
way as virtue is the basic principle of aristocracy and wealth of
oligarchy.[3] That is, it serves both as the criterion for distributing
political rights and as the end towards which the community is
directed. In a democracy all those who are free-born are entitled
to a share in ruling and they rule in such a way as to maximize
freedom, in the sense of the absence of government interference.
Aristotle's fullest account of the democratic conception of liberty
comes in the second chapter of Book VI of the *Politics*. He says
that there are two principles involved in democratic liberty:

> (i) one principle of liberty is for all to rule and be ruled in
> turn and indeed democratic justice is the application of num-
> erical not proportionate equality; whence it follows that the
> majority must be supreme and that whatever the majority
> approve must be the end and the just. Every citizen, it is said,
> must have equality and therefore in a democracy the poor
> have more power than the rich because there are more of them
> and the will of the majority is supreme. This then is one note
> of liberty which all democrats affirm to be the principle of
> their state. (ii) Another is that a man should live as he likes.
> This, they say, is the privilege of the free man since, on the
> other hand, not to live as a man likes is the mark of a slave.
> This is the second characteristic of democracy whence has
> arisen the claim of men to be ruled by none if possible or if
> this is impossible to rule and be ruled in turns; and so it con-
> tributes to the freedom based upon equality.[4]

II

Aristotle objects to the first principle that all men, or more accurately all free males, should share in ruling on two main grounds.
In the first place, he criticizes the distribution of political power
according to an arithmetical proportion, i.e. equally to all men.
Political rights should be awarded κατ' ἀξίαν on the basis of the
individual's contribution to the good of the state which may vary
from person to person and class to class.[5] Aristotle, like Plato, seeks

to prevent equality from being an exclusively democratic ideal by defining it in terms of proportion which allows for both 'arithmetical' (absolute) and 'geometrical' (proportionate) equality.[6] This is a familiar argument and we need not discuss it further.

His other line of attack involves a similar, though more subtle and less well noticed, move with the concept of freedom itself. To appreciate this we must first understand the meaning he himself gives to freedom. From his discussion of slavery we learn that the slave is a possession belonging wholly to the master—'he is not his own but another man's'.[7] He is an instrument of his master, a tool for fulfilling his master's will.[8] By implication, the free man does not belong to, or serve the interest of, anyone else. The same point is made in more general terms in *Metaphysics* A: 'the man is free we say who exists for his own sake and not for another's'.[9] Thus the question of an individual's freedom turns not on whether he is owned as a slave but on whether he has an independent value or, in more modern terms, is an 'end in himself'.

This apparently slight shift of emphasis has important consequences. First, the distinction between dependence and independence can be extended beyond the master-slave relation. Elsewhere in the *Politics,* Aristotle implies that not all men who are 'free' in the sense of not being slaves are really 'free' in the sense of possessing independent value. Just as, in the household, the slave is necessary for the master to live a full and proper life and shares the interest of his master,[10] so, in the community, the class of mechanics (βάναυσοι) and labourers (θῆτες) are necessary to the existence of the community but are not full members of it and should not, in Aristotle's view, be allowed the rights of citizenship.[11] Like the slave, they work not for themselves but for others, in their case the class of fully virtuous citizens. The free man should therefore be careful not to engage in any vulgar work 'because it is the mark of a free man not to live at another's beck and call': ἐλευθέρου γὰρ τὸ μὴ πρὸς ἄλλον ζῆν.[12]

Secondly, by stressing the independent value of the free man rather than his autonomy or freedom of action, Aristotle is able to reconcile being free with being ruled. He distinguishes three main types of political rule—kingly (βασιλική), tyrannical (τυραννική) and 'constitutional' (πολιτική). They are analogous to the three corresponding types of domestic rule, that of the father over his children, the master over his slave and the husband over his wife.[13] Kingly (paternal) rule and tyrannical (despotic) rule are both the rule of a superior over inferiors but they differ in that the king rules in the interests of his subjects while the tyrant or despot rules in his own self-interest. 'Constitutional' rule is the rule over equals and typically involves rotation of office and alternation between ruling and being ruled.[14]

Both kingly and constitutional rule are described as free rule or rule over free men, on the grounds that they are both in the interest of the ruled.[15] Rule is despotic, on the other hand, when it serves the interest of the ruler and not the ruled. This point is obviously closely connected with Aristotle's account of the nature of freedom. The man whose interest is considered by the ruler is being treated as an end and not as a means. He is being ruled for his own sake and not for the sake of another and therefore he is free. Of course, a man of superior virtue is necessary for kingship to be acceptable and such men may be hard to find. The most common type of free rule will therefore be the constitutional type involving the interchange of rulers and ruled. But, nevertheless, there is no logical necessity for the freeman to participate in government so long as his interest is protected.

This is not to say that Aristotle does not value political participation. In his ideal aristocracy, ruling is one of the activities in which the fully good man will exercise his virtue.[16] He finds fault with the nation (ἔθνος) as a political unit because, though it may be fitted for kingly rule,[17] it is too large for the citizens to share effectively in the election of magistrates and the adjudication of lawsuits.[18] He sees some value in the decisions of the many and his polity, the best state in most circumstances, contains an element of democracy.[19] But he puts the main emphasis on what the government prescribes rather than on how it arrives at these prescriptions. The most important thing is to have a government which governs in the interest of the ruled. To allow a measure of popular participation may, in certain circumstances, be the best means of ensuring such a government but if it is not then it may be abandoned without any necessary loss of freedom.

Thus Aristotle does not, like the democrat, make political participation a defining characteristic of freedom. Free men will usually have a chance to share in the process of government but they need not. We can now see the significance of his definition of freedom in terms of rule in the interest of the ruled. It enables him successfully to undermine the democrats' first principle of freedom without surrendering to them the sole right to claim liberty as a political ideal. This sort of move is common in the history of political thought. 'Freedom' carries too many commendatory overtones for it to be safely yielded to one's opponents. The only solution is therefore to retain the word and its evaluative meaning while at the same time changing its descriptive content, that is the objective circumstances to which it refers.[20]

III

Aristotle also objects to the second principle of democratic freedom, the freedom to do as one likes. The democrat sees obedience to the laws as slavery[21] and freedom is therefore the absence of such constraint. This, says Aristotle, is a bad definition (κακῶς ὁρίζονται)[22] and 'mean' (φαῦλον)[23]: 'men should not think it slavery to live according to the rule of the constitution; for it is their salvation'.[24]

Again, in order to understand the point of his criticism, we need to look at the positive side of his theory, at his own view of what the relation between the individual and the laws of his state ought to be. This is especially important because scholars have disagreed about the amount of legal interference which Aristotle allows in the life of the individual citizen. On the one hand, there seems in his political writings to be a marked relaxation of the rigid authoritarianism of Plato. He criticizes the excessive unity of Plato's *Republic* and stresses the value of private property and family life. In the *Ethics*, he places great emphasis on individual choice. 'For him there is no question of that strict intervention in the private sphere which Plato advocates in the state constitution. He not only recognizes individual personality as a fact, but considers it in his ethical theory.'[25] On the other hand, there are certain passages in the *Ethics* which suggest that he is just as much an interventionist as Plato and support Barker's view that neither Plato nor Aristotle was at all concerned to limit state interference.[26] Until this question has been settled we cannot estimate the extent to which he diverges from the principles of the democrat.

Aristotle shared the view of many of his contemporaries that the purpose of the law was to encourage and maintain the virtue of the citizen.[27] In the *Eudemian Ethics* he distinguishes between those aspects of virtue with which the law is legitimately concerned and those with which it is not. 'The private justice practised towards friends depends on ourselves alone, while justice towards all others is determined by the laws and does not depend on us.'[28] However, the suggestion that there is a sphere of virtuous social action outside the scope of law is retracted in the *Nicomachean Ethics*. Of the two types of justice, universal and particular,[29] the former includes all virtue, not absolutely but in relation to others (πρὸς ἕτερον)[30] and is equivalent to action according to law.[31] Thus, all virtuous actions which affect other people, including therefore action towards friends, are prescribed by the laws.

The qualification πρὸς ἕτερον is important because it reflects Aristotle's belief that there is a difference between doing just acts and acting justly. To be fully virtuous it is not sufficient simply to do the acts demanded by virtue. One must also act with the right sort of deliberation and choice which implies the right sort of character: 'But to play the coward or to act unjustly consists not in doing these things except incidentally but in doing them as the result of a certain state of character, just as to practise medicine and healing consists not in applying or not applying the knife, in using or not using medicine, but in doing so in a certain way.'[32] The law can be directly concerned only with the external aspect of just action, the just act which affects others: 'The law bids us do the acts of a brave man and those of a temperate man . . . and similarly with regard to the other virtues, commanding some and forbidding others.'[33]

This distinction reveals a deficiency in certain theories of the state. The state exists, says Aristotle in criticism of Lycophron, not just for the prevention of mutual wrong (i.e. external justice) but for the sake of the good life (i.e. full virtue).[34] Constant performance of virtuous acts is necessary for the formation of virtuous character[35] and it is not sufficient merely to force adults to act virtuously; the process must be begun in childhood. It is easy for children to acquire the wrong habits which are very difficult, if not impossible, to eradicate. Education thus becomes a matter of public concern and Sparta is praised for being one of the few states which pays collective attention to the training of the young.[36] The political community is seen as a massive educational institution designed to force everyone, both young and old, into a common ethical pattern: 'But it surely is not enough that when they are young they should get the right nurture and attention; since they must, even when they are grown up, practise and be habituated to them, we shall need laws for this as well, and generally speaking to cover the whole of life; for most people obey necessity rather than argument and punishments rather than a sense of what is noble.'[37]

Though Aristotle says that law should cover the whole of life (πάντα τὸν βίον) he is not to be taken literally. There are two aspects of human activity which will not be subject to direct legal control. Firstly, in so far as virtuous action is internal, though it may be fostered by legislation, it cannot, as we have seen, be directly enforced. So far we have been concerned with ethical virtue only—that part of virtue which is concerned with relations between men and which is characteristic of the more human side of men's nature. But there are also intellectual virtues, especially wisdom which is exercised in philosophical contemplation, for Aristotle the supreme and most divine activity of man.[38] This sort of virtue is wholly, not just partially, internal. There are no external and enforceable acts of contemplation corresponding to the external and enforceable acts of ethical virtue. The law will still aim to give the right people the right level of material well-being and education necessary for the contemplative life, but it will not be able to regulate the activity of contemplation itself.

Secondly, there will be some mundane matters which, though capable of regulation, will not in fact be regulated. The purpose of the law is to inculcate virtue and though all major spheres of life are relevant to this purpose there are bound to be certain minor matters, for example, details of food or clothing, to which the laws will be indifferent. These two classes of action, wholly internal mental processes and the trivial details of external life, seem to be the only matters which are outside the law. But such exceptions are not sufficient to prove any 'liberalism' in Aristotle, for the liberal is interested in freedom in precisely those activities which are *both* susceptible to coercion *and* morally significant.

The arguments in favour of more substantial, 'liberal' limitations in the extent of legal control in Aristotle are mistaken or at least inconclusive. Firstly, Aristotle's emphasis on individual choice. He does, it is true, stress the internal and voluntary aspect of virtue;[39] the truly virtuous man who has developed the right character will of his own accord freely choose to do the right actions. But this does not imply any lessening of the law's concern with external acts of virtue. Many people will be incapable of choosing the right action and for them legal coercion will always be necessary. In common with many others who have believed that moral questions have correct answers discoverable by reason, Aristotle did not see any point in allowing people to make up their own minds how to act if this was likely to result in morally wrong action. He would not have agreed that the value of choosing to do a good act was in any way diminished by the fact that if one did not choose to do it one would be forced to do it. Free choice was a part of being virtuous but only when it was choice of the right actions. It was better to coerce people to act justly than to let them voluntarily act unjustly. Indeed, only *by* such coercion will they ever learn to choose the right action and so become virtuous.

Secondly, it is true that, in comparison with Plato, Aristotle places greater value on what we would call 'private life', on such things as personal property and family life. But again this does not in itself prove any diminution of legal control. Ethical virtue is to be practised in both the public and the private spheres and therefore both are equally subject to law. We must be careful not to confuse two quite separate uses of the phrase 'private life'. Firstly, it can refer to those activities which are not concerned with the specifically 'political' or 'public' duties of the citizen. This is the sense in which Aristotle uses the word ἴδιος and its cognates.⁴⁰ Secondly, it may mean that part of our lives which is free from interference by the law. These two different 'private lives' are not necessarily coextensive—the private business dealings of the M.P. are still subject to commercial law—nor does belief in the value of one imply belief in the value of the other. Thus, the fact that *some* ethically virtuous action is private in the sense that it is done at home in the company of friends or family is not incompatible with Aristotle's belief that all ethical virtue should be prescribed by law.

Finally, D. J. Allan has recently argued that, in Aristotle's view, 'the requirements of the law in respect of moral action are a minimum. It will rest with the individual to display, for instance, courage and temperance in circumstances, perhaps, where the law does not insist upon it; or in a higher degree than other men when it does so.'⁴¹ The main evidence he offers is Aristotle's statement that the mean, which constitutes the virtuous balance between two immoral extremes, is 'relative to us', πρὸς ἡμᾶς, and not to the 'object' κατ' αὐτὸ τὸ πρᾶγμα.⁴² This implies, he says, that 'the moral mean is relative to persons and not absolute and objective' and therefore that the question of what constitutes the right action in particular circumstances will often have to be left to individual judgment. But this is a dubious argument. The point of the distinction between the mean relative to the object and the mean relative to us is that the former is calculated by averaging two extremes while the latter is not. 'If ten is many and two is few six is the mean taken in terms of the object'⁴³ whereas in the case of the master of any art, the right answer will depend not on the nature of the extremes, but on the individual circumstances. It is significant that Aristotle uses the example of the gymnastic trainer who has sufficient skill to know what is appropriate for each of his pupils. Surely this suggests that the statesman or legislator will similarly be able to decide in particular cases what the right conduct is for the citizen. At any rate, it is very hard to infer from this passage a *denial* of this analogy. It is true that, in spite of the apparent simplicity of the doctrine of the mean, ethical judgments are for Aristotle highly complex. The virtuous man must act 'at the right time, with reference to the right objects, towards the right people, with the right motive and in the right way'.[44] It would therefore be extremely difficult for any legislator to include all acts of virtue in a legal code. Aristotle does, however, realize these problems and does make some allowance for them though not in the way suggested by Allan.

In the *Rhetoric*, he says that there are two classes of just and unjust actions, one covered by written laws, the other unwritten.[45] The latter class is further divided into two categories of which one is the rules of equity. Aristotle was well aware of the limitations in the law due to its generality and of the need to supplement the written law by particular decisions based on equity. 'All law is universal but about some things it is not possible to make a universal statement which shall be correct. In these cases, then, in which it is necessary to speak universally but not possible to do so correctly, the law takes the usual case, though it is not ignorant of the possibility of error. And it is none the less correct; for the error is not in the law but in the nature of the thing, since the matter of practical affairs is of this kind from the start.'[46] There will be cases of just and unjust action which will not be covered explicitly in the written law, and so the law allows the rulers to fill in gaps and make adjustments by use of the legal principles of equity.[47] However, this is a deficiency in the effectiveness more of particular written laws than of general legal control itself.[48] Particular acts of injustice which are condemned by the special decision of a court are no less illegal than those which are clearly contrary to the letter and spirit of a general law.

Aristotle's description of the second type of unwritten justice would appear at first sight to support Allan's argument. It is concerned with 'that conduct that springs from exceptional goodness or badness and is visited accordingly with censure and loss of honour, or with praise and increase of honour and decorations; for instance, gratitude to, or requital of our benefactors, readiness to help our friends and the like.'[49] There will therefore be a class of ethical norms which are backed by what might be called 'social' rather than 'legal' sanctions.[50] But we must be wary of reading any liberalism into this concession. It implies a relaxation in the sort of *means* by which individual conduct is publicly regulated but not in the *extent* of this regulation. Though these rules do not carry typically legal sanctions they were often described as 'laws' (νόμοι) and Aristotle recommends their use by the legislator to control the actions of the citizen. They are simply alternative methods of control.[51]

By these two means, then, equity and unwritten laws carrying social sanctions, Aristotle tries to overcome the inflexibility of a written code. One may still doubt whether the attempt to control all those aspects of the individual's life which are both relevant to the life of virtue and amenable to coercion could be successful even within a small and confined community like the Greek city state. But there is no evidence to suggest that Aristotle thinks such widespread control is either impossible or undesirable.

We can now see the force of Aristotle's objections to the democratic notion that freedom is doing as one likes. To insist, as the democrat does, on the overriding value of acting voluntarily means that it does not matter what actions people do as long as they do them willingly. For Aristotle, this is a principle that applies only to those trivia which are irrelevant to the life of virtue and the democrat is therefore glorifying a characteristic of the least significant and valuable aspect of human existence. Moreover, the democrat wants to extend the area of unfettered choice as widely as possible so that it will include a large number of those activities in which individuals are usually expected to act virtuously. To Aristotle, such a demand would be tantamount to saying that these activities were ethically neutral or indifferent, which they clearly are not. Indeed, as he remarks in the *Metaphysics,* one of the differences between the freeman and the slave is that the former acts in a much less arbitrary way than the latter: 'for all are ordered together to one end, but it is as in a house, where the freemen are least at liberty to act at random, but all things or most things are ordained for them, while the slaves and animals do little for the common good and for the most part act at random.'[52]

The democrat, of course, would not accept the equation of what is not prescribed by the law with the morally neutral or indifferent. Family life, for example, was not to be regulated by law but it was still an important area for the exercise of personal virtue. It was, however, very difficult in Greek to make this distinction between law and morality which is fundamental to any liberal attitude towards the scope of law. The Greek word for law, νόμος, may refer to any common rule of behaviour and not just to those rules which are codified or actually enforced by the courts.[53] The notion of non-legal rules or norms would be odd to a Greek because it would mean that there were νόμοι which were not really νόμοι. True, there was a distinction between written and unwritten laws; but 'unwritten laws' included a wide variety of different rules, legal and judicial as well as social and religious, and so cannot be generally described as 'non-legal' rules.[54] Though there were always some νόμοι which were not in fact enforced, the word νόμος still carried sufficient specifically 'legal' connotations to make it somewhat paradoxical to say that there was a class of νόμοι which *should* not be enforced. Thus the idea that there were social rules which were not the law's business, though it fitted Athenian practice, was theoretically precarious. It is therefore easy for Aristotle to give a philosophical refutation of the democratic position. By arguing that all unjust action is contrary to 'law' and therefore that the statesman or legislator should be concerned with enforcing all ethical virtue, he is able to use ordinary language to reach an extraordinary conclusion.

Aristotle finds this democratic conception of liberty mistaken not only because it is contrary to his view of the proper function of the law but also because it conflicts with the democrat's own interest.[55] Every state has an interest in maintaining its own existence and must therefore avoid any policy which is likely to threaten stability. Extreme democracies, where everything is decided by popular decree without the restraining influence of law and where everyone is allowed to do as he likes are, like tyranny, inherently unstable. This criticism of democracy, that its love of freedom leads it to chaos and anarchy, also occurs in Plato[56] and has become a familiar anti-democratic argument. It is, of course, fallacious when applied to democracies in general. Freedom and stability are not mutually exclusive; more of one does not necessarily imply less of the other. Few, if any, apologists for democracy were outright anarchists advocating the complete absence of coercive rules. Pericles, for example, while upholding the individual's right to freedom in his private life, gives equal weight to the citizen's duty to obey the magistrates and the laws.[57]

Aristotle thus finds the second principle of democratic freedom both morally and politically unsound. Widespread legal control is necessary for the maintenance both of individual virtue and of collective security and should not be regarded as an infringement of personal liberty. We saw earlier that Aristotle answers the democratic argument that freedom involves sharing in the government of the state by defining freedom in terms of independent value. It has been suggested that he offers a further, alternative definition of freedom to replace the second democratic freedom. Newman says that it is 'probable that Aristotle would define freedom as obedience to rightly constituted law'.[58] Barker, clearly using Newman, says that 'one would gather, though he [Aristotle] does not in so many words say, that liberty, on its legal side, is obedience to rightly constituted laws . . . . Aristotle taught the same doctrine which Montesquieu afterwards taught, that "liberty is the right to do as one ought to do and not as one ought not to do" '.[59] This interpretation has subsequently become widely accepted and one often reads that Aristotle advocated the 'rational' or 'positive' view of freedom as doing what is right or commanded by the law.[60]

Yet the evidence for such a redefinition is extremely slight. The democrat, says Aristotle, is led to his definition of freedom because he considers that not to live as one likes is the mark of the slave.[61] Hence, as freedom is the opposite of slavery, freedom must be to live as one likes. Aristotle objects that to live according to the constitution, which is clearly not to live as one likes, should be regarded not as slavery but as salvation (σωτηρία).[62] The Newman-Barker thesis is that Aristotle agrees with the democrats that the distinction between slavery and freedom should be applied to the contrast between obeying the law and doing what one likes but contends that they apply it the wrong way round. Obedience is freedom not slavery; living as one likes is slavery not freedom. But note that he defines living according to the constitution as salvation. Obedience is neither slavery *nor* freedom; it is salvation. We must not read any later notions of personal liberation into the word σωτηρία. It simply refers to the security of the citizen and the state which depend on the existence of law and order.[63] The citizen needs this security and should not disparage it as beneath the dignity of the free man. But there is no suggestion here that Aristotle is amplifying or changing his definition of freedom. Nor does his argument necessarily imply such a change. It is quite logical to say that the free man should obey the law and at the same time to deny that his freedom *consists* in his obedience.

Newman also refers to the previously quoted passage from the *Metaphysics*.[64] Aristotle is there making the point that though everything in the universe is ordered towards a single end, some things (e.g. the heavenly bodies) are more divine and more bound by necessity than other things (e.g. sublunary creatures) whose actions are mainly contingent.[65] Similarly, in the household, the actions of the free man, the master, are largely ordered and ordained while slaves and animals are relatively unconcerned with the common good and therefore act mostly at random. Thus the free man because he is the most concerned with the common good is the least entitled to act according to whim. This argument, as we have seen, helps to explain Aristotle's reasons for objecting to the democratic freedom to do as one likes. But, again, there is no suggestion that the free man is *defined* in terms of his acting according to law or that he is free only *in so far as* he so acts.

We should conclude, therefore, that though Aristotle criticizes the democrat for regarding obedience to the laws as the negation of liberty and claims that such obedience is not inconsistent with freedom, he does not believe that it *is* freedom. The fact that many subsequent political philosophers have combined similar attacks on the 'democratic', or, in more modern terms, 'negative' or 'liberal' conceptions of freedom with a redefinition of 'freedom' in terms of obedience to laws or to necessity need not force us to attribute the same move to Aristotle. He is always unwilling to depart too far from accepted linguistic usage. By saying that the freedom to do what one likes and to go where one likes, which was commonly associated with the status of the free man,[66] was not really to be considered as freedom, Aristotle was already sharply at variance with ordinary language. It is most unlikely that he would want to advocate the even more paradoxical doctrine that acting as one wishes is really slavery. Aristotle's commentators and critics have thus not done justice to the subtlety of his theory of freedom. They have overlooked some of the implications of his earlier definition of freedom which, without radically diverging from customary usage, excludes the artisan class from citizenship and allows free men to accept the rule of exceptionally enlightened men. At the same time, they have unjustifiably credited him with a view of freedom which is probably the least plausible doctrine of modern authoritarianism. That he was an authoritarian is beyond dispute. But he is not guilty of believing that only by subjecting themselves to authority can men be truly 'liberated'.

NOTES

1. See, for example, K. R. Popper, *The Open Society and its Enemies* (London, 1945) ; E. A. Havelock, *The Liberal Temper in Greek Politics* (New Haven and London, 1957).

2. See M. Pohlenz, *Freedom in Greek Life and Thought,* tr. C. Lof-
    mark (Dordrecht, 1966), pp. 1-45.
3. *Pol.* 1294 a 12 ; cf. 1280 a 5, 1281 a 6, 1291 b 34-5, *Rh.* 1366 a 4.
4. *Pol.* 1317 b 2-17. All translations of Aristotle, unless otherwise
    indicated, are from W. D. Ross (ed.) *The Works of Aristotle
    Translated into English* (Oxford, 1909-1952).
5. *Pol.* III, ix-xiii.
6. *Pol.* 1301 b 29, *EN* V iii ; cf. Plato, *Rep.* 558 c, *Gorgias* 508 a-b,
    Laws 757 a-e.
7. *Pol.* 1254 a 14-15.
8. *Pol.* 1253 b 30.
9. *Metaph.* 982 b 25.
10. *Pol.* 1255 b 9-12 ; cf. 1278 b 32-7.
11. *Pol.* 1278 a 1-13.
12. *Rh.* 1367 a 33 ; cf. *Pol.* 1341 b 8-14.
13. *Pol.* 1259 a 37-b17.
14. *Pol.* 1252 a 16 ; but not in the case of the rule of husband over
    wife (*Pol.* 1259 b 4-10 ; cf. *EN* 1160 b 32-5).
15. *Pol.* 1259 a 39-40, 1333 a 3-6.
16. *Pol.* 1277 b 16-21.
17. *Pol.* 1285 b 32-3 ; cf. 1310 b 34-40.
18. *Pol.* 1326 b 12-20.
19. *Pol.* III xi, IV viii.
20. See M. Cranston, *Freedom* (London, 1953) ch. 2.
21. *Pol.* 1310 a 35.
22. *Pol.* 1310 a 28.
23. *Pol.* 1310 a 34.
24. *Pol.* 1310 a 34-6.
25. Pohlenz, op. cit., p. 98.
26. *The Politics of Aristotle,* edited and translated by E. Barker (Ox-
    ford, 1946), p. li.
27. Demosthenes XXV 6, 'The laws desire what is just, good and
    expedient'.
28. *EE* 1235 a 2-4. It is possible that Aristotle is simply mentioning a
    generally received view without actually endorsing it. (ὑπολαμ-
    βάνομεν 1234 b 32.) But, as certain other discrepancies in Aris-
    totle's theory, especially in connection with the scope of political
    science (see R. A. Gauthier and J. Y. Jolif, *L'Ethique à Nico-
    maque* (Paris, 1959), note on 1094 b 11, Vol. II, pp. 10-11) are
    best explained by the hypothesis that Aristotle changed his
    opinions about the extent of law between writing the *Eudemian*
    and the *Nicomachean Ethics,* it is preferable to accept this as
    Aristotle's own view.
29. *EN* V i-ii.
30. *EN* 1129 b 25-7.

31. *EN* 1129 a 34-b1, 1130 b 23-4. This is contradicted by the statement in *EN* VIII that justice is of two kinds, one 'unwritten' and the other 'legal' (κατὰ νόμον 1162 b 21-2). Aristotle is there distinguishing between two types of agreement involving friendship based on utility, the contract with fixed terms and the gentleman's agreement in which payment is left to the friendly feelings of the parties involved. He describes the former as 'legal' (νομική) and the latter as 'moral' (ἠθική). These terms are presumably derived from contemporary usage. At any rate, they do not accurately represent Aristotle's own view for elsewhere he implies that unwritten norms carrying 'social' sanctions are the concern of the legislator (see p. 104).
32. *EN* 1137 a 21-6.
33. *EN* 1129 b 19-24. The two words 'act' and 'action' seem to be the best way of expressing the distinction in English. Aristotle reserves πρᾶξις for the latter and usually uses the neuter article for the former, e.g. τὰ τοῦ ἀνδρείου lit., 'the things of the brave man'. In this passage, however, he uses ἔργα to mark the difference between the external act and the complete action, a point well noted by D. J. Allan, 'Individual and State in the *Ethics and Politics'*, *La Politique d'Aristote*, Entretiens sur l'Antiquité Classique, Tome XI (Geneva, 1965), p. 67.
34. *Pol.* 1280 b 25-31 ; cf. 1280 b 3-6.
35. *EN* 1103 b 21-2.
36. *EN* 1180 a 24-6.
37. *EN* 1180 a 1-4. D. J. Allan has argued that this passage does not fairly represent Aristotle's position because he elsewhere makes a clear distinction between the close supervision necessary for educating children and the much looser legal control of adults. He relies on a supposed distinction in *EN* V ii between two types of law concerning different classes of act. The first deals with those acts 'that are prescribed from the point of view of virtue taken as a whole' (*EN* 1130 b 22-3) which are the commands issued to adults ; the second type are the more all-embracing laws relating to education of the young—'those of the acts punished by the law which have been prescribed with a view to education for the common good and which tend to produce virtue' (*EN* 1130 b 25-6). However, this is a somewhat strained interpretation. Aristotle seems to be describing not two different types of law but the same laws from two different points of view, first as enjoining virtuous acts and second as producing a virtuous disposition. His earlier statement that 'we call those acts just which tend to produce and preserve happiness and its components for the political society' (*EN* 1129 b 17-19) refers, as is clear from the context, to virtuous acts commanded by the laws and suggests that far from distinguishing between moral

education and enforced obedience to laws prescribing just acts, Aristotle holds them to be virtually coextensive.

38. *EN* 1177 b 29-34.
39. *EN* III ii.
40. Cf. *Pol.* 1293 a 7, 1308 b 20, 1309 a 6, 1320 a 28, 1330 a 30, 1337 a 24 (ἴδιος) ; 1273 a 35, b 29 (ἰδιωτεύειν) ; 1272 b 4, 1277 a 25, 1324 a 41 (ἰδιώτης).
41. Op. cit. p. 71.
42. *EN* 1106 a 26- b 7.
43. *EN* 1106 a 33-4.
44. *EN* 1106 b 21-2.
45. *Rh.* I xiii.
46. *EN* 1137 b 13-17.
47. Cf. *Pol.* 1287 a 25-7.
48. Cf. M. Hamburger, *Morals and Law, the Growth of Aristotle's Legal Theory* (New Haven, 1951), pp. 96-9.
49. *Rh.* 1374 a 21-5.
50. Cf. *Rh.* 1375 a 13-20. The phrase 'exceptional goodness or badness' might seem to be a reference to acts of supererogation, acts beyond the call of duty, which we are praised for doing but not blamed for not doing. But the fact that Aristotle mentions the suitability of censure and dishonour rules out this interpretation.
51. 'For public control is plainly effected by laws and good control by good laws ; whether written or unwritten would seem to make no difference' (*EN* 1180 a 34- b 1). Cf. Thuc. ii 37.3 where Pericles includes obedience to the 'code which, although unwritten, cannot be broken without acknowledged disgrace' as part of the law-abidingness of the Athenian as distinct from his freedom in his private life.
52. *Metaph.* 1075 a 18-23.
53. See F. Heinimann, *Nomos und Physis* (Basel, 1945), ch. II. 2.
54. See J. B. Skemp, *Plato's Statesman* (London, 1952) p. 198 n. 3. Athenian democrats were opposed to the enforcement of certain unwritten laws but they did not object to all unwritten law as such ; see Andocides, *De Myst*, 85 ; D. MacDowell (ed.) *Andokides on the Mysteries* (Oxford, 1962), pp. 125-6.
55. *Pol.* 1310 a 25-8.
56. E.g. *Rep.* 557 b- 558 c.
57. 'But all this ease in our private relations does not make us lawless as citizens' Thuc. ii 37.3.
58. W. L. Newman, *The Politics of Aristotle* (Oxford, 1887-1902), note on 1310 a 27, Vol. IV, p. 411.
59. E. Barker, *The Political Thought of Plato and Aristotle* (New York, 1959), p. 355.
60. E.g. Cranston, op. cit. pp. 20-22 ; L. M. McDonald, *Western Political Theory* (New York, 1968), p. 65 n. 43.

61. *Pol.* 1317 b 12-13.
62. *Pol.* 1310 a 36.
63. Cf. *Pol.* 1276 b 28-9, Plato, Laws 715 d.
64. P. 97.
65. See W. D. Ross (ed.) *Aristotle's Metaphysics* (Oxford, 1924), Vol. II p. 401.
66. See W. L. Westermann, 'Slavery and the Elements of Freedom in Ancient Greece', in M. I. Finley (ed.), *Slavery in Classical Antiquity* (Cambridge, 1960), p. 26.

ROME AND GREECE, 196 - 146 B.C.

A. H. McDonald

In 196 B.C. at Corinth, after defeating Philip V of Macedon, Flamininus proclaimed 'the freedom of Greece' and confirmed it by the repulse of Antiochus the Great. The kings had departed from the Aegean. But Rome had entered. In 146, on crushing the Achaean League, Mummius sacked Corinth; at the same time Scipio Aemilianus destroyed Carthage. In fifty years Rome had changed herself and remoulded the political face of the Mediterranean. It is one of the critical periods of world history.[1] We may ask not at first *why* but rather *how* this happened; for if one thing leads to another, motivation and procedure will have interacted. The events call for close study in terms of time and place; that is, we have to examine the chronology and the relation of policy between one theatre of action and the others. This paper is concerned with Greece, but we have to look at Rome and also glance farther afield. The evidence, too, is difficult. Polybius has become fragmentary, our text of Livy stops at 167 B.C. One is tempted to generalize in approaching 150. I shall plot the development before trying to explain it.[2]

In the historical sequence there are three stages: I, 196 - 187 B.C., the first Roman settlement of Greece; II, 187 - 167 B.C., the circumstances leading to the fall of Macedon; III, 167 - 146 B.C., the decline and fall of the Achaean League.

I

In 220 B.C. the Greek leagues and cities lived in tense but familiar relationship with the Hellenistic monarchies. Both sides recognized the scope and the limits of local autonomy, and the weaker states had learnt to play on the balance of Macedon, Syria and Egypt. When Philip V of Macedon and Antiochus the Great of Syria forced the Ptolemaic power back on Alexandria, their success disturbed the Aegean. It affected especially Pergamum, protecting Western Asia Minor, and Rhodes, the commercial guardian of the seas. In Greece Philip's aggression would alienate the Achaean League, while the Aetolian League remained his inveterate enemy. Meanwhile Rome extended her influence over the Adriatic into Illyria. When Philip joined Hannibal she made an alliance with Aetolia and fought the First Macedonian War as long as the Aetolians held out. It was fateful timing at the close of the Second Punic War when Pergamum and Rhodes reported a pact between Macedon and Syria at Egypt's expense, and appealed to Rome to redress the balance of power. Rome intervened to defeat both Philip and Antiochus and confine them to their kingdoms. In doing so she built up a Greek coalition of allies: Pergamum and Rhodes, the Aetolian and Achaean Leagues, and most of the smaller states. Her victory left her to find further trouble among her allies.[3]

The Romans had no reason to be unfamiliar with Greek politics and thought. They had learnt in the past through Etruria and from Campania, as far as they were then capable of learning. They had beaten Pyrrhus and taken over Magna Graecia. They had diplomatic relations with Ptolemaic Egypt, and some connections through Magna Graecia with the Aegean. In driving Carthage out of Sicily during the First Punic War they realized the position of the major Greek cities and respected their autonomy. Their western experience prepared them sufficiently to enter Hellenistic politics. The point is that, however much they understood, they would still handle their policy in their own way.

We have to distinguish diplomacy from personal culture. The Roman nobles in the late third century B.C. might well recall how Odysseus had dallied in the West—at Cape Circeii?—and how Aeneas had made them the latter-day Trojans, to be included in the Greek traditions. That is why Naevius could write successfully. These Romans were no simple 'peasant-soldiers'. Many of them knew their Greek and something of Greek literature: men like Fabius Pictor, Scipio Africanus and Flamininus. At the same time, devoting themselves to politics, administration and war, they followed the principles of their traditional policy.[4]

Roman behaviour included a feature which the legalistic Greeks were slow to appreciate. As patrons in a social convention of 'clientela', the Roman nobles, when they made an agreement on equal terms, still tacitly assumed that the other party would unquestioningly respect their wishes—even in their foreign relations.[5]

'Tacitly' and 'without question'—there was the rub. The attitude had suited Italy, for various practical reasons. It did not suit Greece. The Greeks regarded the Romans as tight-lipped and arrogant; the Romans did not care what impression they gave. As Philip said to M. Aemilius Lepidus, when the latter delivered the Roman ultimatum before the Second Macedonian War in brusque terms, 'I pardon your rudeness for three reasons: you are young, you are handsome, and you are a Roman!'[6]

The Greeks were equally definite about their diplomatic conventions. The kings had tested their statecraft at one another's expense, until they could tell where to draw the line. They failed to see in time that Rome did not know the rules of their power game. Philip's sophisticated aggression, Antiochus' insistence on hereditary claims, failed under the impact of Roman strength; then they accepted the result. But in restoring their kingdoms after defeat even they, and certainly their successors, underestimated the depth of Roman suspicion. The smaller Greek states, even those that had joined Rome, reserved the same right to use their autonomy to press old claims against their neighbours. They relied unduly upon their Hellenistic experience when they were, in fact, dependent ultimately upon the Roman view of policy.

When Rome intervened in Greece to fight the Second Macedonian War, the Senate let the *casus belli* rest on the principle of autonomy.[7] The procedure was familiar since the time of Alexander's successors; it made a popular appeal for support from the leagues and cities against expansionist kings like Philip and Antiochus. Flamininus handled it cleverly. In the negotiations with Philip and the Macedonian peace settlement only the Aetolians saw the strong Roman hand: the others welcomed the proclamation of 'Greek freedom', since it ostensibly suited their interests. Yet it was a Roman peace. There was no sign at this point that they might not be allowed to dispute their local claims in their own fashion but would come under the Italian convention of arbitration by Rome.

It was the Aetolians, the fierce and reckless ones, who raised the issue of independence. 'What are you afraid of?' shouted Flamininus to Philip in the negotiations before Cynoscephalae, as Philip parleyed with the Roman allies from the prow of his ship. 'I fear none but the gods,' replied Philip, 'but I don't trust your Aetolian allies.'[8] Let us examine the course of Roman-Aetolian relations.

First, the treaty of 211 B.C. against Philip in the First Macedonian War. It was fairly drawn up; but the Aetolians violated it in making a separate peace. The Romans held that it lapsed. They refused to help the Aetolian League when Philip resumed his aggression against its cities shortly before the Second Macedonian War. But, once the war began, they took pains to bring the Aetolians, as well as the Achaeans, into their allied coalition. The Aetolian troops distinguished themselves at the battle of Cynoscephalae. Yet Flamininus imposed the settlement. The Aetolians protested, appealing to the treaty of 211 B.C. 'That treaty lapsed,' said Flamininus, 'when you made your own peace with Philip; and even if it hadn't, its terms cannot justify what you claim.' We have Livy (following Polybius) on the original negotiations and a fragmentary inscription that records the terms after ratification with Rome.[9] On the evidence I do not think that we can convict Flamininus of a downright lie. But why did he make his point if the treaty had lapsed? What agreement had he made with the Aetolians when he persuaded them to join in the Second Macedonian War? He must have promised them something, and they would hardly have accepted less than the original terms of military alliance. Is that why they harked back to the treaty? But, whatever was said, it can hardly have been set down formally, and Flamininus felt able to arrange the 'freedom of Greece'. I think he initially hoped to reconcile the sentiment favouring Greek autonomy with Roman policy in the East; but in the face of Aetolian argument he hardened his diplomatic attitude to the legalistic limit of Roman procedure.[10]

The Aetolian League instigated and abetted Antiochus in his invasion of Greece, and they paid the penalty in defeat. The Roman treaty put them out of Greek politics; but their policy had already affected the Senate's attitude towards Greek intransigence in exercising their autonomy against the wishes of Rome.

II

In 189 B.C., after the battle of Magnesia, 'Antiochus' envoys,' says Polybius, 'urged the Romans to use their victory magnanimously, since Fortune had granted them world dominion'; Scipio Africanus replied that victory did not change the Roman terms.[11] But the Senate imposed stricter terms than Scipio's, and the nobles drove Scipio and his liberal diplomacy out of politics.[12] The Aetolian treaty brought Italian practice into Rome's Greek policy. It contained the *maiestas* clause, viz. to follow the dictate of Rome in foreign relations—a special case, since the Aetolian League had

made war on Rome.[13] The historical question remains. How far
would the Senate now act from supreme strength, what scope would
it allow to the autonomous claims of the other Greek states?
The great wars and their aftermath changed the economic conditions of Roman society. The scale of operations in Italy and overseas required an expansion of the trades and crafts in Rome and
the Central Italian cities that supplied the armies and navy. By dis-
placement in the Hannibalic War or by attraction later, labour
moved into the urban centres; this trend enlarged the market for
agricultural produce and encouraged more specialized farming in
Latium and Campania. The spoils of war—whether from the in-
demnities which the Treasury disbursed in public works or by personal gain—provided capital for investment in the new developments, along lines already familiar in the Hellenistic world and
Carthage. It became possible—either by military measures or on
the slave market—to obtain cheap labour to a degree that had not
been seen before. One thinks of Sempronius Gracchus' claim in
176 B.C. that he had killed or captured 80,000 Sardinians, even
before Aemilius Paullus enslaved 150,000 Molossians in 167 B.C.
Polybius in Bk. VI reflects the financial situation and Cato in *De
agricultura* shows the farming side—at a later date, indeed, but the
development must have been under way by 180 B.C. Socially it
brought a more mixed and volatile urban population and a change
in rural conditions that would affect army recruitment.[14]
The Senate set itself the task of returning to normal. In 187
B.C. it repaid 25 years' *tributum,* the war tax, and let money loose
in public works. At the same time it controlled public order, as in
the measures it took to control the Bacchanalian cult. It tried to
regulate the drift of Latins to Rome so as to maintain the levy
of allied troops for the Roman army. We may discern already the
beginnings of a problem that would break out in disorder by 150
B.C., and eventually lead to Marius' army reforms. But *quis custo-
diet ipsos custodes*? The nobles had to maintain their social standing, not only by their public service but through popular appeal.
The answer lay in wealth, by investment in the new agriculture, so
as to support their displaced clients and impress the proletariat by
their liberality in office, and to make even more of a professional
public career. Cato recognized the difficulty, when he appealed for
political morality. A younger generation would adapt the means to
the ends. They had to further what their families wanted, in terms
ostensibly of *virtus* but, in fact, of *fama et gloria.* No great Roman
family would allow its sons—or its daughters in marriage—to neg-

lect their filial duty. 'Why do you ignore me, Polybius?' said the young Scipio Aemilianus. 'Everyone thinks I lack character because I can't take to the law.' When Polybius reassured him, 'Thank you,' he said, 'I shall feel worthy of my family and my ancestors.'[15]

In Greece Philip renounced his external ambitions. His policy was now to restore his kingdom internally and strengthen its position in the north. We need only note his success and indicate the difficulties with Rome. By the Third Macedonian War, indeed, Macedon was as strong in men and money and in military organization as she had been before Rome intervened in Greece. The Senate, with increasing doubt, had watched Philip's policy, and his Thessalian neighbours lost no opportunity of complaining at Rome. Though the commissions included hard men, Philip—on the whole —held his temper. The rivalry of Demetrius and Perseus for the succession encouraged intrigue from the Roman side. When Perseus followed Philip, he did so in disfavour with the Senate.[16]

Perseus ruled Macedon carefully but with a touch of royal ostentation. If he married the daughter of Seleucus IV of Syria and gave his sister to Prusias of Bithynia, this was dynastic practice; it was not welcome to Rome. His prestige played on Greek feeling. In the Greek cities, where economic conditions had declined, Roman policy tended to support the propertied classes, while the proletariat looked towards Macedon. Then Eumenes of Pergamum, who had gained Antochus' influence in Europe as well as in Asia Minor, pressed his Aegean interests against the renewal of Macedonian influence. His testimony was important to Rome. The Senate in the 170's was troubled about the developments in Greece. It could base its policy on the principle of autonomy and find some case on the Macedonian frontier to cite against Perseus, if Rome should decide to attack him.[17]

In discussing the Third Macedonian War we are in difficulty with the sources. Polybius (in his fragments or as rendered by Livy) is anti-Macedonian but at least contemporary. At critical points Livy uses formal Annalistic material, here undoubtedly with a legalistic Roman bias. We may begin with what Polybius reports as the current view of the causes: (1) the primary cause, Perseus' expulsion of the Thracian Abrupolis from his principality, after the latter had raided the Pangaean mines; (2) Perseus' invasion of Dolopia, south-west of Thessaly; (3) the visit of Perseus to Delphi; (4) the plot against Eumenes of Pergamum at Delphi; (5) the murder of Boeotian envoys. Of these charges Polybius takes the first three as προφάσεις, the last two as ἀρχαί of the war itself, while none of them was the αἰτία. The cause, in Polybius' view, lay in Philip's preparation of war against Rome, and Perseus was his posthumous agent. The formulation has a Thucydidean look, and we have to consider the evidence more freely.[18]

(1) The Thracian prince Abrupolis had committed aggression against Macedon in raiding the Pangaean mines. Perseus had a right to repulse him. But had he a right to depose him? Rome did not support Abrupolis at the time, but later took up his case as an 'ally'. It needed only one 'injured ally" to make a *casus belli*.

(2) Philip had taken Dolopia in 190 B.C., without protest from Rome. Dolopia had revolted in 174 B.C. and appealed for Roman arbitration; but meanwhile Perseus regained control. His offence was not so much to have recovered Dolopia but to have done so without reference to Rome.

As for the other charges, Perseus' visit to Delphi was a parade, not an attack. If Eumenes was nearly killed by a rock near Delphi, and if two pro-Roman Thebans perished on the way to Rome, what evidence could prove Perseus responsible? In addition, the pro-Roman chieftain in Illyria, Artetaurus, was assassinated, and the assassins fled to Macedonia—could this implicate the king? Or if he helped Byzantium against its Thracian neighbours, as Philip had done earlier without protest from Rome, was this now a sign of Macedonian expansion?

Most of these charges carry no weight. They represent propaganda rather than evidence—except where Greek diplomacy blurred the distinction. The Senate hardly treated them severally as parts of a case for war. But they supported an impression that Macedon had regained more influence in Greece than was proper under the settlement of 196 B.C.; therefore Rome should intervene again. What satisfaction could Rome demand for this situation? The ultimatum was phrased in terms of 'injury to allies'. But the Senate's aim was to bring Macedon's foreign relations under direct supervision. Perseus could not believe that this was a case for war, and he continued to trust in negotiation. Thus Q. Marcius Philippus was able to gain time for the Roman preparations for a war that the Senate was determined to wage.[19] In the end Perseus had no alternative but to fight, unless he abandoned all claim to rule an independent Macedon.

Just as important in Greek affairs, especially since Aetolia had fallen, the Achaean League upheld its policy in the Peloponnese.[20] In terms of personality Philopoemen did flamboyantly what Philip set about achieving more steadily in the north. We may recall the traditional tension between Achaea, Sparta and Messene. It is enough to note that under the political and social conditions there was little chance of peace, however much Rome might desire it. External influence had played its part in the third century B.C., when the Achaean League was associated with both Macedon and Egypt; then Egypt declined, Philip made his policy intolerable, and the Achaeans joined Rome in the Second Macedonian War. Their policy now involved independent action in the Peloponnese, especially against Sparta. In Sparta since 207 B.C. Nabis held power and directed his policy against Achaea. When Philip, losing the Achaean League, tempted him with the offer of Argos, he accepted Argos; then he, too, saw more advantage in relations with Rome and joined her. What, then, of the autonomy of Argos after the war, under Roman policy? Flamininus forced Nabis to give up Argos and limit his ambitions.[21]

It was Philopoemen who had done most to check Nabis, and he now opposed Flamininus' diplomacy. 'The last of the Greeks', as one Roman said—or, in a more recent judgment, 'the most Roman of the Greeks', a man whose 'spirit forbade him to make it easy for Rome to leave the Greeks really free'. This view has an unduly Roman slant—how free could anyone be under Roman 'patronage'? More plainly, 'Philopoemen was ready to perform the duties of a Roman ally, but he claimed the Achaean right to an independent policy in the Peloponnese'.[22] Yet should not a good ally, if he had any Pan-hellenic feeling, have conceded a little to Roman policy in Greece? A sound Achaean patriot, Philopoemen stood on traditional principles of policy. The Achaeans supported Rome against Philip and Antiochus; the Roman move against Nabis had suited them. On Nabis' death Philopoemen took Sparta into the League. But this policy still left Sparta in disorder, after years of social change. How should exiles return and regain their property and standing? Thirty years later the problem would still be the same. It now baffled the Romans. Flamininus himself, M'. Acilius Glabrio, M. Fulvius Nobilior and Q. Caecilius Metellus all intervened in the Peloponnese. They were hoist on their own principle of Greek autonomy, where the Greeks used it to exploit their local rivalries; then, by Italian practice, they pressed the privilege of arbitration. This procedure, like that of any compromise, gave equal dissatisfaction to all parties; yet in the Peloponnese we have to note how carefully the Senate tried to maintain a balance of interests, and how often it held back in its decisions. Though

Philopoemen checked Rome most openly, the circumstances of dissent were deeply entrenched. It took the sharp Q. Marcius Philippus in 183 B.C. to suggest that Rome should let the Achaean League disrupt itself.[23]

An unhappy feature of the Greek situation was the way in which the states intrigued so keenly against one another in the Roman presence, whether by embassies to the Senate or with the Roman commissions on the spot. Even cities within a league would approach Rome on their own account. It was a dangerous political game, which would incur contempt. It encouraged a tendency to break up the leagues: we should keep this in mind in studying the last years of the Achaean League. The game ignored the Romans' preoccupation with their own aims, their ability to follow suit politically, and their reserve power.

After Philopoemen's death Achaean policy lost the unity which his authority had imposed upon it; Lycortas and his Megalopolitan group were unable to maintain his independent line. It was now that the pro-Roman Callicrates, on an embassy to Rome in 181/0 B.C., advised the Senate to force its wishes on the League. We need not follow Polybius, Lycortas' son, in exaggerating the effect.[24] The Senate certainly expressed its approval of Callicrates; but the Romans already knew the balance of parties for and against their policy. We find little difference in the relations of Rome and Achaea during the next few years.

Rome's repulse of Macedon and Syria from the Aegean did not destroy the old relations of the Hellenistic world. Perseus had his dynastic marriages with Bithynia and Syria. The Achaean League, in diplomatic touch with Pergamum and Syria, kept its connections with Egypt. Eumenes of Pergamum was again active in the Aegean and northern Greece. Rhodes, too, had profited from Antiochus' defeat, even if Rome in 177 B.C. had supported Lycian autonomy against Rhodian control. The Rhodians displayed their navy in escorting Perseus' bride from Syria. There is little of political moment in these details, except with regard to Pergamum; but they serve to remind us, as Rome realized, that the Hellenistic states were still able to live their own life, without a 'patron' from the West.[25]

The Third Macedonian War tested the situation. Syria and Egypt were caught up by their own rivalry in the Sixth Syrian War. They were not likely to influence affairs in Greece; but a decisive victory by one or the other, and especially by Syria, might disturb the Eastern balance upon which Rome relied. Pergamum strongly and Rhodes with some internal dissent supported Rome. Prusias of Bithynia took no steps to help Macedon. The Aetolians split, and the Boeotian cities were so much at odds that their league dissolved. The Achaean League lent help to Rome, yet with obscure complications in which Q. Marcius Philippus played some part; it also kept in touch with Egypt. As the war dragged on, even the Roman supporters lost confidence. In Hellenistic eyes it was, or it had certainly become, a bad and useless war; by their conventions it should be closed in a negotiated peace. Eumenes was suspected of dealing secretly with Perseus, while Rhodes finally decided to mediate at Rome. The sudden victory at Pydna caught them in a fatally compromising position.[26]

On the Roman side the Third Macedonian War brought a crisis of policy. First, Roman commanders began to act so brutally in exacting supplies and claiming local support that the Senate had to decree that this should not be done without its authority. Secondly, it was now difficult for Rome to raise good armies for service overseas, while the Macedonian forces were as strong as they had ever been. The phalanx held the consular legions until Roman morale began to fail. Only L. Aemilius Paullus restored discipline, and he won the battle of Pydna only because a second Roman army had beaten Perseus' ally Genthius in Illyria and was approaching Perseus from the rear. Perseus had to stake the issue on a charge of the phalanx which otherwise he would never have considered. Rome won the war only by deploying her full strength.[27] That is why the Senate, unable to dominate a Greece that contained an independent Macedon, determined to break up the Macedonian kingdom.

It is important to take the point. In peace the Senate would act according to treaty, with the traditional touch of political 'patronage', ready to arbitrate between autonomous allies; often in Greece it had stayed its hand. In war its attitude changed. The Roman command should be supreme—in strategy, in negotiations, tactically in the field, and—with a senatorial commission—in the settlement. For all Flamininus' talk of autonomy, 'Stop quibbling', he had said to the Aetolians; 'I will make the peace terms so that Philip cannot disturb the Greeks.'[28] This was not a legal right but the powerful privilege of leadership. If allies offended against the Roman view of military loyalty by attempting to subvert the conduct of a war, they would pay for it. That is why the Senate's attitude seems to have changed so formidably after Pydna.

Hence the Roman settlement of 167 B.C. Macedon was too strong and Perseus had refused to yield; the Senate removed Macedon from Greek politics. It divided the kingdom in four republics, arranging their local rights and interrelations—but allowing no more. Illyria had threatened Rome's communications with Greece; Illyria was divided similarly in three states. The Molossian part of Epirus had incurred a military penalty, and L. Aemilius Paullus carried it out.[29] As for Pergamum, though Eumenes had helped by informing against Perseus, he had lapsed in loyalty; the Senate humiliated him.[30] Rhodes had even proposed a negotiated peace. She narrowly avoided military subjection, lost influence in Caria and Lycia, and suffered from the activity of Delos now as a free port.[31] The Achaean League paid for its contorted policy. Under charges of pro-Macedonian sympathy a thousand Achaeans, among them Polybius, were taken to Italy; they were not tried but simply held as hostages.[32] Farther east, where Syria was pressing on Egypt, C. Popillius Laenas drew a circle in the sand round Antiochus Epiphanes and ordered him to retire.[33] This was a wartime settlement, applied as broadly as possible to create an Eastern 'protectorate'.

III

Macedon has fallen and Rome has revealed her motives of policy in Greece. We have to study the final stage.[34] Every Hellenistic state in its restricted power had its own problems. Rhodes was not able to control her interests in Caria and Lycia or protect her seas against Cretan piracy. Pergamum had trouble on its Galatian frontier and became involved in war with Bithynia; Eumenes remained suspect at Rome, but on his death in 160 B.C. Attalus II, a Roman favourite, practised a careful policy.[35] Syria, however, like Macedon earlier, had to secure its territory on the north. Antiochus Epiphanes, too, was still suspect; after his death in 163 B.C. the Senate reduced Syria's military strength to the limits laid on Antiochus the Great. Rome did not intervene seriously while the kingdom struggled under dynastic troubles and territorial disruption, and the Parthians gathered in the north.[36] As for Egypt, the Ptolemaic dynasty split in two, and Rome mediated lightly in the division of power. The Macedonian republic fell into disorder; their local freedom did not make good the loss of national unity.[37] In the Peloponnese political and social tension continued, and the Senate could do little to relax it.[38]

The pressure of Roman diplomacy is illustrated by a list of the Senate's commissions:

165 B.C.   Ti. Sempronius Gracchus inspected Pergamum, Rhodes
            and Syria, and reported favourably on their attitude to-
            wards the settlement.

164 B.C.   C. Sulpicius Galus arbitrated on a territorial dispute
            between Sparta and Megalopolis, and inspected Per-
            gamum and Syria.

163 B.C.   Cn. Octavius inspected Macedonia and Galatia, dis-
            armed Syria, and mediated between the Ptolemies.

162 B.C.   T. Manlius Torquatus mediated again in Egypt.

162-1 B.C. Ti. Sempronius Gracchus inspected Greece, mediated
            in Galatia, and inspected Syria.

158 B.C.   C. Fannius Strabo reported on Illyria and Dalmatia.

156 B.C.   P. Cornelius Lentulus reported on war between Bith-
            ynia and Pergamum, L. Appuleius Saturninus inspec-
            ted.

155-4 B.C. C. Claudius Centho mediated between Bithynia and
            Pergamum; L. Anicius Gallus also mediated; Ap.
            Claudius stopped the war.

154 B.C.   Cn. Cornelius Merula intervened between the Ptole-
            mies.

153 B.C.   Roman mediation in a Rhodian-Cretan war; Cato
            mediated between Carthage and Numidia.

152 B.C.   P. Cornelius Scipio Nasica Corculum composed a dis-
            pute between Carthage and Numidia.

150 B.C.   Scipio Aemilianus mediated between Carthage and
            Numidia.

149 B.C.   L. Manlius Vulso tried to check war between Bithynia
            and Pergamum.

The table makes its own case.[39] First, the situation was no longer
one of Hellenistic freedom, directed on occasions by Roman 'patronage', as it had been before the Third Macedonian War. We see
the control of a 'protectorate'. Secondly, since the fiction of full
autonomy was preserved, this did not work satisfactorily; also, it
left the Greeks liable to take undue risks with Rome. Thirdly, by
150 B.C. Rome was deeply involved in the West. If these circumstances should, in the Roman view, create a military emergency,
then the Senate would again expect loyalty regardless of local
problems, and punish anything that threatened subversion. But
would the Achaean League, for instance, appreciate the position?

Consider the Achaean hostages of 167 B.C., such as survived. In 151 the Senate decreed to send them back. It was Cato who made the point. 'Why should some old Greeks,' he said, 'be buried in Italy rather than at home?' Polybius went to see him. 'I think,' he argued, 'that the returning Achaeans should recover their previous honours.' Cato smiled. 'Do you wish, Polybius,' he replied, 'like Odysseus, to go back into the Cyclops' cave to get your cap and belt?' The example is significant. Polybius had made a valid *local* point; Cato knew the *Roman* context.[40]

How far had the changes in Rome itself affected the Senate's diplomacy? My analysis has stressed the application of traditional conventions in a wider political field. There were also personal features of behaviour. Roman nobles were tempted to exploit their authority, relax their diplomatic scruples, find profit in their public service, use overseas affairs for their own advancement at home. Q. Marcius Philippus was not the only Roman to prove as sharp as the Greek politicians on their own ground. The evidence for aristocratic groups does not help in analysing the *nova sapientia*:[41] it was at once general and personal; but we can distinguish old families, for instance, those close to L. Aemilius Paullus, of which the members stayed *moris antiqui memores*. It was the Senate that formulated policy and directed its commissions. Aemilius Paullus in enslaving the Molossians and Scipio Aemilianus at Carthage were undoubtedly under orders. As regards policy the Scipionic group upheld Africanus' liberal attitude in Africa and the East; Cato stood on his Italian principles. But the main body of nobles, whether led by Fulvii or Postumii or both together, adapted the old methods to the fresh circumstances, and perhaps more lightly applied the means to the ends. In Greece this involved an imbroglio of Roman and Hellenistic diplomacy.

Rome was engaged in the West. Ti. Sempronius Gracchus' settlement of Spain in 179 B.C. had broken down, largely through the defects of Roman administration; there was reason for the *Lex Calpurnia de repetundis* in 149 B.C., if only to regain support in Spain. Yet the Spanish wars that began in 153 B.C. could have been liberally settled three years later, had the Senate not insisted upon dictating the terms. Its generals failed, and the military levies met popular opposition.[42] At the same time in Africa the clash of Massinissa with Carthage led to war. We need not follow the details, except later to note Rome's diplomatic methods and her treatment of Carthage in 146 B.C.[43] Problems in Greece became part of a larger military situation.

When Andriscus, claiming to be Perseus' son Philip, first appeared as pretender to the Macedonian throne, he was not taken seriously either in Greece or at Rome. But when he established himself in Macedonia with Thracian help and gained increasing support, Rome sent Iuventius Thalna with a legion in 149 B.C. Andriscus defeated and killed him. With a strong army Q. Caecilius' Metellus crushed Andriscus in the Fourth Macedonian War. It was not so much the pretender as the national feeling he revived that confirmed the failure of the settlement of 167 B.C. The logic of events led to the reduction of Macedonia to provincial status.[44]

The Achaean League still held its position in the Peloponnese, but this was subject to certain critical factors. First, social unrest was affecting the play of parties in the League and its cities. It did not, as elsewhere in Greece, involve direct attitudes towards Rome, viz. the propertied class pro-Roman, proletariat anti-Roman; Achaean policy was already differentiated in its practice. There was no common interest between the Achaean proletariat and, say, Sparta, in face of the traditional rivalry of the states. But popular leaders like Critolaus and Diaeus had less scope for cool calculation, even as far as they were ready to use it; and personal antagonisms became sharper. Secondly, there was tension between the League administration and the constituent cities with their local autonomy; Sparta, for instance, was in the League. At what point would discontent lead to secession? An old problem. Or, more immediately, what right had individual cities to appeal direct to Rome? Another old problem, now accentuated by the Roman supervision. Thirdly, Roman policy had become more disruptive, at least under conditions of military emergency. The Achaean issues were chiefly Peloponnesian, and the Roman commissions had not acted drastically hitherto, even at awkward points; but it was dangerous now to neglect the wider situation.[45]

In 164 B.C., when a Roman commission arbitrated between Sparta and Megalopolis, both in the Achaean League, it acted as if they were independent states. In 155 B.C., when Rhodes and the Cretans were at war, Callicrates checked any move to help either side, so as to avoid Rome's displeasure. The balance swung the other way in the dispute between Athens and Oropus. It was over a matter of taxes, and Oropus appealed to Rome; the Senate appointed Sicyon, a member of the Achaean League, to assess the damages. Sicyon decided heavily against Athens, and Athens appealed to Rome in 155 B.C. to secure a reduction of the damages. Even so Athens still put pressure on Oropus, which now appealed

to the Achaean League. The Achaeans, under Menalcidas who—
though a Spartan—was στρατηγός in 151/0 B.C., moved their army
up to Oropus and forced Athens to withdraw. They did this without
reference to Rome in a case in which the Senate had been involved;
and they had made a military matter of it.[46]

In 150 B.C. a fresh dispute broke out between the Achaean
government and Sparta. Somewhere in the situation we may discern
personal animosity and intrigue that involved Menalcidas (now
back in Sparta), Callicrates and Diaeus, the στρατηγός in 150/49
B.C. In any event Sparta challenged the League's jurisdiction over
her autonomous conditions in a way that threatened secession.
Diaeus reacted violently; his chief Spartan opponents (including
Menalcidas) went into exile and appealed to the Senate. Late in
149 B.C. Diaeus and Callicrates also set out for Rome. Callicrates
died on the way, and Diaeus took a defiant attitude. The Senate
promised a commission. It did not arrive in 148 B.C., but Metellus
from Macedonia warned the Achaeans not to use force against
Sparta before the commission appeared. Meanwhile the League had
attacked Sparta but not pressed the attack home, and Diaeus agreed
to wait. If he had at last seen the danger, it was too late.[47]

In 147 B.C. L. Aurelius Orestes announced at Corinth that the
Senate wished not only Sparta but the cities of Corinth, Argos,
Orchomenus in Arcadia, and Heraclea (near Thermopylae) to be
detached from the Achaean League. Apparently the Senate had
made this decision after Diaeus' appearance in Rome and withheld
announcement of it until Orestes should convey it in person, once
the Macedon situation was under control. It was 'advice' in form,
a direct command in political reality. Secession was an old issue,
but this meant the disruption of Achaean power. Heraclea was an
expendable post in Central Greece; but Corinth (with Acrocorinth)
was one of the strategic 'fetters of Greece', while Argos—especially
if Sparta was independent again—and Orchomenus were essential
to the Achaean position in the Peloponnese. The Senate was, in
effect and—in territorial terms—even more drastically, demanding
what it had demanded of Macedon in 171 B.C., viz. the surrender
of power and policy.[48]

The decision came like a bolt—not quite from the blue, but from
a sky that was not more clouded than it had been at previous
times. The cloud was in the West, overhanging Italy, Africa and
Spain, with some depression over Macedonia. In plainer terms
Rome was in military difficulties that determined her policy in the
Peloponnese. I would judge from the circumstances in Spain. There

we find a dictatorial policy, resting shakily on bad generalship and bad faith, which would continue for twenty years. Rome could not lose, but she had been corrupted—by the exercise of power, by her own social changes, and by her loss of political morality in dealing with other peoples.[49] I have come to the point of generalization; but I have a strict point of procedure in mind. It is connected with 'militarism'. The term is applied to the stage at which what was once a set of strategic calculations is carried on after success, through professional convention, into a situation that should involve the wider responsibilities of politics and government. It was twenty years since the destruction of Macedon and the disruption of the Hellenistic world. The circumstances in Greece might appear similar, calling for loyal support or justifying military punishment. In fact, the Senate had learnt nothing from experience—if, indeed, it wished to do so.

The Achaean politicians had not the steadiness of a Macedonian king, but their choice was the same as that of Perseus. They had to resist or abdicate. First, they prepared to negotiate; but when a second Roman commission under Sex. Julius Caesar did not relax the terms, they cast the die. Critolaus deferred discussion with the Romans and Spartans; then having rallied support he secured a vote of war against Sparta. We may believe that Sex. Caesar, like Marcius Philippus against Perseus, was only set on gaining time for Roman intervention, unless the Achaean League gave in. The Achaeans, too, may have thought that Rome, after all her equivocation, would not apply force to the Peloponnese. The situation was one of force and bluff or, at the best, a tragedy of errors. The League had to face two Roman armies. Critolaus died opposing Metellus in the north, Diaeus lost to Mummius at Corinth, and the ancient city suffered a military fate by decision of the Senate.

If Greece was administered from Macedonia, and the Achaean League regained a weaker form, that is another story.[50]

NOTES

1. This paper was read at the Joint Triennial Classical Conference in Oxford on 7 September 1968. I wrote it for publication in honour of Professor E. M. Blaiklock on his retirement, and I now dedicate it to him.

2. For the Roman perspective: A. H. McDonald, *The Rise of Roman Imperialism* (Sydney, 1940) and *Republican Rome* (London, 1966) ; E. Badian, *Roman Imperialism in the Late Republic,* 2nd ed. (Oxford, 1968). For the Greek setting: M. Rostovtzeff, *Social and Economic History of the Hellenistic World* (Oxford, 1941). For the political history: B. Niese, *Geschichte der griechischen und makedonischen Staaten,* Vols. ii-iii (Gotha, 1899-1903) ; G. De Sanctis, *Storia dei Romani,* Vol. iv, 1-3 (Turin-Florence, 1923-64) ; M. Holleaux, *Rome, la Grèce et les monarchies hellénistiques* (Paris, 1921) and *Cambridge Ancient History,* Vol. viii (Cambridge, 1930), chs. 5-7. Note also J. A. O. Larsen, *Greek Federal States* (Oxford, 1968) ; W. Dahlheim, *Struktur und Entwicklung des römischen Völkerrechts* (Vestigia 8: Munich, 1968). I shall not normally refer to these works in detail below, where I prefer to cite the special studies—but they are basic to the whole reconstruction of events.

3. F. W. Walbank, *Philip V of Macedon* (Cambridge, 1940) chs. 4-6.

4. McDonald, *Repub. Rome,* chs. 3 and 6.

5. M. Gelzer, *Die Nobilität der römischen Republik* (Berlin, 1912) ; H. H. Scullard, *Roman Politics 220-150 B.C.* (Oxford, 1951) ; E. Badian, *Foreign Clientelae* (Oxford, 1958).

6. Polyb. xvi 34.6.

7. Walbank, op. cit. p. 131.

8. Polyb. xviii 1.7.

9. Polyb. xviii 38.6-9 ; Liv. xxvi 24.8-13, xxxiii 13.9-12. On the inscription: McDonald, *JRS* xlvi (1956), 153 ff. (plate xx) ; Walbank, *Historical Commentary on Polybius,* Vol. ii (Oxford, 1967), pp. 599-601.

10. On Flamininus: J. P. V. D. Balsdon, *Phoenix* xxi (1967), 3 ff.

11. Polyb. xxi 16.7-17.2. For the background: E. Badian, *Studies in Greek and Roman History* (Oxford, 1964), pp. 112 ff. (= *CP* liv (1959), 81 ff.) ; H. H. Schmitt, 'Untersuchungen zur Geschichte Antiochos' des Grossen und seiner Zeit', *Historia,* Einzelschr. 6 (1964), chs. 4-5.

12. McDonald, *JRS* xxviii (1938), 153 ff.

13. E. Täubler, *Imperium Romanum,* Vol. i (Berlin, 1913), pp. 62 ff.

14. McDonald, *Repub. Rome,* ch. 5.

15. Polyb. xxxi 23-4. For the setting: R. E. Smith, *The Aristocratic Epoch in Latin Literature* (Sydney, 1947) and *The Failure of the Roman Republic* (Cambridge, 1955), chs. 2-3 ; D. C. Earl, *The Moral and Political Tradition of Rome* (London, 1967), pp. 36 ff. ; A. E. Astin, *Scipio Aemilianus* (Oxford, 1967), pp. 19 ff.

16. Walbank, *Philip V,* ch. 7.

17. P. Meloni, *Perseo* (Rome, 1953).
18. Polyb. xxii 18 ; Täubler, op. cit., pp. 232ff.
19. Walbank, *JRS* xxxi (1941), 86ff.; J. Van Ooteghem, *Lucius Marcius Philippus et sa famille* (Acad. royale de Belgique, classe des lettres, mémoires 55.3, 1961), pp. 70ff.; J. Briscoe, *JRS liv* (1964), pp. 67ff.
20. A. Aymard, *Les premiers rapports de Rome et de la confédération achaienne, 198-189 av. J.C.* (Bordeaux, 1938) ; Larsen, *Greek Fed. States,* pp. 359ff.
21. Walbank, *Philip V,* p. 187.
22. P. V. M. Benecke, *CAH* viii, p. 299 ; Larsen, op. cit., p. 404.
23. Polyb. xxiii 9.8-10.
24. Polyb. xxiv 8-10.
25. J. Seibert, 'Historische Beiträge zu den dynastischen Verbindungen in Hellenistischer Zeit', *Historia,* Einzelschr. 10 (1967).
26. Meloni, *Perseo,* pp. 335ff.
27. Meloni, op. cit., ch. 6. Long ago Prof. Charles Edson showed me how, in strategic terms, the presence of a second Roman army forced Perseus to change from defensive tactics to the attack at Pydna.
28. Polyb. xviii 37, 12.
29. Larsen, *Economic Survey of Ancient Rome* (ed. T. Frank), Vol. iv (Paterson, N. J., 1959), pp. 294ff.; S. I. Oost, *Roman Policy in Epirus and Acarnania* (Dallas, 1954), pp. 83ff; N. G. L. Hammond, *Epirus* (Oxford, 1967), pp. 633ff.
30. E. V. Hansen, *The Attalids of Pergamon* (Cornell, 1947), pp. 117ff.
31. H. H. Schmitt, *Rom und Rhodos* (Munich, 1957), pp. 157ff.
32. Polyb. xxx 13 ; Larsen, *Greek Fed. States,* p. 479.
33. Polyb. xxix 27.
34. De Sanctis, op. cit., iv. 3, ch. 2.
35. D. Magie, *Roman Rule in Asia Minor* (Princeton, 1950), pp. 22, 116, 766, 968.
36. Polyb. xxxi 2, 9-11 ; Niese, op. cit., iii, pp. 243ff.
37. Larsen, *Greek Fed. States,* pp. 295ff.
38. Larsen, op. cit., pp. 483ff.
39. The table is based on T. R. S. Broughton, *The Magistrates of the Roman Republic* Vol. i (New York, 1951 ; Supplement, 1960), under the years of appointment. We need a special study of these commissions, with reference to their powers and political activity in the local conditions of Greece and the East.
40. Polyb. xxxv 6 ; Plut. *Cato* 9.2-3.
41. Briscoe, *JRS liv* (1964), pp. 73ff.; *Historia* xviii (1969), p. 49 ; Scullard, *Rom. Politics,* ch. 14.

42. De Sanctis, op. cit., iv, i, pp. 464ff., iv, 3, pp. 222 ff.; A. Schulten, *CAH* viii, ch. 10; H. Simon, *Roms Kriege in Spanien 154-133 v. Chr.* (Frankfurt, 1962); cf. L. R. Taylor, *JAS* lii (1962), pp. 19ff.

43. B. L. Hallward, *CAH* viii, ch. 15, 1-4; De Sanctis, op. cit., iv, 3, ch. 1.

44. De Sanctis, op. cit., iv, 3, pp. 120ff.

45. At this critical point note for the Achaean setting: Larsen, *Greek Fed. States,* pp. 485ff.; for the events, Niese, op. cit. iii, pp. 337ff., De Sanctis, op. cit., iv, 3, pp. 127ff. the latter especially for political interpretation; their work gives full references to the ancient authorities.

46. On Menalcidas: De Sanctis, loc. cit. (pp. 83, 129 ff.).

47. De Sanctis, loc cit. (pp. 129ff.).

48. On Aurelius Orestes: De Sanctis, loc. cit. (pp. 136ff.).

49. For the play of violence in Roman political thought at home, which sharpened the impersonal effect abroad, see A. W. Lintott, *Violence in Republican Rome* (Oxford, 1968).

50. De Sanctis, op. cit., iv, 3, pp. 171ff.; S. Accame, *Il dominio romano in Grecia dalla guerra acaica ad Augusto* (Rome, 1946); Larsen, *Greek Fed. States,* pp. 498ff.

EVIDENCE FOR LEGISLATION BY TRIBUNES 81 -70 B.C.

D. H. Kelly

It was Mommsen's[1] theory that a law of Sulla the dictator permitted tribunes to bring forward laws only with the prior approval of the Senate. This has been widely accepted,[2] the rival view that Sulla completely abolished the tribunes' power to bring forward laws having found few supporters.[3] As Bloch and Carcopino[4] observe, this point of constitutional law may make little difference if tribunician laws were not a usable weapon in the political struggles of this period. However some consideration of this point may not only assist the dating of certain Roman laws but also throw some light on the assault on oligarchic privilege that reached its successful conclusion in the first consulate of Pompeius and Crassus.

Since in his account of the dictator Sulla's treatment of the tribunate (*BC* i. 100) Appian does not mention any imposing of senatorial control over the tribunes' power to legislate, it is possible to assume that Sulla then reintroduced the short-lived measure that he had carried in 88 (ibid. 59). But the evidence on which Mommsen based his case comprised instances of tribunician laws that were taken to fall within the period 82 - 70.

Of these laws the *Lex Plotia de ui*, if that was the law under which M. Caelius Rufus was tried in 56, may have been passed in 78, but this is far from certain.[5] The *Lex Plotia de reditu Lepidanorum* was assigned by Mommsen to 77.[6] But as Caesar supported this law in his military tribunate (Suet. *Caes.* 5), it can best be dated a year or two before 69, which was the year Caesar was quaestor.[7] Not enough is known of the politics at Rome in the seventies to gauge with precision the point at which an amnesty would have been most likely to be granted to the rebels in Spain. A recent suggestion is that '70 is a highly appropriate year for an amnesty being a year of revolutionary changes and therefore a season for advertising concord'.[8] The *Lex Plotia* was placed in 73 by Maurenbrecher,[9] but this is no more than a guess that at some point in his narrative of this year Sallust prefaced his account of the *Lex Plotia* with some remarks on the amnesty of 77 that included the words '*post reditum eorum quibus senatus belli gratiam fecerat*'.[10] Sallust's words need not refer to a *senatus consultum* authorizing a tribunician law in 77, and the connection between Caesar's military tribunate and the *Lex Plotia de reditu Lepidanorum* points to a date for this in 71 - 70.

If this law came in 70, it does not help establish how Sulla restricted the tribunes' power to bring forward laws, for it may have been passed after the *Lex Licinia Pompeia* of that year.[11] The same applies to the *Lex Plotia agraria*.[12]

The law that is most commonly regarded as falling within the period when Sulla's restriction upon tribunician laws was in force is the *Lex Antonia de Termessibus* (*CIL* I². 2. n. 204). Mommsen placed this law in 72 because it refers to the year *L. Gellio Cn. Lentulo cos.* and because the heading contains the phrase '*de s.s.*'.[13] However, the references to the consuls of 72 need not indicate that they were in office the year the law was passed. A date (1 April) in 72 may have been selected to define the status of Termessus Maior because in this year the consuls passed a law regulating the leasing of property that affected this state.[14]

The names of the ten tribunes who held office in the year the *Lex Antonia* was passed have been established by an inscription (*CIL* I². 2. no. 744) that gives the *consilium* of a *curator uiarum*, L. Volcatius. Of these names three are found in the extant part of the heading of the *Lex Antonia*.[15] The college could not have held office in 71, for it does not include M. Lollius Palicanus, nor in 70, although this is not absolutely certain, for it does not include a Plotius. T. R. S. Broughton[16] assigns this college of tribunes to 68. If it could be shown that tribunician laws could be passed with the Senate's approval before the *Lex Licinia Pompeia*, a date of 72 for the *Lex Antonia* would be made more probable. The phrase '*d.s.s.*' does not of itself establish a date before 70.[17]

The doubts then felt by Last[18] on the possibility of tribunes bringing forward laws in this period were justified. For the dominance of the oligarchy was challenged then by a succession of agitators: Cn. Sicinius in 76, Q. Opimius in 75, C. Licinius Macer in 73 and M. Lollius Palicanus in 71. The meagre evidence for these years suggests that no laws were passed by any of these tribunes, except one. The exception is Quinctius, who seized an opportunity presented by the *iudicium Iunianum*. The law that a reluctant senate allowed him to pass in 74 has so far not been observed. It can be discovered from a close look at part of Cicero's pleading in the *pro Cluentio* and from a passage of the *actio prima* against Verres (*Verr.* i. 46). Here Cicero speaks of a *lex tribunicia* which has not been satisfactorily elucidated, but which can be taken as a *lex Quinctiana*.

In the notorious *iudicium Iunianum* it was common knowledge that money had changed hands. In his prosecution of Verres in 70 Cicero treated it as another flagrant instance of the corruption of senatorial *iudices* (*Verr.* i. 39). He spoke then of one of the *iudices* taking money from both the prosecutor and the defendant. A. Cluentius Habitus, the prosecutor, and his stepfather Statius Albius Oppianicus, the defendant, in this version both resorted to bribery. However in defending Cluentius in 66 when he was prosecuted by Oppianicus' son, Cicero gave out an entirely different version: only Oppianicus, not Cluentius, had used bribery and the bribery had been bungled (*Clu.* 43-116).

In the outcry that had followed the conviction of Oppianicus in 74, the presiding quaestor C. Iunius had been brought to trial and found guilty. Charges of misconduct had played a part in securing the conviction of other senators who had served on the jury that condemned Oppianicus. Cicero's account of the relationship between Cluentius and Oppianicus before the trial in 74 has been shown to be highly misleading.[19] Cicero should also be treated with suspicion when he explains away the conviction of Iunius and others involved in the *iudicium Iunianum* so as to leave nothing to his client Cluentius' discredit.

Cicero made out that the conviction of Iunius was due not to any impression that he had taken bribes but to minor technical irregularities '*quod in legem non iurasset . . . et quod C. Verres praetor urbanus, homo sanctus et diligens, subsortitionem eius in eo codice non haberet, qui tum interlitus proferebatur*' (*Clu.* 91). Of the rest Staienus and Bulbus were convicted of *maiestas* (*ibid.* 97, 99-102); Popilius and Gutta of *ambitus* (*ibid.* 98); Septimius Scaevola of *repetundae* in Apulia (*ibid.* 116). And, Cicero argued, if the *litis aestimatio* mentioned money taken as a bribe, this was due only to the carefree way the *litis aestimatio* was, as usual, made up after the important issue had been decided (ibid. 115-6).

Cicero dealt with these disreputable senators only to show that the aftermath of the scandal of Oppianicus' conviction was not to be taken as showing that Cluentius had used bribery then. He fol-

lowed the same line in dealing with Iunius and one of the *iudices,*
C. Fidiculanius Falcula. The latter was tried and acquitted under
the same law under which Iunicus had been found guilty. He was
then tried for *repetundae,* which, Cicero pointed out, was the normal way of prosecuting a *iudex* accused of taking bribes (ibid. 103-
4),[20] and he was acquitted.

The same point could have been raised about Septimius Scaevola,
so Cicero carefully made his prosecution for *repetundae* refer only
to misdeeds in Apulia, not to judicial corruption. In insisting that
the indictments against the other *iudices* did not formally concern
judicial corruption, Cicero misleadingly ignored the misdeeds that
their prosecutors must have elaborated on: these would have included a great deal about the *iudicium Iunianum.* In this way he
obscured the issue about those *iudices* believed to have taken
bribes. In dealing with those believed to have secured an unjust
condemnation by bribery, Iunius and Falcula, he had a more in-
genious plea. If Iunius had been charged with corruptly securing
Oppianicus' conviction, he would have been prosecuted under the
same law as Cluentius was being prosecuted under in 66 (ibid. 89-
90), that is, the *Lex Cornelia de sicariis,* which included a provision
'*ne quis iudicio circumueniretur*' (ibid. 151. cf. 148).

In dealing with the law and the court before which Iunius and
Falcula were tried Cicero is evasive and abusive. The prosecutor
of both these had been L. Quinctius, tribune in that year and
counsel for his friend Oppianicus. According to Cicero this arrogant and seditious tribune then began to exploit the ill-repute of the
senatorial *iudicia,* holding turbulent *contiones* and for once shaking
the Roman people out of its usual torpor (ibid. 77, 79, 90-96, 103,
137-8). It was Quinctius who prosecuted Iunius and then Falcula.

Under what law were these two tried? It was neither the *Lex
Cornelia de sicariis* nor the *Lex Cornelia repetundarum* and so was
neither of the two laws that dealt with judicial conspiracy and
corruption respectively. In establishing Cluentius' innocence of
malpractice in the *iudicium Iunianum* Cicero repeatedly emphasizes
the prejudice, hostility and mistaken notions that the agitation of
Quinctius had produced. With considerable exaggeration he speaks
of *contiones* by a tribune as now having a revival for the first time
since Sulla's dictatorship (ibid. 110). Sicinius and Opimius at least
must have held these, but neither of them had, it seems, found
such an opportunity as Quinctius had.

Cicero's references to Quinctius' activities were meant to account
for the *inuidia* against his client and at the same time to create

inuidia against the prosecution in turn. So he gave very little information about how Iunius and Falcula were tried. Iunius' trial was simply too turbulent to be a proper trial (ibid. 96). Falcula was acquitted on his first prosecution because feeling had died down and sedition and rioting were absent (ibid. 103). From Cicero's arguments elsewhere in the *pro Cluentio* something can be learnt of the law that was used against these two.

Cicero also disputed the prosecution's interpretation of a *senatus consultum* that allegedly declared that the jury in the *iudicium Iunianum* had been bribed (ibid. 136). He maintained that it was not specific but was only meant to placate popular feeling by condemning corruption in general terms. He asked the prosecutor (ibid. 137) whether any law in accordance with that *senatus consultum* had been passed by Lucullus (consul 74) or by the consuls of the following year, to whom the senate had referred the matter. Peterson[21] took '*istam legem ex isto senatus consulto*' as a sarcastic phrase for a non-existent law. But the readiness of Cicero to dismiss this whole matter ought to make us suspect that he had something to conceal. The argument in 136-7 is to be connected with the emotive plea in 145-160 for the jury to frustrate the prosecutor Accius' attempt to extend the provision of the *Lex Cornelia* against 'circumvention' from senatorial to equestrian *iudices*. The feelings of the *equites* could run high on this, as later incidents show,[22] and the prosecutor could hardly have been so obtuse as to offend the *equites* on the jury.

Probably Accius' argument was that among the good reasons for condemning Cluentius for poisoning was that Cluentius had himself used bribery to secure the conviction of Oppianicus on the same charge. This would be quite in the way of a Roman orator. Accius must have given a full account of the *iudicium Iunianum*, using all possible ways of showing that Cluentius had used bribery. He would have dealt with the *senatus consultum* of 74 in this way and mentioned attendant circumstances that Cicero had to ignore. The law about which Cicero interrogated his rival would have come up here, when Accius described how Iunius had got his deserts. On the other hand Cicero concentrated on the opinion of respectable statesmen who thought that nothing was to be done, especially that of L. Lucullus, whose crushing of Quinctius in that year won him fame or notoriety (Plut. *Luc.* 5, 4; 33, 5; Sall. *Hist.* iii 48. 11 Maurenbrecher; cf. iii 17 and iv 71).

Quinctius' moment had been brief. He got Iunius but failed with Falcula. Then Lucullus opposed him successfully and the consuls of the following year did not think it necessary to reintroduce any legislation in accordance with the senatus consultum (ibid. 137).[23] Lastly, the Roman people was moved by the spectacle of Iunius' weeping son to reject a law setting up a *quaestio*.

The *quaestio* in question must have been a special one to deal with judicial corruption, like the one proposed (*Att.* i 17.8) after the acquittal of Clodius. In 73, when the question of this *quaestio* came up again, the matter was dropped, as the mood of the people had changed. The year before, at the height of Quinctius' agitation, the Senate had been forced to authorize the tribune Quinctius to propose a law establishing a *quaestio* to deal with those involved in the *iudicium Iunianum*. However the acquittal of Falcula seems to have enabled Lucullus to get the upper hand over Quinctius. The *quaestio* was probably set up for a short time only. The matter of its renewal would then have been referred by the Senate to the consuls elect (ibid. 137). They did nothing, and Iunius' son probably appeared at a *contio* held to explain why.

This reconstruction from the *pro Cluentio* of the events 74-3 may be supported by the passage from Cicero's speech against Verres (*Verr.* i 46): '*nunc autem homines in speculis sunt; obseruant quem ad modum sese unus quisque uestrum gerat in retinenda religione conseruandisque legibus. uident adhuc post legem tribuniciam unum senatorem uel tenuissimum esse damnatum: quod tametsi non reprehendunt, tamen magno opere quod laudent non habent. nulla est enim laus ibi esse integrum, ubi nemo est qui aut possit aut conetur corrumpere.*'

This passage comes after Cicero has been reminding the jury of senators of two unpalatable but unavoidable developments of that year. The corruption of the jury courts had become such a scandal that the people clamoured for the restoration of the tribunate (ibid. 2, 43-5); cf. *Diu. Caec.* 8, which shows that the appointment of the censors too was demanded for the same reason. For censors could degrade or stigmatize those guilty of judicial corruption: the censors of this year expelled from the Senate P. Lentulus Sura for this very reason (Plut. *Cic.* 17.3), one of them stigmatized Popilius for taking bribes in the *iudicium Iunianum* (*pro Cluentio* 131-2) and both punished Cluentius (ibid. 133-4). This show of severity came too late to silence the demand for reform of the *iudicia* (*Diu. Caec.* 1, 8-9), so Cicero could present the prosecution of Verres as a senatorial jury's last chance to redeem the order's good name.

In *Verr.* i 37-40 Cicero alluded briefly to flagrant cases of corruption. These had made Pompieus' promise to restore the tribunate acceptable to the people (ibid. 45). In Cicero's list those involved in the *iudicium Iunianum* have pride of place, but Iunius is not mentioned. He is however alluded to in the passage quoted above. The *legem tribuniciam*[24] of that passage is the *Lex Quinctia* passed in 74 to set up a special *quaestio*. Its only victim was Iunius, the single impoverished senator.[25]

The measures provoked by the *iudicium Iunianum* had not been effective in checking judicial corruption. The convictions of men involved in other courts helped keep the issue alive, as did the scandal of the coloured voting tablets used at the trial of Varro.[26] Then came the misgovernment of Sicily by Verres who as urban praetor in 74 had had a hand in the shady business in the *iudicium Iunianum*.[27] Verres injured prominent Sicilians, clients of Pompeius, but in spite of protests in the Senate remained in power.[28] Enemies of the oligarchy found sacrilege a subject that needed attention and prosecuted *nobiles* for liaisons with Vestal Virgins.[29] Under fire from many directions, with its foreign policy collapsing[30] and the slave revolt in Italy likely to get out of hand, the oligarchy was helpless to correct even the domestic abuse that Quinctius had highlighted and others had kept in prominence. In 66 Cicero could commend those senators who were ready to maintain *concordia* with the *equites* (*Cluent.* 152). There had been a breach in 74, when the *equites,* indifferent perhaps to what senatorial *iudices* did to senators, had been incensed at the corrupt conviction of one of their *ordo* as prominent as Oppianicus. The neglect of judicial corruption was a serious mistake, for it would alienate those who expected better of the ruling class. The conviction of Verres can be seen as a last, unsuccessful attempt to placate feeling against the oligarchy on this score. Class-solidarity and dislike of Quinctius and his methods led the oligarchy to frustrate the *quaestio Quinctiana* without taking any positive action to correct the abuse that laid them open to attack. No mere passing storm,[31] Quinctius' agitation had revealed a grave weakness in the Sullan settlement. The oligarchy's indifference to judicial corruption contributed to the tribunate's recovery of the power to legislate that Sulla had hedged around with a severe restriction and no doubt intended should remain dormant.[32]

NOTES

1. *Römische Staatsrecht* (181-8, repr. 1952) Vol. ii p. 372; iii 158.

2. E.g. by G. W. Botsford, *The Roman Assemblies* (1909), 413; Drumann-Groebe, *Geschichte Roms* (2nd ed., 1899, repr. 1964), 2.411 n. 3; F. B. Marsh, *A History of the Roman World 146-30 B.C.* (3rd ed. 1963), 130; F. de Martino, *Storia della Constituzione Romana* (1961), 3.81; J. Bleicken, 'Das Volkstribunat der Klassichen Republik' (*Zetemata* 13, 1965), 12 n. 1; 14.

3. E.g. G. Long, *The Decline of the Roman Republic* (1866), 2.399-400; G. Ferrero, *The Greatness and Decline of Rome* (Eng. trans. 1909), 1.114; H. Last *CAH* 9 (1932), 292-3, 896 (an important discussion).

4. G. Bloch-J. Carcopino, *Histoire Romaine Vol. II: La Republique romaine de 133 à 44 av. J.C.* (1940), 464 n. 49.

5. Cic. *Cael.* 1, 70 with the discussion and bibliography ad. loc. in the edition of R. G. Austin 3rd ed. (1960), 42-3. For Mommsen's view see *Römische Strafrecht* (1899, repr. 1955), 654 n. 2.

6. *Römische Strafrecht* ibid. (This untenable view is a retrogression on that of *Römische Geschichte* (repr. Phaidon n.d.), 671, which places the law after the death of Perperna.)

7. E. Badian, *JRS* 49 (1959), 87 n. 53.

8. R. Syme, *JRS* 53 (1963), 57-8.

9. *Sallustii Historiarum Reliquiae* (1891, repr. 1967), 1.78 n. 8, 2.126.

10. Sall. *Hist.* 3.47 Maurenbrecher. A Plotius was active in 73 in the trial of the Vestal Virgins: See Plut. *Crass.* 1.2 and *Cat. Min.* 19.3 (where Πλώτιος should be read for Κλώδιος). But he was not necessarily the author of the *Lex de reditu Lepidanorum* or the *Lex agraria,* or, if he was, he may have held more than one tribunate.

11. Cf. H. Last, op. cit. (n. 3), 896.

12. For this law see R. E. Smith, *CQ* 7 (1957) 82; P. A. Brunt *JRS* (1962), 69 n. 3.

13. 'tr. pl. de. s. s. plebem . . .'. For Mommsen's view see *Römische Staatsrecht* 2.1, 312 n. 1, CIL 1 p. 114.

14. 'ac ne locentur <sancitum est sanctione q>uae facta est ex l<ege rogata L. Gellio Cn. Lentulo cos . . .' (Col. 1. uu. 21-23. The restoration in these lines seems plausible; cf. Col. 1. uu. 4-5.)

15. Viz. C. Antonius, Cn. Cornelius and C. Fundanius.

16. *MRR* 2. 141 n. 6. But 69 is excluded, since the three tribunes known to have held office in that year do not occur in the college of ten.

17. The phrase is thought to have been in the gap in the *codex unicus* of eight to ten letters in the heading of the *Lex Quinctia de aquaeductibus* (Front. *Aquaed.* 129). V. Ehrenberg and A. H. M. Jones, *Documents illustrating the reigns of Augustus and Tiberius*

2nd ed. (1955) 124, tentatively fill the gap with [*d e s(ua)* *s(ententia)*?] For the use of the abbreviation see *CIL.* I *Index Grammaticus III*, p. 612: it means *de senatus sententia.*

18. Op. cit. (n. 3). H. H. Scullard, *From the Gracchi to Nero* (1959, 2nd ed. p. b. 1963), 84, 403 n. 33 leaves the question open, as does Lengle in *R.E.* 6A. 2484-5.

19. G. E. Hoenigswald, *TAPhA* 93 (1962), 109-23.

20. Cf. U. Ewins, *JRS* 50 (1960), 94-100. cf. A. N. Sherwin-White, ibid. 42 (1952), 46 n. 23.

21. W. Peterson, *Pro A Cluentio Oratio* (1899), 218.

22. Cic. *Att.* 1.17.8 ; *id., Rab. Post.,* 8-19.

23. The MSS reading *referendum* was altered to *ferendum* by Manutius (see A. C. Clark's *apparatus*), a change accepted by Peterson (op. cit. (n. 21), 219.), because of his belief that no law had been passed in 74. The interpretation of *referendum* as *denuo, rursus ferendum* is Orelli's (see G. G. Ramsay, *Cicero: Pro Cluentio* 2nd ed. (1869), 218).

24. Ernesti, *Ciceronis Opera* (London, 1799), 8.31, explained *legem tribuniciam* as the Sullan law restricting the tribunate, but for the proper sense of *tribuniciam,* 'passed by a tribune (or tribunes)', see e.g. *leg. agr.* 2.21. W. E. Heitland and H. Cowie *Ciceronis in Q. Caec. Diuinatio et in C. Verr. Act. Prima* (1876, repr. 1898) ad loc. take the phrase to refer to the *Lex Licinia Pompeia*, which again gives an anomalous and unparalleled sense to *tribuniciam.* This view, as old as Ps.-Asconius (p. 220 Stangl), was also held by Mommsem (*Römische Staatsrecht* 2.1, 311 n. 3).

25. In *Clu.* 79 Cicero speaks of him as a man who had held the aedileship and had every chance of a praetorship. In *Verr.* i 46 Cicero is concerned to damn this solitary conviction with faint praise, and so stresses the man's poverty. Ps.-Asconius (p. 221 Stangl) took the senator to be 'Dolabella' (Cn. Dolabella, praetor 81: *RE* 4 s.u. Cornelius, n. 135).

26. *Diu. Caec.* 24 ; *Verr.* i 40 ; *Verr.* ii 2.79 ; ibid. 5.173 ; *Clu.* 173 (which establishes the date *paucis postea mensibus, sc.* the *iudicium Iunianum*).

27. *Verr.* i 39 ; *Clu.* 91. The reticence in *Verr.* ii 1.157-8 about Verres' *subsortitio* can be due only to Cicero's desire not to contradict too blatantly the version he gave out in the *pro Cluentio*: a sign then of the time of writing the undelivered *actio secunda.* Cicero had already had occasion to explain away his remarks in the *actio prima* (*Clu.* 138-42).

28. E. Badian, *Foreign Clientelae (264-70 B.C.)* (1958), 282-4.

29. Both Crassus and Catilina were involved: D. R. Shackleton Bailey, *Cicero's Letters to Atticus* (1965), 1.319.

30. Badian op. cit. (n. 28), 279-81.

31. H. Grundel in *R.E.* 24. s.u. Quinctius, n. 12, 1003, realized in general terms the importance of his agitation: 'Es sich hierbei zweifellos um eine hoch-politische Sache handelte, die in der Tat zu einer wirklichen Sensation führte.'

32. I should like to thank Mr G. T. Griffith and Dr A. H. McDonald for their guidance.

AMBITION IN THE *GEORGICS*: VERGIL'S REJECTION OF ARCADIA[1]

Robert R. Dyer

> And through my troubled spirit goes
> the shadow of an old despair.
>
> A. R. D. Fairburn

E. M. Blaiklock, analysing the Stoic elements in the character of Aeneas, comments that Vergil must have become dissatisfied with his earlier Epicureanism: 'Epicureanism, nobly mediated through Lucretius, had once made a strong appeal to Vergil, but he had come to realize that a Roman needed something more, and that his mystic's mind could not rest in so firm a materialism. It is impossible to trace a coherent spiritual development, although part of the trail can be picked up in the Fourth *Georgic,* but Vergil reached something like acceptance of Stoicism. The evidence is Aeneas himself, although Bowra goes too far in asserting that the hero is "built on a Stoic plan".'[2]

In the continuing dialogue of teacher and student I should like to offer him in this present volume an attempt of my students and mine to trace this trail through the *Georgics.* It has seemed to us that Vergil became dissatisfied with the ideals of Lucretius and the *Eclogues* through observing the involvement of his young contemporaries, Cornelius Gallus and Octavian Caesar, in political action, and through formulating for himself a major commitment, the *Aeneid.* The dissatisfaction of Vergil with his earlier career is sharply, if urbanely, focused in the concluding lines of the *Georgics*:

> Haec super aruorum cultu pecorumque canebam
> et super arboribus, Caesar dum magnus ad altum
> fulminat Euphraten bello uictorque uolentis
> per populos dat iura uiamque adfectat Olympo.
> illo Vergilium me tempore dulcis alebat
> Parthenope studiis florentem ignobilis oti,
> carmina qui lusi pastorum audaxque iuuenta,
> Tityre, te patulae cecini sub tegmine fagi. (iv. 559-66)

We must consider the goals of Octavian's conquest, to bring civilization to the underdeveloped East, as praiseworthy and superior to the leisure pastimes of an *ignobilis*. When we next read Vergil his own goals will have escalated. And within the *Georgics* Octavian's goals run as a constant thread. He is addressed three times, and mentioned twice, always in a context of ambition.[3] Commentators who have regarded these invocations as insertions, perhaps motivated by the private audition with Octavian at which the poem was read, certainly at least by Maecenas' patronage, and as quite irrelevant to the structure of the poem,[4] have underestimated the strong contrast within this structure between the small cares of the farmer and the grand ambitions of Octavian and Vergil.

The *Georgics* is a didactic poem about farming only on the most superficial level. We cannot be certain what sort of poem Vergil set out to write when he began it around 36 B.C.,[5] but the poet who had so praised the utopian farmer's rustic *securitas* in the *Eclogues* may well have set out to write a hymn which would praise the real Italian farmer and show his unbroken, uncorrupted closeness to the simple gods of the countryside. There are traces of such a poem in our present text, notably Book II with its idyllic picture of the Italian countryside, the *Saturnia tellus* (136-176), and of the farmer on holiday (519ff.). The world which Vergil's *fortunatus agricola* enjoys is the Golden Age of Saturn (538), before banquets, war and the other examples of ambitious *curae*.

The ideal picture is reminiscent of the idealized Arcadian and Sicilian shepherds of the *Eclogues,* who enjoy their *securitas* in music and tales of love. The references to the Saturnian Age take us back to the *Fourth Eclogue,* suggesting that the farmer is alone in enjoying the pleasures which were once shared by all and is therefore a precursor of the new Golden Age promised there. It follows that Vergil was urging his contemporaries to return to the land and become pioneers of the new Golden Age. Indeed Vergil and Horace both did retire to live on small farms in the neighbourhood of cities. In this retreat from the cares and ambitions of life at Rome both writers were demonstrably under the influence of Epicureanism. If we may accept poems 5 and 8 of the *Catalepton* as authentic, and the assertions of Servius (ad *Ecl.* vi. 13) and of the *Vitae* as independent evidence, Vergil actually studied the doctrine with Siro.[6] Even if the worst were to be true and this evidence is entirely fabricated, we yet know that the *Georgics* is strongly influenced by Lucretius, and was written in or near Naples, where Siro must have been a dominant intellectual figure. Praise of the

simple farming life in Italy seems a natural development for a
young Epicurean poet who has made his literary mark by pastorals
on the Arcadian and Sicilian shepherds in the manner of Theocritus.
Yet if this was Vergil's original purpose, the poem he finally
composed is of quite a different character. If he once thought to
praise Epicurean *securitas* he finally asserts that *labor,* the most
obvious Latin rendering of πόνος,[7] is a goal and necessity of human
life. 'The lesson inculcated by Vergil is directly opposite to that
state of quietism and pure contemplation in which Lucretius finds
the ideal of human life.'[8] If he once thought to encourage a return
to the Italian soil he eventually wrote a work which downgrades
the farmer's life to a meaningless slavery to a cruel and uncompre-
hended universe.

Vergil may have profited, during his years of composition, from
observing the frustrations and failures of those who followed his
earlier utopian dream of finding in rural Italy the rustic Saturnian
Age. We New Zealanders understand the frustrations of trying to
realize Arcadia as well as any people alive.[9] Most of us are descendants of settlers who followed this dream away from the indus-
trializing Britain of the mid-nineteenth century. We read their dis-
illusion, struggle and resignation in their memoirs and correspondence.

Vergil introduces his farmer in early spring (G. i. 43ff.)[10]—appropriately, as a calendar of prescriptions for farming begins with the
first signs of spring and ends with the dead of winter. Yet spring is
also the season of natural growth when man has his highest hopes
and easiest labour. So Vergil hymns it at ii. 323ff.

> parturit almus ager Zephyrique trementibus auris
> laxant arua sinus; superat tener omnibus umor,
> inque nouos soles audent se gramina tuto
> credere ... (330-3)

The world itself must have been created in spring. How could the
newly-created things have endured the toil of creation except in
the springtime of a Golden Age?[11]

> nec res hunc tenerae possent perferre laborem,
> si non tanta quies iret frigusque caloremque
> inter, et exciperet caeli indulgentia terras. (343-5)

The new farmer, whom Vergil asks us to imagine in need of his
precepts on this first day of spring, is able to enter on his year's
work with energy because he sees everywhere around him the co-

operation of nature, the *caeli indulgentia*. Yet it is quickly clear that he must toil if he is to make a success of the farm. As the Golden Age of plenty came to an end, man's food supply failed and he was forced to struggle against blight and thistle (i. 150-2). If he fails to repel the threat he will gaze in vain on the produce of others and have to ward off starvation by gathering acorns. Yet he can be assisted in two ways: by precepts such as those of the *Georgics* (e.g. i. 79 *sed tamen alternis facilis labor*) or by the instruments and skills he is forced to develop (imaged at 160ff. as if military weapons and techniques). Hard toil is *improbus*: 'deformed, uncivilized, damned'; yet through *labor* come the various skills of the human race, for in it lies man's power to resist decay:

> tum uariae uenere artes. labor omnia uicit
> improbus et duris urgens in rebus egestas. (145-6)

The toil of man is easily destroyed, by geese, cranes, succory, shade (i. 118ff.), by time and human error (197), by rainstorm (325); degeneration is a law of nature. Only man's ceaseless effort can withstand these pressures. He is like an oarsman struggling against a swift current; the moment he relaxes he is swept away:

> sic omnia fatis
> in peius ruere ac retro sublapsa referri,
> non aliter quam qui aduerso vix flumine lembum
> remigiis subigit, si bracchia forte remisit,
> atque illum in praeceps prono rapit alueus amni. (199-203)

We should not, however, overstress the positive features of *labor* in the *Georgics*. It is not the redemptive force which Brooks Otis sees: 'Man must deserve and atone if he is to get the co-operation of nature.'[12] All the love and energy man may put into his *labor* may be swept away effortlessly by fate and the gods. As the bullock collapses under disease before his owner, both beast and man have reason to cry before the face of the gods:

> quid labor aut benefacta iuuant? quid uomere terras
> inuertisse grauis? (iii. 525-6)

They can find no sin or impiety in their lives to explain sudden disaster. Similarly Orpheus, stirred by love to use the magic of his song to save Eurydice, will look back as she vanishes, lost by a moment's carelessness:

> ibi omnis
> effusus labor atque inmitis rupta tyranni
> foedera, terque fragor stagnis auditus Auerni. (iv. 491-3)

Fate and the gods are the cruel forces of Euripides which punish
blindly both sinner and faithful and thus disqualify themselves from
the love and worship of mankind. They do not judge *labor* in the
balance of their decisions.

In the utopian dream rural life offers an escape from this
cruelty. Surely living close to the rural gods of the Golden Age
man can read the signs and avoid disaster:

> fortunatus et ille deos qui nouit agrestis
> Panaque Siluanumque senem Nymphasque sorores . . .
>
> (ii. 493f.)

Vergil devotes *Georgics* i. 203-497 to describing the farmer's obser-
vation of signs. We are warned at once that our hopes of finding
easy salvation in country worship and lore are to be disappointed.
The farmer observes the signs of coming storm. Yet, as he watches
his ripe grain or his harvested piles he cannot, for all his knowledge, save them from destruction and, as the steep sky breaks
loose in downpour, the fertile hopes of his spring sowing, the
labours of his cattle, disappear before him:

>   ruit arduus aether,
> et pluuia ingenti sata laeta boumque labores
> diluit.   (i. 324-6)

Indeed, he saw the signs foretelling the Civil Wars. He was power-
less to avert them. As Vergil looks around at the chaotic world of
civil war, he no longer sees any solution in the farmer's life. He
prays to the gods to allow 'this young man' to come to the aid of
an age overturned (i. 500-1). The book closes with a world in
chaos, imaged by a four-horse chariot which leaves the starting-
gate in disorder and has no hope of success.

The *Second Georgic* is a panegyric to the happy life of the man
who cultivates trees or vines. The farmer should see that his land
does not lie idle (37), and should consider which plants are best
suited for which situation (109ff.), but his life is comparatively
easy. The book contains a hymn to Italy as the land of continual
spring and summer (*hic uer adsiduum atque alienis mensibus
aestas* (149)), the land of the Saturnian Golden Age, *magna parens
frugum, Saturnia tellus, magna uirum* (173-4). A second hymn
(319-345) portrays spring as the easiest season, the temperate
season when life was (and is) created on earth. The book ends with
a picture of the farmer on holiday, leading the life of the Saturnian
Age.

The last eighty-five lines (458-542) deserve closer study. Here Vergil twice contrasts the *fortunatus* in the country with the ambition and luxury of urban life. However, the lines are interrupted by an account of Vergil's purposes as a poet and by his own sense of a work unfinished. The structure may be analysed as follows:[13]

1. Farmers as lucky men, with peaceful *securitas* (458-60).
They are lucky if they do not have to live in the Roman throng, marvelling at the luxury of the wealthy and corrupted by imported customs (461-6). They have a quiet life (*secura quies et nescia fallere uita*) and reverence for gods and elders. Justice lingered here before she left men at the close of the Golden Age (467-74, cf. *Ecl.* iv).

2. Vergil's wishes for himself. He has committed himself to being a servant of the Muses and wishes that the Muses may teach him an understanding of the universe (475-82):

> me uero primum dulces ante omnia Musae,
> quarum sacra fero ingenti percussus amore,
> accipiant caelique uias et sidera monstrent . . .

But if he cannot aspire so high he hopes he can find pleasure, if less glory, in the fields, rivers and woods (483-9).

3. The truly lucky man. Lucky is the man who was able to learn the causes of things and conquer the fear of death: *felix qui potuit rerum cognoscere causas* (490-2).

4. Another sort of lucky man. Lucky also is the man who knows the country gods (*fortunatus et ille* . . . 493-4). He cannot be moved by terror or war; he has no blind ambitions or jealousies (495-512); while the ambitious man is pursuing his empty ambitions the farmer has finished his year's work (513-22); portrait of the successful farmer on autumn holiday (523-40).

5. Clausula. I have worked hard; it is time to rest the weary horses (541-2).
Clearly central in this structure is the *felix*. Vergil grades his own highest purpose as to be a man who understands the universe. *Felix*, from the same root as *fecundus*, *fetus*, implies a man both fortunate and successfully productive. The man who is *fortunatus*, blessed by fortune, is on a lower scale, and Vergil accepts rustic life as a second best. Moreover, there is something ambivalent in describing the farmer as *fortunatus*. In the *First Georgic* we saw

that the earth does not pour forth an easy livelihood, that the farmer's life is not necessarily *secura quies et nescia fallere uita* and that the end of his year's work is not necessarily prosperous. We can only conclude that the farmer of the *Second Georgic* is *fortunatus* also in comparison with other farmers. It is thus obvious that the conditional clauses are important in lines 458-66. Farmers are lucky *if* they achieve the life of the *Second Georgic*.

The farmer's holiday can now be seen in perspective. The farmer has reached, thanks to *Fortuna*, a point where he can relax. The poet joins him and observes that together they have covered a vast amount of ground; it is time to rest their horses. Although their horses have covered many *spatia*, they have not competed in a race. It is implied in the image that they are being worked for some purpose; the purpose is not yet clear.

Much of the *Third Georgic* is taken up with the training of horses and cattle. This section is deliberately opened by the clause 'If anyone, marvelling at the rewards of the Olympian crown, raises horses or anyone raises strong bullocks for the plough' (48-9, cf. 180-1). The task of the farmer breeding horses or cattle for the yoke is largely to break the beasts to their function. A section is thus appropriate on curbing their sexual instincts. Vergil begins:

> sed non ulla magis uiris industria firmat
> quam Venerem et caeci stimulos auertere amoris,
> siue boum siue est cui gratior usus equorum. (209-11)

The bull or stallion should be kept alone to conserve his energy, for the mere sight of the female saps his strength, making him forget the woods and his grazing through her allurement; the scent of the mare makes the stallion uncontrollable; mares may kill their charioteer or race off to the mountains in their passion.

In the section on *caecus amor*, which appears at first a digression, Vergil analyses two other sorts of *amor* by which the irrational impulses of the animals are disciplined. Vergil here exemplifies the contrast between undisciplined ambition and two sorts of disciplined commitment which will be further analysed in the *Fourth Georgic*. He makes it clear that love is a madness common to all animals, including man; hence the animals may be taken as exemplifying human love.

The first commitment is one discovered by the animal himself after he has failed in the passion of blind love. Vergil describes the furious battle of two bulls fighting for a cow. The loser goes into exile, mourning his lost love, and practises his fighting until he returns having *collectum robur uiresque refectae* and charges like an ocean roller on his unsuspecting rival. He has not succumbed to the lover's frustration; he has found an active response —what the New Zealand poet C. K. Stead calls the *discipline* of love:

> So bondage holds me, but commanding love
> (Itself a discipline) is free to move.
> Prisoned by walls of stone war-prisoners built,
> I know myself more bound by what love yields
> Than by the laws that thought so often melts
> As hand obeys; so seem a slave to commands
> I most despise, while yet all thought moves free
> Into your greater serfdom, binding me.[14]

Vergil had already himself observed, and been impressed by, the active discipline of love. In the *Tenth Eclogue* he shows Gallus moving from lonely lovesick self-indulgence to an active surrender to love: *omnia uincit amor: et nos cedamus amori* (69).[15]

In the main part of the poem Gallus speaks (31-69), responding to advice he has just received and to the Arcadian dream-world in general (described 9-30). Around this are set two eight-line poems. The first announces the subject, *sollicitos Galli dicamus amores* (6); the second concludes the poem abruptly, maintaining the pastoral convention that the poet is a goatherd, weaving a wicker-work basket under a juniper as his goats graze. He thus opposes the trivial but necessary cares of his *securitas,* the grazing goats and the coming of night, to the passionate struggle of the lover with his disease.[16]

Gallus reacts to three different attitudes. The Arcadian shepherds find him alone, deserted even by the Naiads, and ask with interest but total non-involvement, *Unde amor iste?* Next Apollo gives him the facts of Lycoris' desertion and asks rhetorically, *Quid insanis?* as if the facts alone will bring him to his senses. Finally, Pan, *deus Arcadiae,* tells him to put a limit to weeping, not because love is a sickness, but because love is cruelly indifferent to tears (*Amor non talia curat,* 28). In the first response (31-43) Gallus finds consolation that the Arcadians will turn his suffering into song, for they are *soli cantare periti,* and he turns first to three subjunctive worlds, which represent three ways of accepting Arcadian escapism:[17] the future after death, when the Arcadians preserve the memory of his romantic love; the might-have-been-past, when he would have enjoyed only their carefree loves; the might-have-been-present, when he and his love—now Lycoris—would be lying together in the country. But the memory of Lycoris shocks him back into reality.[18] He now shifts to considering remedies for his *insania* (44-60). As he thinks of how the girl will suffer in the cold climates to which she goes, he begins to plan for his own cold future. He will cure his love by hunting and by inscribing his love on the forest trees. But he breaks off abruptly in mid verse: *tamquam haec sit nostri medicina furoris, / aut deus ille malis hominum mitescere discat* (60-1). As he rejected escapism, so he now rejects the other philosophical remedy for love, repression. In acknowledging the victory of *amor* (62-9), he returns to the advice of Pan. Love is victorious when man realizes he cannot escape and when it disciplines him to obey its orders.

Gallus' surrender to *amor* is not a passionate abandonment to *caecus amor*. Like the young bull he seeks new strength; his love gives birth to a reasoned commitment. In the *Tenth Eclogue* Vergil first conceptualizes a positive opposite to self-indulgence and *securitas*, the *amor Galli*. It may not be unreasonable to see in the sucker from this love which grows in Vergil's mind[19] the first foreshadowings of the ambitions which guide Vergil in the *Georgics* and in conceiving the *Aeneid*. In the *Georgics* he commits himself to the love of the Muses (ii. 475-6) and of *Parnassus* (iii. 291-2). In using the Muses he reminds us that the discipline of poetic creation comes in his mythology from outside him, from the bond to an object of affection and ambition, just as the lover's discipline does. However, the disciplining of *amor* to a higher will recurs more importantly in the *exempla* of the *Fourth Georgic*.

The second commitment by which *caecus amor* may be disciplined in the *Third Georgic* is that imposed on the animals by human training. The horse must be trained to curb its sexual instinct if it is to become a functioning part of the racing chariot team. We are reminded of the figurative use of this discipline in Plato's *Phaedrus* (246a-57a), where τὸ ἐπιθυμητικόν and τὸ θυμοειδές are imaged as two chariot horses which must be controlled by reason (λόγος) as charioteer if the soul is to continue harmoniously in its search for the good. The team makes use, in its higher pursuit, of the horse which is of its own accord τιμῆς ἐραστής or has been disciplined to abandon its baser instincts. Yet Vergil's point in the *Third Georgic* is not allegorical. The purpose of the chariot team is ambitious—victory at the games—as Vergil has already made clear in his description of the chariot race (iii. 103-12), ending *tantus amor laudum, tantae est uictoria curae*. The horse has been trained to curb his *amor* in order to further the ambitions (*amor laudum*) of the chariot team.

Vergil will come back to the worker whose *amor* and *labor* are, of his own free will, subordinated to those of his superiors in his picture of the bees in the *Fourth Georgic*. There it will be clear that the role of the bee is servile. It thus appears that the training of the horse is man's attempt to control its independent instincts and enslave it to his ambitions. At this point Vergil passes no philosophical judgment on these ambitions. It is only elsewhere in the poem that the well-disciplined chariot team appears a model of successful and praiseworthy ambition. Vergil there implies the Platonic theory that in the harmonious pursuit of social goals there is a discipline of reasoned commitment over the other appetitive instincts.

The chariot is disordered when the horses are out of the charioteer's control. He must discipline them to obey his command. Vergil uses this as an image for the disordered state in an important simile in the *First Georgic*:

> hinc mouet Euphrates, illuc Germania bellum;
> uicinae ruptis inter se legibus urbes
> arma ferunt; saeuit toto Mars impius orbe;
> ut cum carceribus sese effudere quadrigae,
> addunt in spatio, et frustra retinacula tendens
> fertur equis auriga neque audit currus habenas. (i. 509-14)

The simile is complex and needs to be conceived within its context, the actual start of a chariot race at the *ludi*. That Vergil has the start of a real race in mind may be seen from his choice of a phrase from racing jargon (*uox propria circi*, Servius), *addunt in spatio*, which has only recently been adequately interpreted.[20] 'As when the four-horse teams have poured from the starting gates, they come on to the course proper one by one, and, holding the reins in vain, the charioteer is carried along by his team and the chariot does not hear the bit.' The discord which rages on the track results not only from the fierce contest but from the failure of at least one chariot team to obey the charioteer's control. A charioteer who has lost control over his horses has little chance until he can restore their racing rhythm.[21] The team must function in harmony if it is to be victorious in a lawless contest.

It is clear in context that Vergil is inviting Octavian to give up his present ambition for private triumphs and to assume control over the disordered chariot of the Roman state in its pursuit of higher ambitions, its national destiny. He prays the Roman gods to allow the young Octavian to come to the aid of a world over-turned (*saeclo euerso*): 'Already the heavens envy us your presence and complain you care for the triumphs of men, as in a place where right and wrong are reversed' (i. 503-5). His ambitions are blind so long as they are private and inharmonious; when disciplined by the divine will for Rome and employed in restoring order to the dis-ordered state they will be praiseworthy. His goals must be in har-mony with those of the gods and of the state.

Thus where the first sort of discipline is a model of how the rational man should pursue his goals, the second discipline is a model of how society may function harmoniously in the pursuit of social goals. *Amor* is not a metaphor or symbol for these pursuits; it is a synecdoche, a poetic shorthand, for all those appetitive in-stincts of which love is one. In the digression in the *Third Georgic* only *caecus amor* is bad.

The destiny of Rome herself requires a charioteer. When the charioteer has brought the state into harmony, they will be victori-ous in the strife of nations and entitled to impose the laws of civiliz-ation, found naturally in the harmonious state, on the conquered states. In this Platonic mythology of a social order the inferior elements must either voluntarily or by training accept the leader-ship of the man and nation of destiny.

Octavian is not yet that man of destiny. That much is clear from the chariot image in the *First Georgic*. Vergil offers him the goals to which he might as leader dedicate himself. Some are com-paratively simple and involve bringing order to the distant pro-vinces: 'Caesar, who now as victor on the furthest shores of Asia keeps the unwarworthy Indian from the Roman citadels' (ii. 170-2); 'while Caesar hurled the thunderbolt by the deep Euphrates and gave civilization (*iura*) to willing peoples' (iv. 559-61); and a list of the Eastern triumphs which Vergil will engrave on the gates of his Octavian temple (iii. 26ff.). None of this has yet been achieved. Likewise, Octavian has not yet made his way to Olympus, as he is said to be doing at iv. 561, nor has he chosen over which sphere to become god or where he will become a constellation (i. 24ff.). These things are set before him as goals to which he may commit himself, and the gods are asked to allow him to be-come controller of the Roman destiny to bring the competing ambi-tions of its members back into order. To be sure, there is much urbanity in the thought of the *imbellem Indum* and of the Scorpion drawing back in the sky and leaving the young soldier *caeli iusta plus parte* (i.35)—no doubt through fear of his savagery. Yet these are real goals, and, whether Octavian has yet formulated anything like this or not, Vergil urges him to commit himself to guiding Roman destiny and Roman campaigns against the East.

Moreover, Vergil in the prooemium to Book III identifies himself with Octavian's goals. Octavian's Eastern triumphs (iii. 26-36) will be engraved in gold on a triumphal temple, centred around Octavian, which Vergil will build, together with the Roman lineage from Troy and the great underworld sinners. Vergil must search for a way to become victorious on the lips of men; he imagines how he will triumph, in dream images where he leads the solemn triumphal procession with an olive crown, riding on one of a hundred four-horse chariots by the river Mincius (17-8). At his Mantuan games, in honour of the Muses which he will have brought from Greece to settle there, Greece will compete in triumphal games. The scenes on the temple of Octavian Caesar correspond, he makes clear, to the battles he will describe in his poems and which will bring him glory (46-8). Thus Vergil's envisioned triumph is intimately bound with Octavian's.

Yet Vergil does not imagine he can triumph without *labor*. He identifies his work as *labor* at ii. 39 (*tuque ades inceptum una decurrere laborem*, to Maecenas, cf. iii. 41) and iv. 116 (*atque equidem, extremo ni iam sub fine laborum,/uela traham*), cf. iv. 6, iii. 289-90. His *labor* is clearly not undertaken from external pressure (*egestas*, i. 146), but from his ambition to be a great poet, his *amor Parnasi*. His praise of the great scientific poet as *felix* at ii. 477-82, 490-2, portrays the success which he envies. This is apparently a second sort of *labor* differentiated from the meaningless and uncertain *labor* of the farmer (whether *fortunatus*, as in the *Second Georgic*, or not) by being employed for higher goals.

At the end of the *Second Georgic* Vergil saw his pause in his uncompleted task as resting weary horses from training around the track (ii. 541-2). He thus comes to identify his own work and ambition as similar to the chariot team, whose ultimate goal is triumphant victory, but which must be long trained and finally undergo the long hard race under the firm control of the charioteer. The chariot image has taken on new moralistic symbolism for man and means in the pursuit of glory.

Thus the training of the racehorse and the bullock in the *Third Georgic* (discussed above) takes on a new universal symbolism for man searching to control the appetitive instincts, including *caecus amor*, within him in pursuit of high and important goals.

Vergil has undoubtedly conceived his personal goals by watching
what appeared to him in 30-29 B.C. as the resounding triumph of
his young contemporaries' commitment to political goals and the
welfare of Rome.

Yet Vergil ends the *Third Georgic* with a return to the pessimism
of the *First Georgic*. A farmer watches his cattle die of plague. As
the bullock collapses at the plough the world of man and animal
collapses. All the happy sights of the farmer's life cannot move
farmer or bullock. His toil, his kindness to the cattle, the bullock's
toil and willingness to work, their simple life on grasses and water,
their famed *securitas*—all collapse as the great bull neck flows on
to the ground (522-30). This is the ultimate failure of all those
utopian dreams with which Vergil's farmer began his career. His
ambition to escape from it all is no different from other ambitions;
his blind *labor* on his farm may result in disaster as absolute as that
which befalls the man given over to blind ambition. This is a
Euripidean world in which the pure in heart is as subject to the
irrational whims of the gods as the sinner. And so, Vergil embarks
on the *haud mollia iussa* of Maecenas with Euripidean echoes ring-
ing in his ears:

> uocat ingenti clamore Cithaeron
> Taygetique canes domitrixque Epidaurus equorum,
> et uox adsensu nemorum ingeminata remugit (iii. 43-5)

Are the voices of ambition which summon him the same sounds
which Pentheus heard before his destruction, Actaeon as he left
for his ill-fated hunting expedition, and Hippolytus as he drove his
horses from Epidaurus?[22] The Euripidean fear, that divine anger
may overtake one and all, receives its most terrifying expression
from a poet who felt that fear for his own ambitious undertakings,
rises to its extreme of tragic beauty in Vergil's portrait of the
ploughman loosing his bullock from the yoke as it grieves at its
brother's death. It is once more clear that man is a pawn in an
incomprehensible universe.

If the *Georgics* ended at this point we would take Vergil simply
as a Roman pessimist in the Euripidean mould. But in the *Fourth
Georgic* he appears to venture on a solution, or, rather, several
solutions, of which one will emerge as man's salvation from a cruel
destiny.

The portrait of the bees has been taken as a portrait of ideal
society. The bees lead a life undistracted by sexual love or any of
those *curae* which might distract them from their *labor*. Their toil

is coincidental with their *amor*: *tantus amor florum et generandi gloria mellis* (205, with an echo of the charioteer's *tantus amor laudum, tanta est uictoria curae*, iii. 111), *Cecropias innatus apes amor urguet habendi, /munere quamque suo* (177-8). This equation between *labor* and *innatus amor* enables them to lead a peaceful life, useful to the beekeeper, who preserves social order among them by killing off any rival *rex* who arises to threaten the supremacy of the queen bee. The picture is at first intellectually satisfying. It is only when we come to allegorize the figures that its inherent tragedy emerges, and we see that man, if his role in the eyes of the gods is that of the bees, has no more freedom than a slave. Their society is another Arcadian escape from personal responsibility, and the happiness they claim for themselves in their fatalistic surrender is only illusory.

The *Fourth Georgic* ends with two *exempla* of men who strive to escape from this enslaved society to achieve goals apparently denied them in this pessimistic view of natural order. Central in this final tableau is Orpheus, driven by *amor,* his total commitment to the love of his dead Eurydice, to attempt to conquer death and bring her back. He learns the conditions under which he may restore her to life and almost succeeds, but his irrational love escapes from rational control and he forgets these conditions. He looks back at her in love, no longer totally committed to the job in hand, restoring her to life. As he does so he loses all the toil he put into his undertaking: *ibi omnis/effusus labor* (490-1). His tragedy is like the ploughman's. He has no second chance, as his failure originates in his forgetful failure to observe the conditions given him by the gods. Eurydice complains that his love was a *furor,* a madness which disobeyed the commands of reason. Orpheus retreats to the self-indulgent world of self-pity which Gallus had once endured but rejected, and eventually dies.[23]

The story of Orpheus is placed in the midst of the story of Aristaeus. Aristaeus has suffered the same disaster as the ploughman at the end of the *Third Georgic.* He has lost his bees by disease and famine (318). The beekeeper is asked to remember this story if he ever loses his swarm (281-5). Vergil relates, in all apparent seriousness, how the Egyptians of the Nile delta breed bees out of carcases (285-314). In this account even the dead cattle of the *Third Georgic* prove to be useful for something. But the purpose of this account is less to give farmers helpful hints than to contrast how Aristaeus overcame his apparent disaster with the failure of the farmers in Books I and III and of Orpheus.

Aristaeus cries before the face of the gods words of accusation reminiscent of those spoken by the *tristis arator*: *quid labor aut benefacta iuuant? quid uomere terras/ inuertisse gravis?* (iii. 525-6):

> en etiam hunc ipsum uitae mortalis honorem,
> quem mihi uix frugum et pecorum custodia sollers
> omnia temptanti extuderat, te matre relinquo. (iv. 326-8)

He addresses his mother, Cyrene, a Naiad (like Arethusa and the Naiads addressed in the *Tenth Eclogue*), in words based on those of Achilles to Thetis (*Iliad* i. 352ff.), when he asks why she bore him to be dishonoured. He challenges her to uproot his entire farming livelihood, including his *felicis siluas* (an echo of the happy *Second Georgic*). But Cyrene, Arethusa and the Nymphs hear his cries and wail aloud. Arethusa tells Cyrene:

> 'Cyrene soror, ipse tibi, tua maxima cura,
> tristis Aristaeus Penei genitoris ad undam
> stat lacrimans, et te crudelem nomine dicit.' (353-5)

Cyrene admits him to her underwater home where all the rivers meet, gives him the magic gift of ambrosia, and tells him to ask Proteus for the solution to his problem (395-6). She explains how he is to wrestle with Proteus. Proteus tells Aristaeus that he is paying for the crime of causing Eurydice's death[24] and relates the Orpheus story. Cyrene at once interprets this as a solution to Aristaeus' *curae*:

> 'Nate, licet tristis animo deponere curas,
> haec omnis morbi causa.' (531-2)

She instructs him to pray to the Nymphs, for they will pardon him and abandon their anger (536), and to sacrifice, among other things, four bulls. He at once obeys the will of the gods (558-9). As a reward for his willing and unquestioning *pietas* the bees swarm from the carcases on the ninth day, a miracle.

So the *Georgics* ends, with the clausula quoted at the beginning of this paper. Whatever allegories are to be sought in the contrapuntal situation of Aristaeus and Orpheus, the *Georgics* ends with one man who triumphs, with the help of the gods and with *labor*, over divine punishment which had swept away the *uitae mortalis honorem*. Aristaeus does not simply get his bees back; he discovers a way to survive the catastrophe of nature. Turning with infinite reliance to his gods, seeking out and atoning for his sins, and finding in unremitting *labor* against the degenerative tendencies of nature a truly human spirit of endurance,[25] Aristaeus emerges as the committed man, seeking to be *pius,* as the Greek hero sought to be εὐσεβής, and willing to endure toils, the necessary condition of *auctoritas,* as the traditional Roman had always been. He brings his commitment under the control of reason and the gods and moves to a human status which the gods bless with miracles. Thus Aristaeus is linked firmly with that public image which Augustus wished to project and which was perhaps his real motivation, as he assumed the ambitious reins of Rome's discordant destiny. Vergil intends that our compassion and admiration of Orpheus' brilliant failure should be overshadowed by the success of Aristeaus' dedication in surviving disaster and becoming the recipient of divine love made manifest in miraculous *benefacta.*

Vergil is now psychologically ready to begin the *Aeneid.* He understands in himself the ambition which urges him to seek fame, his *amor Musarum* (G. ii. 476), and its relationship to *labor,* in the two senses of hard recurrent work and the ability to fight against disaster and decay to achieve a rhythm—as the charioteer or the oarsman must fight to establish *moderatio* if he is to succeed, and the farmer stubbornly performs his annual maintenance. He further understands, or believes he understands, the characteristics of ambition and *pietas* which motivate the man of destiny to lead his country out of disaster towards visionary goals. The sense of survival exemplified by Aristaeus will now be translated into higher and more socially significant situations. Aeneas' commitment is his *amor patriae* (*Aen.* iv. 347: *hic* (sc. *Italia) amor, haec patria est);* he is fired with dedication to Rome's coming glory (vi. 889).

Returning again to the human ambition and passion of Orpheus Vergil will show us in the final climactic scene of the *Aeneid* how Aeneas, reaching out to the moment of achievement which destiny has allowed him, is freed for one second to react with human love and anger as he liberates his guilt and sorrow for the death of Pallas by killing without mercy the man who had killed his friend. In this moment Pallas is more than Aeneas' friend; as prince of the Arcadian city on the Tiber he also symbolizes the hopes and dreams of Arcadia and all that has been destroyed by Aeneas' restless search for a stable home for his descendants.[26] His decision to follow Aeneas is symbolic of the decisions of Gallus and Vergil to reject Arcadia in favour of Octavian's dreams and ambitions. Aeneas' vengeance is in turn some vicarious absolution for the guilt that must have haunted Augustus when he looked back on his road to power—at Cicero, at Gallus, at how many more?

The action of Aeneas in the last lines of the *Aeneid* is often misunderstood and cannot perhaps be clearly grasped in all its curious counterpoint against the character of Aeneas elsewhere and the themes of the epic.[27] It can best be understood by comparing it to the dying words of Hippolytus in Euripides' tragedy. The Greek playwright shows us cruel, irrational gods who destroy the fabric of the rational world in which Hippolytus tries to live and Phaedra tries to bury her obsession beneath her sense of shame. As the gods bring them to their terrible chessboard doom, death itself liberates Hippolytus for one moment to act with love and compassion towards his father, the only character left to continue the fearful, uncertain life of Euripidean man, with a desolation nowhere paralleled in literature unless by the *tristis arator* of *Georgics* III. Euripides, in the few dying words of Hippolytus (1449ff.), balances against his manic pessimism about the human condition a gleam of faith in man's nature in those moments when it is free from destiny's dictates. So Vergil humanizes his character for one final brilliant moment, as he escapes from playing the role of queen bee to his keepers and can avenge, with the passion of an Orpheus, the death of his Eurydice. Vergil must mean us to understand that death is not the sole moment when man is free of the human condition, for he *can* reach, by following his sense of destiny towards his ambition, a moment of power when he is free to assume his own human nature. Thus the justification of Aeneas lies not only in his success in bringing to pass the destiny of Rome but in finding the level of existence where free will is possible.

Vergil advances, in reply to Euripidean pessimism about the gods, not the quietistic solutions of the Epicureans and Stoics, but a programme of active *amor* and *pietas* which will bring man to a level of achievement where his will is no longer subject to the gods. It is thus, in Vergil's opinion, that men of destiny like Augustus become equal to the gods, and a writer may, even at that late date, rival Homer in creating an epic to embody the spirit of a national way of life and give it new direction and impetus. Strong personal commitment to action, the *amor Galli,* rejecting Arcadia and the philosophies of quietism, finally triumphs in the peace of Augustus and the brilliance of the *Aeneid.* All the failures and betrayals of that road to triumph receive symbolic catharsis in the avenging of the dead Arcadian.

Vergil opens the way for the Christian ethic of modern Europe and the New World, that the man who commits himself with all his faith and energy to his reasoned ambition can, no matter what his private failures, if he listens within success or disaster for the will of a loving God, lead society forward and achieve personal liberty. The society which seeks to return to the Arcadian dream, whether of escapism or of organized socialism, with its underlying fatalism, has lost the meaning of the Vergilian myth.

NOTES

1. In the preparation of this paper I owe a special debt to the members of my graduate Vergil seminar, Fall 1967, particularly to Louise Fortson, Susan Severn and T. J. Stewart, and to the members of the Indiana Classical Seminar who discussed a preliminary version of my ideas on *caecus amor*. I am grateful for constructive and destructive points made there by Glanville Downey, James W. Halporn, David L. Sigsbee, Gordon Williams, and John R. Wilson. In particular, Silvio Skefich points out that 'ambition' now implies not only the active seeking of goals but also some degree of public irresponsibility. 'Emotional commitment' and 'involvement' more accurately render my point and have been used in the text of this paper to translate the non-sexual uses of *amor*, although I have retained the simpler word in my title.

2. *The Hero of the 'Aeneid'* (University of Auckland Bulletin No. 59, classical series no. 3, 1961), p. 18.

3. *G.* i. 24-42 ; 500-14 ; iii. 8-48 ; cf. ii. 170ff.; iv. 558-65.

4. On the structure see the editions by de Saint-Dénis and Richter ; E. Burck, *Hermes* 64, 1929, 279-321 ; K. Büchner, *P. Vergilius Maro, Der Dichter der Römer* (1955, reprinted from Pauly-Wissowa) ; Brooks Otis, *Virgil: a study in civilized poetry* (Oxford, 1964), ch. 5 ; and the work of F. Klingner and L. P. Wilkinson. On the invocations see U. Fleischer, 'Musentempel und Octavianehrung des Vergil im Proömium zum dritten Buche der Georgica', *Hermes* 95, 1960, 280-331 ; Gordon Williams, *Tradition and Originality in Roman Poetry* (Oxford, 1968), pp. 93-6, etc. I regret that the last-named arrived too late for me to digest its many incisive insights into Vergil.

5. The familiar theory that Maecenas instructed Vergil to attempt a didactic poem encouraging the resettlement of veterans from the Civil Wars was first proposed by Edward Gibbon, 'Essai sur l'étude de la littérature' (*Miscellaneous Works*, ed. John, Lord Sheffield, London 1814, vol. IV 1-93, first published 1761), pp. 32ff.

6. Servius *ad Buc.* 6. 13: *Nam uult (sc.* Silenus) *exequi sectam Epicuream, quam didicerant tam Vergilius quam Varus docente Sirone.* According to the *Vita Focae* Vergil studied with Siro in Rome, but Siro is known to have taught in Naples and Vergil

may refer to philosophical pursuits in Naples at *G.* iv. 563
(*studiis florentem ignoblis oti*). Perhaps he then lived in the
uillula quae Sironis erat (*Catalepton* 10).

7. The central duty of the Epicurean *sapiens* was to avoid πόνος and
achieve ἀπονία or ἀταραξία. Lucretius and other Roman Epicureans did not use *labor* as a translation of πόνος, no doubt from
fear of offending Roman prejudice. They chose instead the word
cura, together with *securitas* for ἀπονία. Vergil first uses *cura* in
this sense at *Catalepton* 5.10, where it is directly linked with the
docta dicta Sironis. His most sophisticated use of the concept is
in *Aeneid* IV, where Dido surrenders to it and Aeneas shows
Epicurean *pietas* in overcoming it.

8. W. Y. Sellar, *The Roman Poets of the Augustan Age: Virgil*
(Oxford, 2nd ed. 1883), p. 214. In his elegant analysis of Vergil's
use of Lucretius (ch. vi, pp. 199-260), Sellar argues that the
apparent inconsistencies may be explained in that Vergil 'was
nullius addictus iurare in uerba magistri, and that he accepted
certain results of science which impressed his imagination, without
caring for their consistency with others which he equally accepts'
(213). This view appears to me a misunderstanding of Vergil's
intentions. For Lucretian echoes in the *Georgics* see also E.
Paratore, *Atene e Roma* 41, 1939, 177-202.

9. In choosing to offer Professor Blaiklock in this volume an essay
which has allegorical implications for the predicament of the
modern New Zealand intellectual I wish to pay tribute to a man
who has never seen classical scholarship, particularly in so remote
and so new a culture as ours, as divorced from the social and
intellectual problems of our time and place.

10. For a sensitive account of the particularity of this farmer and this
spring day see R. Beutler, *Hermes* 75, 1940, 410ff.

11. There is a continuing ambiguity in Vergil between springtime and
the Golden Age, centring around his faith that Rome is about to
emerge from civil war into a second Golden Age (*Ecl.* iv) under
the leadership of Octavian's piety (cf. *Aen.* vi. 791ff.). For
Horace's impressive rejection of this identification see my article,
'Diffugere Niues: Horace and the Augustan spring'. *G & R* 12,
1965, 79-84.

12. Op. cit. (n. 4), pp. 162-3, cf. 153ff. et passim.

13. See F. Klingner, *Hermes* 66, 1931, 159ff. (*Studien zur grieschi-
schen und römischen Literatur,* Zurich and Stuttgart, 1964, pp.
252ff.) ; and Gordon Williams, op. cit., pp. 165-6, 616-9.

14. 'Night Watch in the Tararuas', from *Landfall,* Sept. 1954, p. 153
(cf. *The Penguin Book of New Zealand Verse,* p. 296).

15. On this eclogue note particularly C. G. Hardie, 'The Tenth
Eclogue', *Proceedings of the Virgil Society* 6, 1966-7, 1-11, and
Gordon Williams, op. cit. (n. 4), 233-9.

16. The Epicureans pursue only those sexual liaisons which are easy (cf. Lucr. iv. 1037ff. and, for the impact of this theory on Roman love poets after Catullus, Kenneth Quinn, *Latin Explorations* (London, 1963), pp. 144ff.). Other sorts of love are *curae* to be avoided (cf. n. 7). What Apollo here means by sick or obsessive love, in the context of Arcadia, may be judged from *Ecl.* ii. 68ff.: *quae te dementia cepit? . . . inuenies alium, si te hic fastidit, Alexim.* On romantic love in Vergil see J. Perret, *Maia* 16, 1965, 3-18.

17. On the dream-world aspects of Arcadia see Bruno Snell, 'Arcadia: the discovery of the spiritual landscape', in *The Discovery of the Mind* (trans. T. G. Rosenmeyer, Oxford, 1953), ch. 13.

18. Lines 44-5 are ambiguous, as befits the speech of an *insanus: nunc insanus amor duri me Martis in armis/ tela inter media atque aduersos detinet hostis. Duri Martis* may be construed as dependent on *insanus amor* (so C. G. Hardie, op. cit., and most editors) or on *in armis* (so D. A. Kidd, 'Imitation in the Tenth Eclogue', *BICS* 11, 1964, 54-64 ; Gordon Williams, op. cit., 236). I know of no good study of ambiguity and symbolism as a mark of the disordered mind, just as clarity is a mark of the *sapiens,* although it is so used from the Greek tragedians on. In Vergil cf. *Aen.* 4. 550-1, 590-1, and Kenneth Quinn, op. cit., p. 55 ; 'Syntactical Ambiguity in Horace and Virgil', *Aumla* 14, 1960, 36-46 ; *Virgil's Aeneid: a critical description* (Ann Arbor, 1968), pp. 394-414. It is unclear whether Gallus' obsession is with war or with Lycoris, whether he plans to continue as a soldier, as a lover, or as both. Yet the sentence brings the *insanus* back to a reality which makes death, escape and a happy life equally impossible. His obsession detains him in active arms.

19. Cf. my note, 'Vergil *Eclogue* 10. 73-74 and the suckering habit of the white alder', *CP* 64, 1969, 233-4.

20. H. A. Harris, 'The Starting-gate for Chariots at Olympia', *G & R* 15, 1968, 113-26. For details of racing at the Constantinople hippodrome see Phaidon Koukoules, *Byzantinon Bios kai Politismos* (Athens, 1949) III, pp. 7-80.

21. See Nonnus 37. 197-201. Nonnus' description of the chariot race (103-484) is the clearest available to us. However, despite Nonnus and the detailed study by Ph. Koukoules, many aspects are obscure to us. All modern authorities assume that the teams galloped, e.g. R. C. Bronson, 'Chariot Racing in Etruria', in *Studi in Onore di Luisa Banti,* ed. G. Becatti et al. (Rome, 1965), pp. 89-106 ; J. K. Anderson, *Ancient Greek Horsemanship* (University of California Press, 1961), p. 37. Racing horses are conventionally shown in a half-rear, as if in mid-gallop, in all monuments from Hittite times, cf. S. Reinach, 'La représentation du galop dans l'art, ancien et moderne', *Revue Archéologique* 1900, I 216-51, 441-50 ;

II 244-59 ; 1901, I 27-45 ; II 9-11. However, no great weight can be placed on this convention, and we have evidence that the racing breeds were trained in a high-stepping trot. I here assume that chariot teams trotted, as I believe it impossible for four horses to gallop free when closely yoked together, two to the yoke-pole, two trace-horses to the inner horses by short leather yoke-bands (familiar to us from vase-painting), particularly around sharp turns and over a course of six to eight miles. Apparently the only disciplined gait known in antiquity was the trot. Trotters will break into a gallop quite frequently at the beginning of a race and must be slowed to allow them to find their racing gait. Four yoked horses breaking would be spectacular, and it is to this real phenomenon I judge Vergil to allude.

22. Vergil did in fact have misgivings about his plan to write the *Aeneid*, as we may judge from his letter to Augustus, quoted by Macrobius, *Sat.* i. 24.10: *tanta incohata res est, ut paene uitio mentis tantum opus ingressus mihi uidear.* We see echoes of his Epicurean youth in this doubt about his ambitions and haunting images of attendant disaster.

23. Servius tells us that the Orpheus episode replaces a passage on Gallus and that these *laudes Galli* originally occupied the second half of the *Fourth Georgic* (ad. *Buc.* 10.1 ; but cf. ad. *G.* iv. 1, where he says they were replaced by the *Orphei fabula*). It is generally assumed that the first version of the *Georgics* was read to Octavian and published in 29 B.C., but that the *Fourth Georgic* was substantially revised after Gallus' death in 27/6 B.C. It is tempting to argue that the figure of Gallus remains allegorically hidden in Orpheus, while his relationship to Octavian Augustus is paralleled by that of Orpheus to Aristaeus. When Vergil presented the poem first to Octavian, Gallus was in his first year as governor, engaged on that long-sought prize of Roman politics, the settlement of Egypt, and no doubt sending exciting letters to his two old friends, Octavian and Vergil. His later fall from favour gave Vergil another example of ruined ambition. The failure of Orpheus provided Vergil with an *exemplum* of such failure and he deliberately forged a meaningful link with the success of Aristaeus. Aristaeus should be a triumphant figure ; our lack of sympathy for him may reflect Vergil's real sentiments to Augustus at the time of Gallus' death. Yet he openly states that the nymphs, patronesses of the *Eclogues* and thus of Gallus, will pardon Aristaeus for his crime against Orpheus, in recognition of his *pietas*. The bees will swarm again for their keeper, who will once more exercise his benevolent yet firm control over their society. The contrast between Orpheus and Aristaeus (on which see G. Ramain, *RPh* 48, 1924, 117-23) reveals Vergil's growing belief in men of destiny, favoured by the gods for their dedication to the divine will. His

sympathies lie with the victims of their destiny, with Gallus and Pallas and Dido, but reason and reality presented him with Augustus as the true man of destiny, following goals as intangible as false dreams (cf. *Aen*. vi. 893ff.), yet miraculously to be realized. It was just this sense of destiny which carried many great German thinkers in the blind steps of Hitler, while yearning for friends and a way of life which he had swept aside.

24. This link appears to be Vergil's invention: E. Norden, 'Aus Vergils Werkstatt', *Sitzb. Preuss. Akad. Wiss.*, 1930, 355ff., and 'Orpheus und Eurydike', ibid., 1934, 626ff.; J. Heurgon, 'Orphée et Eurydice avant Virgile', *Mélange arch. et hist. Ec. fr. de Rome* 1932, 6-60.

25. Cf. P. McGushin, 'Virgil and the Spirit of Endurance', *AJP* 84, 1964, 225-53.

26. See W. R. Johnson, 'Aeneas and the Ironies of *Pietas*', *CJ* 60, 1965, 360-4, for further discussion of the death of Pallas as symbolizing for Aeneas 'all the waste and horror of war as well as his failure to avert that waste and horror.' Other echoes of the Arcadian pastoral world in the *Aeneid* were analysed by W. S. Anderson in a paper delivered to the American Philological Association at Toronto, 29 December 1968; cf. R. A. Hornsby, 'The *Pastor* in the Poetry of Vergil', *CJ* 63, 1968, 145-58.

27. For literary analysis of this scene see Agathe Thornton, 'The Last Scene of the *Aeneid*', G & R 22, 1953, 82-4; Kenneth Quinn, 'Some Dying Words: tragic insight in the *Aeneid* and the question of Virgil's competence', *Aumla* 22, 1964, 178-90 (cf. *Maia* 16, 1964, 341-9; *Virgil's Aeneid*, pp. 252ff.). The last five years have seen a rapid growth in our understanding of the tensions in the character of Aeneas and Vergil's attitude to them, e.g. Wendell Clausen, 'An Interpretation of the *Aeneid*', HSCP 68, 1964, 139-47 (reprinted with an introduction and other articles taking a similar view in *Vergil: a collection of critical essays*, ed. Steele Commager, Englewood Cliffs, N.J., 1966); Michael Putnam, *The Poetry of the Aeneid* (Harvard University Press, 1965); R. D. Williams, 'The Purpose of the *Aeneid*', *Antichthon* 1, 1967, 29ff.; J. R. Wilson, 'Action and Devotion in Aeneas', G & R 16, 1969, 67-75.

PRIMUM FACINUS NOVI PRINCIPATUS?

J. D. Lewis

Most scholars would I think agree that the rule of Tiberius had some merit at first, but deteriorated later. Tacitus held this view (*Ann.* iv 6, vi 51), though he believed that Tiberius, even in the early period of his principate, had evil tendencies which were held in check only by fear of public opinion or the influence of Germanicus, Drusus, or Livia. This belief makes it easier for Tacitus to impute evil motives or actions to him in the early period: the tendency to evil was always there. Some of these imputations are probably false (as I hope to show), and if so are due to anti-Tiberian bias in Tacitus or his sources.[1] Where this bias is at work it should be recognized for what it is. It is plainly evident in the account of the death of Augustus and the execution of Agrippa (*Ann.* i 5-6). I trust that an essay which explores this topic will be a fitting tribute to the scholar who first introduced me to the study of the *Annals* of Tacitus. If the essay does not reveal much that is new (except perhaps in some minor details) I hope this will be forgiven in a field which has been so often worked over. Perhaps it will persuade some readers to return to what I believe is the sound interpretation of this passage—which has recently in some respects been wrongly expounded. Of course certainty in such matters is impossible of achievement. It may be that at the very time of the execution of Agrippa even men of high position and close to the imperial house were doubtful as to who had given the order for execution. Probably no official or public statement was ever made: but probably also those who looked carefully at the facts drew the correct conclusion. Some no doubt drew the wrong conclusion, and no doubt the lack of a public statement gave rise then and later to some false rumours. But enough evidence has survived to show where probability lies.

The account of the death of Augustus and of the execution of Agrippa Postumus form a sinister preface to the reign of Tiberius,[2] emphasizing particularly the wicked scheming of Livia.[3] The sinister preface makes the generally sinister picture of the reign of Tiberius more credible.

In a recent discussion of *Annals* i 5-6, D. C. A. Shotter has denied that these chapters 'prejudice our interpretation of the rest of the reign', or that the disposal of Agrippa Postumus is 'contrived to serve as an ominous opening for the reign'.[4] These chapters are rather designed 'to show Tiberius' character through his actions—to illustrate the pressures that public opinion imposed upon a ruler, especially one who was new and of a highly susceptible temperament'.

Now whether or not Tacitus so intended, it can hardly be denied that the first chapters of Book I do in fact provide an ominous opening for the reign. This of course springs to some extent from the facts themselves, e.g. the execution of Agrippa. But a contribution is also made by Tacitus' assertion that Tiberius and Livia share the guilt of the deed, and by the rumours which lend this assertion a cloak of credibility. In fact, as I hope to show, the assertion of guilt is almost certainly false. Tacitus not only gives the reign of Tiberius an ominous opening: he also distorts the truth in order to do so.

Shotter may be correct in assuming that, in the second half of chapter 6, Tacitus' primary aim is to point out that Tiberius had not yet realized the need to accept responsibility for the actions of subordinates, and to draw a veil over them when necessary: and there may have been some justification for the reported remarks of Sallustius Crispus to Livia. But to accept this is not to accept that Tiberius was in fact responsible for the execution of Agrippa. The most likely assumption is that he was not.

Agrippa's execution is mentioned at the beginning of chapter 6: '*primum facinus novi principatus fuit Postumi Agrippae caedes*'. Of course '*principatus*' does not specifically accuse Tiberius, as would '*principis*' (though in fact Tiberius was not yet '*princeps*'). But the next sentence leaves little doubt what is meant: '*nihil de ea re Tiberius apud senatum disseruit: patris iussa simulabat*'. 'He pretended that the command was his father's.' If the command did not come from his adoptive father, Augustus, it can only have come from Tiberius. (Livia will not have had the authority to give it. This was not yet the principate of Claudius.)

So far there is, in Tacitus' words, no doubt about Tiberius' guilt, though the statement is not completely precise. Then, to one's surprise, doubt appears: *'neque credibile erat'* that Augustus was responsible: *'propius vero'* it was Tiberius and Livia. The almost definite statement of guilt as an unquestioned fact has become a doubtful probability, obviously based upon subjective inference. Tacitus had no better basis for his inference than the statement: *'ceterum in nullius umquam suorum necem duravit, neque mortem nepoti pro securitate privigni inlatam credibile erat.'*[5] Paladini,[6] who argues for the guilt of Tiberius, says, 'Tacito da parte sua non ha dubbi': but in fact it seems clear that Tacitus did have doubts which he thrust out of his mind for insufficient reason.

Of the other sources only Dio (lvii 3.5) has no doubt that Tiberius was directly responsible for the execution of Agrippa. He mentions three other theories which were subsequently invented without factual basis: they blamed either Augustus, or the centurion, or Livia. Paladini argues,[7] from the fact that none of these three inventions blames Tiberius, that they were in fact spread from the palace. Dio's word εἴα may reinforce this argument, as Paladini says, but the following λογοποιεῖν surely tells against it. It is unlikely that Dio had any better evidence than had Tacitus or Suetonius. If they were not sure, he has no right to be.

I now turn to Suetonius, whom Paladini claims as a supporter (along with Tacitus) of the complicity of Tiberius. Suetonius (*Tib.* 22) begins with a statement which appears to implicate Tiberius, but need not: *'excessum Augusti non prius palam fecit [Tiberius] quam Agrippa iuvene interempto.'* 'Tiberius did not announce the death of Augustus until the young man Agrippa had been killed.' This ought to mean[8] that Tiberius at least knew in advance that Agrippa would be killed, perhaps having been told by Augustus in their final talk.[9] Who gave the order for the killing? In his third sentence Suetonius says there was a doubt whether Augustus left the order as he lay dying, or whether Livia dictated it *'nomine Augusti'* (to Sallustius Crispus? *Ann.* i 6): and in this case whether Tiberius knew of it or not. If this statement of Suetonius exhausts all the versions of the story known to him (as it should), there cannot have been any evidence that Tiberius either initiated the order or knew of its initiation. The most that Suetonius should mean is that Tiberius learnt of it before Agrippa was killed and delayed his announcement of the death of Augustus until he had heard that Agrippa had been killed.

Suetonius goes on to relate that the military tribune[10] guarding Agrippa slew him 'when he had read the order' (*lectis codicillis*).

This phrase of Suetonius is most naturally taken as implying that
the order had been left under seal with the tribune at Planasia, to
be opened and read only on further instructions or news of Augustus' death:[11] if Suetonius meant that the order had just arrived
at Planasia he might rather have written *'acceptis codicillis'*.[12]
Tacitus' words (*Ann.* i 6.1) fit the assumption that the order had
been lodged under seal at Planasia: *'ne cunctaretur Agrippam
morte adficere quandoque ipse supremum diem explevisset'*. If this
assumption is correct it can surely only have been Augustus who
lodged an order in advance for Agrippa's death.

On this assumption Tacitus' statement, *'is [Sallustius] ad tri-
bunum miserat codicillos'* would refer to the original (conditional)
order for execution, or possibly to the despatch of a message an-
nouncing Augustus' death and commanding the opening of the
sealed order. If this suggestion of a sealed order is not acceptable
(because of the obvious danger of premature revelation) we must
assume that Sallustius on Augustus' death despatched the (one and
only) order for execution signed by Augustus, which Augustus had
previously authorized.

Livia of course may have known of the order, and if so no doubt
approved of it. But if Augustus gave the order Tiberius did not:
and in spite of Suetonius' first sentence in chapter 22 there are good
grounds for believing that he did not even know of it. These grounds
are to be found in Tiberius' reply to the tribune: *'Tiberius renun-
cianti tribuno factum esse quod imperasset, neque imperasse se, et
redditurum eum senatui rationem respondit.'* Tacitus (*Ann.* i 6.3)
has almost the same words. Of course these words, and those of
Sallustius reported by Tacitus, may not actually have been spoken.
If they are sheer invention there is no argument. But sheer invention of the whole incident seems unlikely. Why should anyone invent Tiberius' proposal to refer the matter to the Senate? It seems
reasonable to assume that something like the words reported were
actually spoken. Probably there were witnesses (perhaps including
Sallustius) when the centurion reported to Tiberius—and probably
it was through one of these that the conversation was recorded. If
there were no witnesses, the survival of the words is more difficult
to account for: but the centurion may have told others of
Tiberius' reaction, or Tiberius himself may have told Sallustius
of the incident. It is more difficult to account for the survival of
Sallustius' alleged words to Livia. Were they spoken or written—
perhaps in a letter? One can only guess.[13] It is perhaps more important to ask why Sallustius turned to Livia with his complaint of

Tiberius' indiscretion. Livia may well have known of the execution order, and it may have been because of this that Sallustius complained to Livia: but her involvement need not have been any deeper. One cannot use Sallustius' actions to prove that Livia initiated the order—as has been said, she did not have the necessary authority. Nor, probably, did Tiberius give the order in spite of the centurion's words, *'factum esse quod imperasset [Tiberius]'*. A writer who wished, for whatever reason, to blame Tiberius for the execution of Agrippa would find it easy to mould the words of the centurion to fit his case (i.e. to change *'imperatum esset'* to *'imperasset')* : or one might argue that the centurion wrongly believed that the order had been given by Tiberius because it arrived, or was acted on, after the death of Augustus.[14]

In fact the story of the centurion, if authentic, gives good reason for exculpating Tiberius. Had Tiberius plotted the death of Agrippa, would he not have provided against anyone making a public report to himself of the deed? (As has been said, it seems most likely that the centurion made his report before others.) If Tiberius had asked for a report, surely he would have asked for it to be made in secret. But a stronger argument is this: had Tiberius and Sallustius shared complicity in the deed, surely they would have arranged together what to do and say when the news became public. That Sallustius was involved seems certain: Tiberius, most unlikely.

Moreover would Tiberius, if an accomplice, have suggested an investigation by the Senate[15] which would probably have brought to light his own complicity—especially if he had been responsible for the *codicilli* which Sallustius sent off? Sallustius in self-defence would have found it difficult not to reveal the complicity of Tiberius. No, if Tiberius had known of the deed, he would, on hearing of it, have made better use of his customary taciturnity. His remark sounds more like that of a man surprised—by news however welcome.

Tiberius' recommendation of a senatorial enquiry was the natural reaction of one who, without feeling himself involved, respected constitutional procedure. It perhaps also owes something to the fact that the Senate had confirmed the banishment of Agrippa to Planasia (as Hohl pointed out[16]). The idea of a senatorial enquiry was probably dropped when it was realized that Augustus was in fact responsible. Tiberius' respect for Augustus is well attested.[17] He may also have wished to avoid making trouble for Sallustius: perhaps he was influenced by Sallustius' advice.[18] It might have been better for Tiberius' reputation had he proceeded with the investigation—this might have scotched the rumours we now find in Tacitus, Suetonius, and Dio. Sallustius' recommendation of secrecy may not have been wise.

Suetonius gives Tiberius' motive in threatening the centurion with a senatorial enquiry: *'invidiam scilicet in praesentia vitans.'* *'Invidia'* here need not mean 'the odium which was rightly his' because he had given the execution order (as Paladini believes[19]): it may mean 'the odium which would be unfairly cast upon him' (even though he had not given the order).

My conclusion about chapter 22 is that Suetonius had not got his thoughts clear before he wrote. One should not conclude from his words that he believed that Tiberius had initiated the execution order. The third sentence seems to rule him out altogether.

Velleius (ii 112.7) mentions the adoption of Agrippa, his fall from favour, and his death. His language is vague (e.g. *'in praecipita conversus . . . dignum furore suo habuit exitum'*). The sentence comes strangely in the middle of Velleius' account of the war in Pannonia in A.D. 6. The ostensible reason for placing it here is that this is the year of Agrippa's first fall from favour. It has sometimes been argued[20] that Velleius is deliberately vague in his account of Agrippa's death because he is concealing the complicity of his patron Tiberius. This may be so, and Sir Ronald Syme[21] may be right in saying that Velleius has for the same reason deliberately given the impression that Agrippa was executed in the reign of Augustus. But these are not necessary conclusions. In regard to the charge of deliberate vagueness about the date of execution, it was natural for Velleius, having mentioned Agrippa's fall from favour in A.D. 6, to go on to mention his death. He could not hope to deceive his contemporaries, many of whom would remember the simultaneity of the deaths of Augustus and Agrippa. Similarly the vagueness about the manner of execution may not be due to ulterior motives: the banishment of Agrippa to Surrentum and his military confinement on Planasia are treated with an equal vagueness. If the vagueness *is* deliberate, it is even possible that Velleius suspected that Tiberius was responsible for the execution of Agrippa, but wrongly. Later writers—Suetonius, Tacitus—were not sure where the truth lay. Velleius may have been mistaken. His evidence is not enough to convict Tiberius.

There was I believe in the ancient sources at least room for doubt about the guilt of Tiberius. But these doubts would be lessened if certain rumours (related in *Annals* i 5-6) were true, e.g.

that Augustus had wished to reinstate Agrippa, and had even had a secret friendly meeting with him on the island of Planasia; and that when this came to the ears of Livia through the indiscretion of the wife of Fabius Maximus, Augustus' companion on the voyage to Planasia, Livia hastened the death of Augustus in order to prevent the supplanting of Tiberius, and with Tiberius contrived the death of Agrippa. Was there any truth in these rumours? Dio (lvi 30) accepts as fact the voyage to Planasia, and mentions a suspicion that Livia poisoned Augustus by smearing poison on his favourite figs. Suetonius has nothing to say of Livia hastening Augustus' death and ignores the rumoured reconciliation—rightly. Augustus was 76 years old, and in ill health. It is true that he liked travelling by sea on short coastal voyages, but not by night.[22] A voyage to Planasia involved more than a short coastal voyage— and seems unlikely. Moreover was his absence of several days, which must have been known to many accomplices—slaves, freedmen, soldiers, sailors—kept from his wife Livia (though she was presumably tending his health, and also supposedly on the watch for any attempt to supplant Tiberius) until she learnt the secret from the wife of Augustus' voyage-companion? The whole story is most unlikely, and even Tacitus gives it only as a rumour.[23] The story perhaps arose from the incident referred to by Plutarch and Pliny.[24] In them there is no mention of a voyage to Planasia, nor of the execution of Agrippa. Plutarch tells the story as a warning against talkativeness. Fabius overheard Augustus complaining that only a stepson would suceed him. Fabius told his wife, who told Livia, who told Augustus—whose subsequent coldness so depressed Fabius that he went home determined to commit suicide. But his wife anticipated Fabius and killed herself before his eyes. Some of the details here need not be correct—Tacitus makes the wife weep over the pyre of her husband, who has mysteriously died, perhaps by suicide: but the basic story may be true. Had the incident had any connection with a voyage to Planasia or the execution of Agrippa, these matters are unlikely to have been altogether omitted by both Plutarch[25] and Pliny—the latter of whom gives a list of the misfortunes suffered by Augustus. He does, it is true, speak of the *cogitationes* of Livia and Tiberius which arose from the indiscretion of Fabius—and which were Augustus' last *cura*. But he says nothing of any deeds.[26]

There is another argument against the veracity of the rumour of the reconciliation—to be found in Augustus' will. Agrippa was apparently not named amongst the heirs.[27] If there had been a reconciliation, surely Augustus, in view of his age and ill-health, would have found time[28] to alter his will in Agrippa's favour, if only to the extent of naming him among his heirs? It may of course be true that he wished to do so but that Livia either prevented him from making a new will, or was successful in foisting an earlier will upon an unsuspecting public—but there is no hint of this. Augustus did not alter his will because there had been no reconciliation.

Perhaps Agrippa's apparent absence from the will can be pressed further. According to Roman law, failure to mention by name a living son '*in potestate*' invalidated a will.[29] If this provision applied in the time of Augustus (as it appears to have done) the will would seem to have been invalid. E. Hohl argues[30] that Augustus ordered Agrippa to be executed immediately after his own death, and so knew that Agrippa would be dead when the will was opened. If this reasoning is correct we have here a proof that it was Augustus who ordered Agrippa's execution, a decision probably made by April in A.D. 13[31] when he drew up his last will. But there is a difficulty. It is more likely that, for the will to be valid, Agrippa had to be dead, not at the time of the opening of the will, but at the time it was made,[32] or at the time of Augustus' death.[33] In any case Augustus could not know that his will would be opened after the death of Agrippa.

Had Augustus earlier taken steps which made it unnecessary to mention Agrippa in his will? Suetonius (*Aug.* 65.3) says that soon after Agrippa had been adopted (in fact probably in A.D. 6[34]) Augustus '*Agrippam . . . abdicavit seposuitque Surrentum*'. Pliny (*Nat. Hist.* vii 150) uses the word '*abdicatio*' to refer to the same action. What is meant by '*abdicavit*' and '*abdicatio*'? Did '*abdicatio*' cancel the adoption? The Greek practice of ἀποκήρυξις, which involved expulsion from the family, is said not to have been recognized by Roman law.[35] The results of the Greek ἀποκήρυξις seem to have been virtually the same as those of the more elaborate three-fold Roman *emancipatio*[36]—but this is not the word which Suetonius and Pliny use. '*Abdicatio*' is mentioned a good deal in Quintilian and Seneca the Elder, apparently with the force of ἀποκήρυξις, but apparently also only in imaginary cases invented in the rhetorical schools, often from Greek life.[37] Where the word clearly has a real Roman context, the meaning appears to be more restricted. In 141 B.C. T. Manlius Torquatus, having decided that his son was guilty of misconduct as governor of Macedon, '*filium condemnavit abdicavitque*'[38] (Livy *per.* 54): and Valerius Maximus makes Torquatus explain what this meant: '*Et republica eum et domo mea indignum iudico protinusque e conspectu meo abire iubeo.*'[39] This may have been all that '*abdicatio*' meant in the case of Agrippa, i.e. there may have been no cancellation of adoption, or severance of family ties.

But there was another step in the decline of Agrippa. Suetonius (*Aug.* 65.9) says that Augustus sent ('*transportauit*') him to Planasia and placed him under military guard, and that the Senate decreed that he should stay there forever. Dio at lv 32.2 appears to lump together both the first and the second step in Agrippa's decline. In fact it is only Suetonius (*Aug.* 65) who explicitly mentions the sojourn at Surrentum. He also says that it was brief: hence it was easy to run the two together. Dio says: ἀπεκηρύχθη, καὶ ἥ τε οὐσία αὐτοῦ τῷ στρατιωτικῷ ταμιείῳ ἐδόθη, καὶ αὐτὸς ἐς Πλανασίαν . . . ἐνεβλήθη. ἀπεκηρύχθη probably refers to the '*abdicatio*' (or Roman form of ἀποκήρυξις) mentioned by Suetonius and Pliny as part of the first step. The confiscation of property (in fact presumably a '*peculium*') of which Dio speaks is more likely to belong to the second step and to the severer set of punishments. This property may have consisted of, or included, Agrippa's inheritance from his father which, according to Dio lv 32.2, he had earlier accused Augustus of wrongfully withholding from him.

Pliny (*Nat. Hist.* vii 149-150) speaks of '*relegatio*' for Agrippa after '*abdicatio*' (he also uses the word '*ablegatio*' without making it clear whether this is a synonym for '*abdicatio*' or '*relegatio*', or a 'blanket' word for both). '*Relegatio*' was sometimes not for life: and it was usually only when '*relegatio*' was for life that confiscation of property (such as that mentioned by Dio) was also imposed.[40] Was the penalty now imposed on Agrippa in fact '*relegatio*'?

This might seem likely, especially in view of Pliny's use of the word: but this supposition does not account for all the circumstances. Is it possible that Agrippa suffered '*deportatio*', the severer form of exile? When these punishments became standardized, '*relegatio*' did not normally involve loss of citizenship, '*deportatio*' did. It also normally involved perpetual banishment and confiscation of property, both of which were exceptional in '*relegatio*'. Suetonius and Dio each say that one of these two punishments was imposed on Agrippa. If he suffered also loss of citizenship ('*capitis deminutio media*') this would explain his apparent absence from the will: as a '*peregrinus*' he could no longer be '*in potestate*' or inherit.[41] It seems possible then that Agrippa suffered '*deportatio*' in fact if not

in name (*'deportatio'* is usually said to have been initiated by
Tiberius). There is positive evidence of two forms of punishment
normally associated with *'deportatio'*—perpetual banishment and
confiscation of property: there is inferential evidence of the third
(loss of citizenship would explain Agrippa's omission from the
will). Suetonius' word, *'transportauit'* (*Aug.* 65.9) might hide
'deportatio'.

Of course caution is necessary here. The evidence of Suetonius
and Dio is not strong. But there is another argument which helps
the belief that Agrippa suffered a severer punishment than *'relegatio'*. It was not only as an heir that Agrippa apparently received
no mention in the will. Suetonius (*Aug.* 101.5) tells us that Augustus banned both Julias (Agrippa's mother and sister) from his
tomb—again no mention of Agrippa. Was this because he had lost
his citizenship and was therefore no longer in any legal sense a
member of Augustus' family? Cancellation of the adoption would
leave him grandchild of Augustus, like his sister Julia: but his
status seems lower than hers. Was there no longer any reason at
all for his sharing Augustus' tomb? The Julias had apparently both
suffered *'relegatio'*,[42] but they, unlike Agrippa, had to be specially
excluded. It is possible then that Agrippa had suffered the severer
'deportatio', or at any rate loss of citizenship. This would also mean
loss of family rights.

Probably another possibility should be considered—was the disposal of Agrippa's body provided for in the order for his execution?
Tacitus (*Ann.* ii 39.3) says that the slave Clemens, having arrived
too late to save his master Agrippa, stole his ashes, apparently from
Planasia. Had Augustus ordered that Agrippa's body be burned,
and that the ashes be retained at Planasia forever (*'in perpetuum'*
—Suet. *Aug.* 65.9)? This may explain why Agrippa did not have
to be excluded from Augustus' tomb.

To conclude this long discussion of the will: one or both of the
two apparent failures to mention Agrippa may be due to one or
more of the several possibilities suggested. Only *'abdicatio'* (=
ἀποκήρυξις?), and *'relegatio'* have any support in the sources:
but whatever the legal formula was, it seems likely that Augustus,
before he made his last will in A.D. 13, had taken some step that
rendered Agrippa neither his *'filius'* nor a claimant to share his
tomb. Neither failure is adequately explained by Hohl's suggestion that Agrippa is not mentioned because Augustus knew he
would be executed soon after his own death. Nor can one use the
omission of Agrippa to prove that Augustus ordered the execution:

but one can use it to show that there was no reconciliation. It then becomes more likely that Augustus did order the execution. The will lends no support to the theory that it was Tiberius and Livia who engineered the removal of Agrippa. They had no need to. There has been no reconciliation with Agrippa—though perhaps Augustus sometimes spoke longingly of an heir of his own blood. But it was probably he who gave the order for the execution of Agrippa.

If the Tacitean rumour of the voyage to Planasia is unlikely to be true, it is easier to make a decision about the cause of the death of Augustus, and the circumstances in which it took place. Tacitus (*Ann.* i 5) says that there was a suspicion that Livia had caused the ill health which led to Augustus' death. When death drew near Livia recalled Tiberius, who had set out for Illyricum. (It is a weakness in Tacitus' story that Livia did not cause Augustus' death while Tiberius was at hand.) Tacitus says that the evidence was not clear as to whether Tiberius returned to find Augustus alive or dead: but he asserts as fact that Livia set guards on the palace and the roads, and, while sending out optimistic bulletins, delayed the announcement of the death of Augustus until the necessary arrangements had been made for Tiberius to take control. All this fits Tacitus' general picture of the scheming Livia.

Dio lvi (30-31) agrees with Tacitus in some respects. He mentions the suspicion that Livia administered poison, the delay in the announcement, and the doubt whether Tiberius was present at Augustus' death, though he affirms that most writers, and those the more trustworthy ones, said that he was not present.[43] The alleged delay in the announcement is hardly consistent with Dio's statement that Augustus made his (presumably final) wishes known to his friends (εἰπὼν αὐτοῖς ὅσα ἔχρῃζε - lvi 30.3). And Suetonius (*Aug.* 99) gives a different account of Augustus' last interview with his friends. There was obviously some variety in the tradition.

Of the melodrama there is no hint in Suetonius' account (*Aug.* 97-99).[44] Suetonius relates that (presumably early in August—Augustus died on the 19th)[45] Augustus, though in ill-health, accompanied Tiberius en route to Illyricum as far as Beneventum (such attention hardly fits a recent reconciliation with Agrippa—but it can scarcely have been much earlier as Fabius Maximus was alive on 14th May in A.D. 14).[46] As he returned from Beneventum he took to his bed at Nola, sent for Tiberius,[47] and had a long private interview with him. Did Augustus now tell Tiberius of his order for the execution of Agrippa? Suetonius has a good deal of information about Augustus' last day of life. He took care over his toilet, received some friends and some visitors from Rome, and then, apparently while the latter were still present, suddenly died, though not before giving to Livia a last kiss and a last exhortation. The account of Velleius (ii 123) is in essentials the same. Tiberius was recalled by Augustus and returned in time for a last fond embrace.

This picture is very different from that of Tacitus.[48] One might claim that it is the official version invented to give an air of normality to what was really the last act of a melodramatic plot, and an air of legitimacy to Tiberius' seizure of the fruits of his mother's contriving. The account of Velleius (probably completed and published in Tiberius' lifetime) is especially open to this charge because of his known dependence on Augustus and Tiberius (e.g. Velleius ii 124.4) and the perhaps over-harmonious picture he gives of the death-bed scenes (*'circumfusus amplexibus Tiberii sui'*— *'subrefectus primo conspectu alloquioque carissimi sibi spiritus'*— ii 123.2). But his account need not be basically wrong.

In an era of much propaganda and suspicion arising from bitter family intrigues and violent animosities the official version of events was hardly likely to survive for long after the death of those in whose interests it was created, unless it was closely related to what was generally believed to be the truth. On the other hand the melodrama which Tacitus hints at or asserts is improbable. If there was no reconciliation with Agrippa, there was no need to hasten Augustus' death by poison or other means. Both Dio and Tacitus mention this possibility only as a rumour. Seneca the philosopher and Pliny the Elder seem to show no knowledge of or belief in any such rumour. If it were true it would be odd—though not necessarily inconsistent—that Livia should later be made a priestess of the deified husband she had poisoned.[49] Suetonius disregards it altogether: and I prefer to regard Suetonius' picture as seeming normal because it records what actually happened—the peaceful death of a great statesman in full command of his senses and of his country, and after giving his last instructions to his chosen successor. The normality of Suetonius is the truth. Velleius merely gives the truth an 'official' gloss.

If then Augustus died peacefully (and naturally) in the arms of his wife and even of Tiberius, whence arose the other picture preferred by Tacitus? How did the story taken up by Plutarch get transformed into the Tacitean version? Charlesworth points out[50] that those who would have benefited from the accession of Agrippa, Julia his mother, Julia his sister, and Agrippina his sister and the wife of Germanicus, would have welcomed such a transformation: and it may well have been made by some of their adherents. Agrippina the Younger also, mother of Nero, would be likely in her Memoirs to have made much of any suggestion that Augustus would have liked to reinstate Agrippa. No doubt in her view, just as Augustus should have been succeeded by his grandson Agrippa, so Claudius should be succeeded by Nero, the great-great-grandson of Augustus, and not by her stepson, Britannicus. Those who thought in this way will also have inclined to vilification of Livia, who could be blamed for the succession of her son Tiberius. The murderous stepmother of Tacitus does not appear in earlier writers. Velleius (ii 130.5) accords Livia high praise. Seneca (*De Clem.* i 9.5) praises her influence for clemency. The Elder Pliny's only hint of evil is the *'cogitationes'* of *Nat. Hist.* vii 150. Even Suetonius (e.g. *Tib.* 22 and 51.2) has only some improbable gossip to bring against her. It seems likely that the Tacitean Livia took shape in propaganda of the Julian faction, made public presumably after the death of Tiberius, and perhaps intensified later—though one hesitates to think that the (probably) murderous Agrippina the Younger would have liked much made of the allegedly murderous Livia. If there is anything in this line of thought it means that Tacitus did not himself invent the false picture of Livia and her involvement in the death of Agrippa—and also that it may not even have been rumoured in A.D. 14. But he or his source may have been persuaded to believe in the existence of the treacherous stepmother Livia because they saw clearer evidence of the treacherous stepmother Agrippina. Agrippina, having arranged for the poisoning of her husband Claudius, put guards round the palace and sent out optimistic bulletins until she had made the necessary arrangements for her son Nero to displace her stepson Britannicus.[51] Her actions are very like those falsely attributed to Livia.

The similarity of situation may account for the verbal similarities between, on the one hand, *Annals* i 6 and i 10.8 and, on the other hand, *Annals* xii 66 - xiii 1, and also the surprising use of 'Nero' for Tiberius at *Annals* i 5.4.[52] This was perhaps intended to recall not only the imagined similarity of situation, but also the incident described in *Annals* xii 41, when Britannicus, perhaps unintentionally,[53] addressed Nero as Domitius, thus apparently ignoring Nero's adoption by Claudius.

Another possible influence on Tacitus' account of the last days

of Augustus has recently been suggested by Syme[54]—the accession
of Hadrian with the suspicion of poisoning and the doubtful adoption. This would account for the discussion of the *'capaces imperii'*
in *Annals* i 13, for which there is a Trajanic parallel, and which
may be a later insertion in the text. Koestermann approves of the
suggestion.[55] It is perhaps easier to accept contemporary events as
an influence on Tacitus' interpretation of earlier history. But the
already mentioned verbal similarities point rather to the death of
Claudius being in Tacitus' mind when he was describing the death
of Augustus.

Augustus had good reasons of state for removing Agrippa,
reasons which will have outweighed considerations of humanity.
Augustus had finally chosen Tiberius as his successor, believing
him to be the best man then available. Agrippa might be a danger:
he were best removed, if possible in such a way as would bring no
odium on Tiberius. In fact Augustus as *paterfamilias* had the power
to order the execution of a son or a grandson.[56] If Agrippa was still
subject to his *'patria potestas'*, it would not be surprising if he
made use of it. Why did he not have Agrippa executed before he
himself died? Tacitus' statement,[57] *'ceterum in nullius umquam*
suorum necem duravit', may be true to the extent that Augustus
could contemplate the execution of Agrippa after his own death,
but not before. Is it possible that he hoped that the young man's
violent nature might cause his own death if he, Augustus, lived
long enough?

It is then highly probable that Augustus ordered the execution
of Agrippa. The rumoured reconciliation and the rumoured poisoning of Augustus by Livia are false. Even Tacitus gives them only
as rumours. Such restraint by one who so obviously disapproved
of Tiberius and Livia can be taken as showing his consciousness of
the weakness of the evidence. Why does Tacitus reproduce the
rumours? 'To illustrate the pressures that public opinion imposed
upon a ruler', as Shotter says?[58] Were such rumours prevalent at
the time, or did they rather spring up later,[59] as a result of anti-
Tiberian and pro-Julian propaganda? Did anyone in A.D. 14 seriously consider Agrippa as a rival to Tiberius? True, Agrippa was
the grandson of Augustus, and had been adopted as his son in
A.D. 4: but then he had been disgraced and sent off to Surrentum,
later to military confinement on Planasia.[60] Surely Augustus would
not have taken these steps without good reason? Agrippa was
probably quite unfitted for authority. How could he be rival to
Tiberius—though Tiberius was merely Livia's son? Tiberius, like

Agrippa, had been adopted by Augustus in A.D. 4, but he had later been granted *'tribunicia potestas'* and *'imperium procon-sulare'*.[61] At Augustus' death Tiberius' powers were virtually equal to those of the princeps. Tiberius had successfully led large Roman armies in several major campaigns, each lasting several years—though one would not think so from Tacitus' words *'omnisque per exercitus ostentatur'*, later modified, it is true, by *'spectatum bello'*.[62] Tiberius thus had considerable experience of administration and leadership—and the official support of Augustus. What had Agrippa—in disgrace, in confinement, nothing achieved, no public position held—to offer against this? It is true that there had already been attempts to free Agrippa, but the freeing of his mother Julia was also attempted:[63] and the organisers seem to have been non-entities or adventurers (possibly secretly encouraged by, or seeking to win the favour of, the faction of Germanicus and Agrippina). Also the mysterious slave Clemens, having heard that Augustus was dead, sought to carry off Agrippa to the armies of Germany—but was too late: and in A.D. 16, now impersonating his dead master, attempted to raise a revolt.[64] Tacitus reports that equites and senators *were said* to have supported him, Dio (lvii 16.3) speaks of his gaining strong support in Gaul and Italy, Suetonius (*Tib.* 25.2) speaks of a *'non contemnendam manum'* (apparently confusing the attempt of A.D. 16 with that of A.D. 14). But the ease with which the conspiracy collapsed on the execution of Clemens (whose arrest was contrived by Sallustius Crispus) should probably be taken to show that it was a matter of little importance (cf. Tacitus' words (*Ann.* ii 40.1) *'an inanem credulitatem tempore ipso vanes-cere sineret'*). Agrippa in himself cannot have been a real threat to the succession of Tiberius, as Koestermann says.[65] Yet if there were discontent with Tiberius' rule, or if Agrippa's sister Agrippina and her husband Germanicus raised a faction against Tiberius, Agrippa could be a rallying point. Agrippa could be a greater danger to Tiberius than he was to Augustus. If Augustus wished to remove dangers to the succession, Agrippa was better out of the way. But it is also worth saying that so far there had been no example of succession to the principate by right of birth: and Augustus himself had been adopted by Julius Caesar. The heredi-tary right of succession was far from being established.

One may doubt then whether the rumours reproduced by Tacitus were prevalent at the time. One may also doubt whether Tiberius was much influenced by rumour. He was of course new to the lonely eminence of rule: but it would be very surprising if his long

years as military commander had not given him some immunity
from the pressure of public opinion (if only the public opinion of
large armies), and some understanding of the duties and responsibilities of a man in authority.[66]

Tacitus did not introduce the rumours 'to illustrate the pressures
that public opinion imposed upon a ruler'. He introduced them to
make plausible the story that Tiberius attained the principate only
through the machinations of Livia, and that Livia and Tiberius
were responsible for the death of Agrippa, for motives made more
credible by the rumours given.[67] This is in accord with the accepted
principle of Tacitean composition: non-factual material is presented
in a way that persuades the reader to accept Tacitus' interpretation
of the factual material.[68]

The death of Augustus no doubt ushered in a time of considerable public anxiety, and the news of the execution of Agrippa
naturally set tongues wagging. But the gloomy, plot-laden atmos-
phere of the early chapters of the *Annals* is not all authentic. Augustus did not think of reinstating Agrippa, but ordered his execution. Livia had no need to hasten the death of Augustus. Tiberius,
his clearly designated successor, was at his bedside receiving his
last instructions. Tacitus was misled by his sources and his own
misconceptions. The execution of Agrippa was not the '*primum
facinus*' of the principate of Tiberius: it was the '*ultimum facinus*'
of the principate of Augustus.[69]

NOTES

1. G. A. Harrer, 'Tacitus and Tiberius', *AJPh* xli (1920), 57-68, points
   out that there was in the sources, from Seneca the philosopher on,
   an attitude critical of Tiberius. Tacitus did not create this attitude.
2. Compare M. P. Charlesworth, 'Tiberius and the Death of Augustus', *AJPh* xliv (1923) 145-57, esp. 146: and Syme, *Tacitus* I 306-7.
3. See E. Koestermann, 'Der Eingang der Annalen des Tacitus',
   Hist. 10 (1961), 330-355.
4. D. C. A. Shotter, *Mnemosyne* 18 (1965), 359.
5. This statement is not seriously invalidated by Suet. *Aug.* 65.8:
   'ex nepte Iulia post damnationem editum infantem agnosci alique
   vetuit.'
6. M. L. Paladini, 'La Morte di Agrippa Postumo e la Congiurra di
   Clemente', *Acme* 7 (1954), 313-329, esp. 318.

7. Paladini, art. cit., 319.
8. I have considered and rejected the possibility that there is merely a temporal connection between the two ideas in this sentence (i.e. 'the execution happened before the announcement'). Sometimes prius . . . quam + participle does in Suetonius convey merely temporal connection, e.g. *Cal.* 27.4, but it seems most unlikely that in writing the sentence under discussion he did not have in mind a purposeful delay (as perhaps in *Galba* 11). However he may have been wrong in this belief.
9. Suet. *Tib.* 21.1.
10. Tacitus (*Ann.* i 6.1) speaks of a centurion. Possibly both Tacitus and Suetonius are correct. The tribune in charge ordered a centurion to do the deed.
11. As Charlesworth also assumes, art. cit., 156.
12. Cf. 'accepto nuncio', Suet. *Otho.* 12.2.
13. Sallustius probably adopted the second husband of the younger Agrippina, Passienus Crispus: see Stein, *PW* 1A 2 1955. Did Sallustius' words reach Agrippina because of this relationship, and were they reported in her Memoirs? For Tacitus' use of these see *Ann.* iv 53.3. Her mother also may have been a writer in Augustus' lifetime: Suet. *Aug.* 86.10. See also note 52 below.
14. A. E. Pappano, 'Agrippa Postumus', *CPh* xxxvi (1941), 30-45, esp. 44, argues that the 'codicilli' must have carried the authority of Tiberius because the centurion reported to him. But after the death of Augustus, to whom should a report be made? Pappano also believes in a definite plot to free Agrippa which became known just before or after Augustus' death. In his view it was this which moved Sallustius to send the order for execution in the name of Tiberius. But a difficulty for both these tenets of Pappano is the probability that Augustus lodged the order for execution on Planasia well before his own death (see p. 168). Pappano gives a thorough and detailed treatment of the early life of Agrippa Postumus.
15. This is stressed by Willrich, 'Augustus bei Tacitus', *Hermes LXII* (1927), 77.
16. Hohl, 'Primum facinus novi principatus', *Hermes* LXX (1935) 350-355, esp. 350. Suet. *Aug.* 65.4 mentions the senatorial decree.
17. Tac. *Ann.* iv 37.4.
18. Tac. *Ann.* i 6.6.
19. Art. cit. 319.
20. E.g. by Paladini, art. cit. 322. Paladini links Velleius' phrase 'in praecipitia conversus' with the αὐτογνωμονήσας of Dio lvii 3.6 as evidence of a charge of revolutionary tendencies made against Agrippa by the imperial house: but it is doubtful whether Velleius or Dio had revolutionary tendencies in mind.

21. Syme, *Tacitus,* I 367, n. 9. See also Koestermann, 'Der Pannonischdalmatinische Krieg, 6-9 n. Chr.', *Hermes* LXXXI (1953), 345-377, esp. 357, n. 2, who believes that Velleius wished to avoid mentioning the fate of Agrippa when dealing with the accession of Tiberius. Could he not have refrained from saying anything at all about Agrippa?

22. Suet. *Aug.* 82.3, 97.3.

23. As Shotter points out, art. cit. p. 359.

24. Plut. *de Garrulitate* 11 ; Pliny *Nat. Hist.* vii 150. Plutarch has 'Fuluius' instead of 'Fabius'.

25. Even so it seems likely that the tradition which Plutarch is following represents an intermediate stage in the growth of the anti-Claudian legend. Agrippa is in exile ἐκ διαβολῆς τινος: Livia fears enmity and strife if Agrippa succeeds Augustus. Paladini, 'Tacito *Ann.,* i 5.2-4', *Latomus* 24 (1965) 425, n. 3, points out that *Epit. de Caes.* 1.27, seems to be following the same tradition as Plutarch and Tacitus (though it makes Livia responsible for Agrippa's 'relegatio'). It is unlikely that Augustus exiled Agrippa because of 'a false accusation' (διαβολή) or that Livia was responsible for the 'relegatio'.

26. For which reason Willrich, art. cit. 77, argues (not very cogently) that Tacitus' version was invented after A.D. 77, the date of publication of Pliny's *Natural History.*

27. Suet. *Aug.* 101.2.

28. Tacitus (*Ann.* i 5) says that the rumour was that the voyage to Planasia took place 'paucos ante menses' (before Augustus' illness).

29. W. W. Buckland, *A Text Book of Roman Law from Augustus to Justinian* (Cambridge, 1932), p. 322 and note 3, where it is suggested that the rule probably existed in Cicero's time (Cic. *de Orat.* i 38.175 and 57.241) ; also J. L. Strachan Davidson. *Problems of the Roman Criminal Law,* pp. 85-95.

30. Art. cit. esp. 352-353.

31. Suet. *Aug.* 101.1.

32. P. F. Girard, *Manuel Elémentaire de Droit Romain,* 6th edn. (Paris, 1918) p. 868. "Les éléments de validité du testament sont nécessaires au moment de sa confection."

33. W. A. Hunter, *Roman Law,* 2nd edn. (London, 1885), p. 776.

34. Vell. ii 112.7.

35. 'Abdicatio, quae Graeco more ad alienandos liberos usurpabatur et *apokeryxis* dicebatur, Romanis legibus non comprobatur' (Cod. viii 46(47)6): Leonhard, RE I 1, 24, 'Abdicatio'.

36. Just. *Inst.* i 11.3 shows that 'emancipatio' was sometimes used as punishment.

37. Quint. *Inst. Or.* iii 6.96 (quoting a law, 'abdicatus ne quid de bonis patris capiat'), and vii 4.27. vii 4.11 is a warning against taking such cases as authentic: 'nam quae in scholis abdicatorum, haec in foro exheredatorum a parentibus et bona apud centumviros repetentium ratio est'. Spalding's note (31) in iii 6.96 is misleading because he mistakenly has the tense of 'usurpabatur' as present. See also Sen. *Controversiae* i 1 for another case of 'abdicatio'.
38. Livy *per.* 54.
39. Val. Max, v 8.3: Cic. *de Fin.* i 7.24, with note by J. S. Reid in his edition. Cf. also Val. Max. v 7.2 where 'nota pellere' ('domo') is the equivalent of 'abdicare'.
40. Kleinfeller *RE* I A i 564-5, 'Relegatio' and *RE* V, 1.231, 'Deportatio in insulam'.
41. Buckland, op. cit., p. 97, n. 7 and p. 135, and Strachan Davidson, op. cit., p. 57.
42. Vell. ii 100.5, Suet. *Aug.* 65.1. Tac. *Ann.* i. 53.1, iv. 71.6, and Dio LV 10.14 are less explicit.
43. C. Questa, *La Parola del Passato,* LXIV (1959), 41-54, esp. 45 sees in Dio's verbs γέγραπται and ἔφασαν a difference between sources before Dio as he writes (said to be more trustworthy) and others known only indirectly.
44. Though the first sentence of *Tib.* 22 perhaps implies some.
45. Suet. *Aug.* 100.1.
46. Acta Arvalium CIL VI 1.2023a. Tacitus (*Ann.* i 5) says that the rumour was that the voyage to Planasia took place 'paucos ante menses' (before Augustus' illness), and that Fabius died not long afterwards.
47. Perhaps Livia sent the message, which would explain Tacitus' words (*Ann.* i 5.3), 'properis matris litteris'.
48. Some scholars have believed that it was written to correct Tacitus e.g. H. Willrich, *Livia* (Leipzig, Berlin, 1911), p. 5.
49. Dio lvi 46.1.
50. Art. cit. 153-4, supported by C. Questa, art. cit. 51-52.
51. Tac. *Ann.* xii 66-69, Suet. *Claud.* 45.1.
52. Discussed by Martin, *C.Q.* (N.S.) V (1955), 123-128, and by H. Willrich, art. cit., 76-77. Shotter, art. cit., 359-360, disagrees with their conclusions. Walter Allen Jr., 'The Death of Agrippa Postumus', *TAPA* 78 (1947) 131-139, points out another coincidence of words at Tac. *Ann.* i 3 'Agrippam Postumum nullius flagitii compertum,' and *Ann.* iv 11 '(Drusum) nullius ante flagitii compertum.' Allen argues that Tacitus' apparent lack of confidence in the respectability of his source in the second passage may point to Agrippina the Younger, who may well have used of Agrippa the words quoted from *Ann.* i 3, The words quoted from *Ann.* iv 11 appear to be part of Tacitus' own comment on an unlikely

explanation of the death of Drusus, but they may have been borrowed from his source. See also note 13.
53. Cf. Suet. *Nero* 7.4.
54. R. Syme, *Tacitus,* I 306ff., II 482ff., 692ff.
55. E. Koestermann, *Tacitus Annalen,* p. 80, note on 5.1.
56. Hunter, op. cit., p. 190 ; Buckland, op. cit., p. 103.
57. *Ann.* i 6.2.
58. Art. cit., 361.
59. Dio lvi 46.1 ταῦτα (rumours about Augustus and Tiberius) μὲν δὴ οὖν ὕστερον διαθροεῖν ἤρξαντο.
60. Suet. *Aug.* 65.3 and 9, Vell. ii 104.1, ii 112.7, Dio LV 32.1-2. For a full discussion of Agrippa's character see Pappano art. cit. 33.
61. Tac. *Ann.* i 10.7, i 7.5, Suet. *Tib.* 21.1, Vell. ii 121.1.
62. Tac. *Ann.* i 3.3, 4.3.
63. Suet. *Aug.* 19.2.
64. Tac. *Ann.* ii 39-40. For a fuller (but insufficiently sceptical) discussion see J. Mogenet, 'La Conjuration de Clemens', *L'Antiquité Classique,* xxiii (1954) 321-330.
65. Art. cit., 333. Dio lvii 4.1 regards Germanicus as a much more serious rival.
66. Cf. Suet. *Tib.* 18.
67. Tac. *Ann.* i 6.2: illum (Tiberium) metu, hanc (Liviam) novercalibus odiis, suspecti et invisi iuvenis caedem festinavisse.
68. See B. Walker, *The Annals of Tiberius* (Manchester, 1952), esp. pp. 33-34, 158. A similar principle may be seen in the attempt in the first sentence of *Ann.* i 6 to arouse sympathy for Agrippa.
69. Cf. Hohl, art. cit., 355.

THE PORTRAYAL OF AUTOCRATIC POWER IN PLUTARCH'S *LIVES*

B. F. Harris

It is not without reason that the *Lives* of Plutarch are still studied predominantly as historical material, for often they describe men and periods about which we are poorly informed elsewhere, and this has led to intensive work on Plutarch's sources and his methods of composition. This historical work[1] has been of great value to those whose interest in Plutarch is also literary and philosophical, who study the *Lives* in the setting of his other extant writings and, more broadly, of the Greeks who lived under the early Roman Empire.

This paper belongs to the latter class, and aims to explore one broad theme, that of autocratic power, as Plutarch depicts it in a number of representative *Lives*. It will be relevant first briefly to consider his biographical method and its tradition, and also his own political attitudes.

I

Plutarch was a moralist and literary artist; as a biographer he disclaims the writing of 'pragmatic history'.[2] Rather, his interest is in character. He portrays the 'signs of the soul' in notable men, like a portrait painter who selects certain features only of his subject to convey the essential impression.[3] Plutarch is fully aware that he is working at second hand, historically speaking. In the preface to the *Nicias* he says he will rapidly traverse the writings of Thucydides and Philistus on this topic, to show that he bases himself on a reliable historical framework, and cannot be charged with carelessness or laziness. However, he also claims to add extra material from ancient decrees about Nicias, οὐ τὴν ἄχρηστον ἀθροίζων ἱστορίαν, ἀλλὰ τὴν πρὸς κατανόησιν ἤθους καὶ τρόπου παραδιδούς. This one remark epitomizes his whole attitude. This is far from an academic exercise. Plutarch believes in the wholesome effect of the contemplation of great characters, and summons his readers to active participation. History, he says in the *Timoleon,* is a kind of mirror by which a man may adorn his life in accordance with virtue. In his own researches (as, he hoped, in his reader's experience) he 'lived a common life' with his subject, 'entertaining him as a guest'.[4] The *Pericles* expounds the same view in more philosophical terms. The soul, says Plutarch (writing as a Platonist) is by nature φιλομαθής καὶ φιλοθέαμος, and must fix on worthy objects, that is, virtuous deeds. Whereas in other areas of perception such as works of art we remain detached, virtue inevitably arouses emulation; it implants an impulse towards action and a settled moral purpose.[5] The corollary of this, stated in the *Timoleon* and the *Demetrius,* is that the soul is naturally repelled by what is malicious or ignoble, and thus it is also salutary to view some historical figures notable for their vices.[6] But Plutarch takes a lenient view of moral faults, remarking in the *Cimon* that he prefers to call them 'deficiencies in virtue',[7] and we shall observe how this materially affects some portraits in the *Lives.*

This belief about the purpose of historical writing has affinities with the Greek and Roman historians. There is a strong didactic note in Thucydides and Polybius, in Sallust and Livy and Tacitus, and the attitude to human character in Plutarch was widely held. It goes back to the *Nicomachean Ethics,* when in defining moral virtue Aristotle began with the natural impulses present in all men, which by means of repeated actions (πράξεις) develop into a fixed moral disposition (ἕξις).[8] Hence the stress in all Peripatetic biography on actions as the key to character; historical study from this angle was an integral part of the young politician's training outlined in the *Rhetoric* and *Politics.*

The effect of this doctrine in Greek and Roman historiography has recently been described by Professor Gordon Williams. He points out that 'it harmonised perfectly with that curious substantial and mechanistic view of character held by the ancient world . . . Instead of regarding the concepts of virtue and vice as a convenient method of classifying human actions, there seems to have been a tendency to regard character as a constituent element of a human being, something actual and given like the physical features, a determinant of his actions, such that every action reflected a basic trait of character.'[9]

In biography, the early successors of Aristotle had developed the study of character found in the *Ethics*. Theophrastus' *Characters* is most familiar because of its survival, but it was Aristoxenus his contemporary who established the literary genre in the wide scope which Plutarch much later inherited.[10] How did he go about the composition, however, of individual *Lives?* The only sure means of determining this is to have before us the same historical source or sources as Plutarch can be proved to have used in a particular case, and to deduce this method thereby. But the analysis of Plutarch's sources has been found a very complex matter, and there have been extremes of interpretation. Earlier German scholars, who did pioneer work in analysis (particularly in the use of the 'chronographische-eidologische' distinction in the narratives) often became too sceptical of Plutarch's standards and ability. If there were considerable differences, for instance, between Plutarch's fifth century *Lives* and Herodotus or Thucydides, the assumption tended to be that he was not following the original authorities at all but recasting an existing biography of the Hellenistic school,[11] and the use he repeatedly makes, on his own information, of *Apophthegmata* or collections of sayings, seemed to support this view. But Plutarch has been rehabilitated in this group of *Lives*, by the memorable discussion of A. W. Gomme in particular,[12] who concludes 'I do not in fact believe that a man, universally declared to be widely read and universally admitted to be honest, used only one or two books for an essay or a *Life*, keeping closely to their form and content, using all their learning (which may also be second or third hand) pretending to quote from so many authors, criticizing some of them, and suppressing the name of one author in particular—the one from whom he took nearly everything he knew.' Having regard to Plutarch's own comments and his relative isolation at Chaeronea from the major libraries, he pictures him as writing with a limited number of books around him, relying on the voluminous notes of his previous reading and beyond that on a capacious if sometimes inadequate memory.[13]

In certain other *Lives* it has been possible to locate Plutarch's main sources with some confidence and thus follow his method. Thus J. E. Powell argued from the similarity with Arrian's history of Alexander that he and Plutarch followed a common *Life,* and Plutarch in addition the spurious Letters of Alexander, but even here it is risky to limit Plutarch to these sources only.[14] More recently D. A. Russell has analysed the *Coriolanus*[15] on the assumption, widely held, that Plutarch's sole historical source here was

Dionysius of Halicarnassus *Roman Antiquities* V-VIII, and that the other elements, antiquarian and philosophical, can be fairly readily identified. Russell is therefore able to look at these expansions and alterations of Dionysius where Plutarch is 'applying criteria of psychological probability to his source-narrative': that is, where the biographer, dissatisfied with Dionysius in matters of ἤθη καὶ πάθη, gives his own reconstruction. It becomes apparent that Plutarch finds the key to Coriolanus' character in his φιλοτιμία and ὀργή, and that he has used his sources with considerable freedom, relying on his own character evaluation and supplementing Dionysius with material from his own wide reading.

It has thus been possible, by the consideration of a representative number of the *Lives*, to test the accuracy of Plutarch's own description of his aims and methods. There can be no doubt that what he says in general terms is perfectly true—he is selective in his historical material, he does not deal exhaustively even with the selected episodes in his subjects' careers; οὔτε γὰρ ἱστορίας γράφομεν, ἀλλὰ βίους, οὔτε ταῖς ἐπιφανεστάταις πράξεσι πάντως ἔνεστι δήλωσις ἀρετῆς ἢ κακίας, ἀλλὰ πρᾶγμα βραχὺ πολλάκις καὶ ῥῆμα καὶ παιδία τις ἔμφασιν ἤθους ἐποίησε μᾶλλον ἢ μάχαι μυριόνεκροι καὶ παρατάξεις αἱ μέγισται καὶ πολιορκίαι πόλεων (*Alex.* 1.2). This may exaggerate the case, but it makes it plain that as he read his sources Plutarch made a constant habit of analysing men's actions so as to form a 'model' in his mind of their moral constitutions. To this extent one might call his method inductive. But he took the process further. Having decided what the major springs of a man's actions were, he then chose his material so as to illustrate his thesis.

II

Although there is this concentration on ἤθη καὶ πάθη, Plutarch's political attitudes entered into his total estimate of character. It was against the background of the constitutional propriety of a man's position, in Plutarch's eyes, that many of his actions public and private were to be judged, and this was particularly so with the exercise of autocratic power.

It is not difficult to find from the *Lives* themselves, and also the political *Essays*, where Plutarch stood. As a Platonist he took an aristocratic view of government, with the familiar picture of the philosopher-king as his starting point. In the *Ad principem inerudi-*

tum and the *Maxime cum principibus philosopho esse disserendum* Plutarch sets forth the qualities of good rulers, blending his Platonism with shrewd commonsense. The ruler embodies the divine law on earth,[16] and the secret of greatness is self-rule, which is the opposite of the popular misconception that the primary advantage of kingly power is freedom from the rule of others. The king has not come to this moral eminence unaided—it is the philosopher who has inspired in him the qualities of enlightened rule. Prominent among these are εὐβουλία, δικαιοσύνη, χρηστότης, μεγαλοφροσύνη.

This political ideal in Greek thought had been adapted to the reality of the Roman principate before Plutarch's age, and it is instructive to study his *Essays* alongside Pliny's *Panegyricus,* and the four *Speeches on Kingship* of Dio of Prusa, which are documents of the same period.[17] Plutarch accepted the Roman Empire philosophically, and speaking of the roles of Τύχη and Ἀρετή in this regard, could say εἰκός ἐστιν αὐτὰς σπεισμένας συνελθεῖν καὶ συνελθούσας ἐπιτελειῶσαι καὶ συναπεργάσαθαι τῶν ἀνθρωπίνων ἔργων τὸ κάλλιστον.[18]

It was thus as a monarchist in the Platonic tradition that Plutarch approached the widely differing political situations in which his characters moved, Greek, Roman and barbarian, and of course a serious weakness in his historical appreciation was his inability to gain a deep understanding, even of Greek democracy in the fifth century.[19] But for our purposes his view of the influence of power on individual character is more important, and his discussion in the *Praecepta gerendae rei publicae* is very useful in this regard. It is a curious mixture of advice to a young man entering public life: at some points, writing with an aristocratic flavour, he seems to assume a career of eminence in the context of Greece centuries before. Thus he lists as prime qualifications ἀρετή, φρόνημα, λόγος, and warns against the habitual sins of φιλαρχία, φιλοκέρδεια, ὑπεροψία. This is all for a young Pericles. More frequently, Plutarch gives his advice in the realistic setting of the Greek provinces of the early Roman Empire: he points to a *modus vivendi* with Roman governors whereby a Greek with a statesman's gifts can retain some of the true dignity of office, and at the same time show proper deference towards his rulers.

It is here that his general comments on φιλοτιμία are instructive, for in the *Lives* this is a central motif. Ambition has its source in many virtues and abilities, but is innate in men of robust and impetuous spirit and 'the wave that comes from the mass of men, raising it aloft and sweeping it along by praises, often makes it uncontrolled and difficult to manage'. It is not outward honours that the true statesman should covet, but Plato's 'gold of one's own, mingled in the soul', and Plutarch gives this the aristocratic interpretation as that virtue which a man inherits by his birth.[20]

III

We shall first consider two examples of Plutarch's portrayal of τύραννις of the 'conventional' kind, the *Artaxerxes* and the *Dion*.

The *Artaxerxes* lies outside the series of parallel Greek and Roman *Lives,* but displays some of the motifs we shall observe to be prominent in them. Artaxerxes in his early career is the benign τύραννος, contrasted strongly with his brother, the stormy Cyrus, whose outstanding natural qualities become submerged beneath his ὀργή—resentment at his older brother's accession to the throne. Thus Cyrus is λαμπὸς τῇ ψυχῇ, πολεμικὸς διαφερόντως, φιλέται-ρος, but also highly-strung and impetuous. His supporters believed he possessed the φρόνημα and φιλοτιμία essential in the king. Artaxerxes is a much milder man, and like his father was known for his πραότης and μεγαλοψυχία. The first motif is therefore two conflicting aspects of tyranny, and Cyrus attempts to wrest power from his brother. But his evil ambition predestines him to failure. In the background, as frequently with such conflicts in Plutarch, another pair are contrasted. The long resentment of Parysatis against her daughter-in-law Stateira breaks out in the incitement of her favourite Cyrus. One woman is beautiful and noble, the other an embittered schemer. The narrative gains momentum with the recklessness of Cyrus' revolt and the violence of his death in battle against his brother.

The second motif has as its starting-point the ἀνέλπιστος εὐτυχία of Cyrus' death for the fortunes of Artaxerxes. It is the μεταβολή of this *Life,* a frequent ingredient in Plutarch's narra-tives, particularly in a tale of autocratic power.[21] We now read a study of the deterioration in a king whose rule is unchallenged. Artaxerxes, not content until he himself has the credit of killing Cyrus, reveals typical vices of an Eastern despot: he is inconstant and hideously cruel, and plays into the hands of Parysatis with her plots to remove her personal enemies. Stateira is poisoned (although Plutarch rejects Ctesias' account of Parysatis' responsibility). The king wards off the Greek threat to the 'empty vaunt' of his Empire by bribery, and the shameful 'Peace of Antalcidas', but later betrays the Spartan whom he once called his guest-friend. Darker deeds now mark his decline—the incestuous marriage with Atossa and delusions of his divinity as Law incarnate. The only redeeming feature is Artaxerxes' endurance of hardships on the expedition to Egypt: but his failure brings on what Plutarch regards as the most ruinous quality in tyrants, δειλία. Only its opposite, θαρραλεότης, can lead to a rule where the tyrant can afford to act generously (25 fin.).

The stage is now set for the third 'act', which itself arises from Artaxerxes' deterioration into despotism—the rivalry of his sons Darius and Ochus for the throne. There are complexities here similar to those in the earlier struggle of Artaxerxes and Cyrus. Darius is declared the future king, but his mistrust in his father is inflamed by the tempestuous Teribazus (ἀνώμαλος καὶ παράφορος) who displays in a minor role the fatal flaws of a tyrant's character. Artaxerxes removes both by a counter-plot, but is faced by the even more menacing Ochus, who is now consolidating his own position by the removal of another brother Ariaspes (who by contrast is πρᾶος δὲ καὶ ἁπλοῦς καὶ φιλάνθρωπος). The narrative concludes with the despairing death of the aged Artaxerxes, and the murderous cruelty of Ochus.

Within the familiar framework of barbarian tyranny, Plutarch's narrative is marked by these dominant motifs. He was fascinated, it seems, with the outworking of φιλοτιμία, good and evil, in contrasting pairs of aspirants to power, and with the seeming inevitability of corruption and decline in the despotic character. This was the 'model' which determined the choice of material from his sources.

Amongst the Greek *Lives* the *Dion* provides the best parallel, for Syracusan tyrants were in some ways as fickle and barbarous in Plutarch's eyes as the Persian. The pattern is more complicated, for the personal rivalries for power are matched by the contrasts of political systems, monarchical, tyrannical and democratic. Viewed in this light, the story has two main motifs. First there is the strong contrast Plutarch portrays between Dionysius the Elder and the young Dion. The former is a tyrant of the mould described in Chapter 7—ruined in his youth by the flatteries of courtiers, absorbed in pleasures and amours, and thus cloaking for a time the cruelty of his rule. Dion, however, is a man of spirited and philosophic temperament: ὄγκος, παρρησία, μεγαλοψυχία, σεμνότης, ἐγκράτεια are the keynotes, but there is a streak of τραχύτης in his dealings also, and his enemies speak of ὑπεροψία and αὐθάδεια. With youthful idealism he enlists Plato in the effort to civilize the older tyrant, but Plato is expelled, and he turns his attention to Dionysius the Younger. The latter is not naturally harsh like his father, but his character has already been perverted by the time Dion tries to reform him through Plato's advice. At this point Plutarch draws out the king-tyrant distinction through the mouth of Dion: 'the adamantine bonds of power were not, as the Elder had said, fear and force, a large navy and a huge garrison of barbarians, but rather goodwill and enthusiasm and the favour which was engendered by virtue and justice.'

A second theme thus develops, and Dion is cast in the role of physician of Syracuse, an ailing city which Dionysius wished only to make 'the tomb of his falling tyranny'. In the series of struggles between the two their fortunes are swayed by the fickleness of the Syracusan *demos,* and the democratic motif is introduced. Plutarch has remarked earlier (12 fin.) that Dion, while holding as his ideal for the city a healthy aristocracy, would acquiesce in a democracy if this could not eventuate, and Heraclides now enters the narrative. He is the returned exile who is elected naval commander by the Syracusans in opposition to Dion, a projection of the *demos* in his character—οὐκ ἀραρὼς τὴν γνώμην, ἀλλὰ πρὸς πάντα κοῦφος, ἥκιστα δὲ βέβαιος ἐν κοινωνίᾳ . . . (33.2). The picture is filled out with colourful descriptions of the undisciplined mob, given over to premature rejoicings during the temporary restorations of popular rule.

Dion's exercise of power in Syracuse is the theme of the latter section of the *Life.* His philosophical bias is now evident, after extreme vicissitudes of fortune, in his ἐγκράτεια. He is generous, lives simply, dresses modestly, 'as though he was eating with Plato in the Academy' (52.2). But he also retains his innate σεμνότης and aloofness towards the common people. By contrast, the submissive Heraclides still reveals his vices; he is ταραχώδης καὶ εὐμετάθετος καὶ στασιαστικός, and out of this situation arises Dion's single but fatal error. He yields to those who wanted any lingering threat from Heraclides removed, and allows him to be murdered. This, Plutarch believed, was the μεταβολή in Dion's career, and the *Life* concludes on a dramatic note. He becomes the victim of his one folly, for his former associate Callippus plots his death in revenge for Heraclides. Dion has portentous visions, declares his willingness 'to die many deaths', and his murder takes on something of a ritual aspect (57.3 fin.). Thus Dion, who in all other aspects exercised a kingly rule, yielded at a crucial point to a tyrannical deed. The story towards the end has overtones of the tragic drama.

It is apparent that the characterizations in the *Dion* are more subtle than those of the *Artaxerxes*. Plutarch is moving on the more familiar ground of Greek history, and his Platonic loyalties come out in the contentions of rival political systems at Syracuse. A benevolent monarchy is his ideal, with an equal distaste for the excesses of tyranny and democracy, all of which is depicted in contrasting character portraits. There are three generally accepted sources for the *Dion*, of which two, the Letters of Timonides and the Platonic Epistles (especially the Seventh) are contemporary with the events. The third, the history of Timaeus which Cornelius Nepos also used, gave a strongly biased view of the Sicilian tyrants, and there is good evidence that Plutarch used Timaeus intelligently. That is, source criticism of the *Dion* bears out what the narrative itself leads us to conjecture, that Plutarch formed his own view of these rulers and the dramatized story bears the imprint of his personality.[22]

Of other *Lives* in the Second Series, the *Alexander* and *Caesar* are the most illuminating studies of autocratic power.[23] Here was the opportunity *par excellence* to compare the outworking of φιλοτιμία, and it will be noticed that the external struggles for power which mark these *Lives* are matched fully by inner moral contentions, and the reader becomes absorbed as much in the 'signs of the soul' in Alexander and Caesar as in the outward course of their careers.[24]

The dynamism of Alexander's personality is the major impression at the beginning of this *Life*. It is φιλοτιμία, τόλμη, μεγαλοφροσύνη which impel him onwards towards the youthful goals of δόξα and ἀρετή: he wants to receive from his father not a kingdom of wealth, luxury and pleasures, but ἀγῶνας καὶ πολέμους καὶ φιλοτιμίας. The first 'contest' Plutarch describes is in Alexander's own development. On the one hand there is the philosophical training under Aristotle, when Philip saw he was amenable to following the path of reason towards his royal duties, on the other the quarrels between father and son over the women of the Macedonian court, and then between Alexander and his half-brother Arrhidaeus.

At the outset of the reign Plutarch stresses his resolve to rule the turbulent kingdom boldly, and a vivid picture is rapidly built up of Alexander's invincibility, both in purpose and action. The Delphic acknowledgement of his power (14.4) followed by the portents before his expedition is the prelude to victory at the river Granicus. From this point in the narrative Alexander's generalship is matched by the benevolence of Fortune, and there is much emphasis on the conqueror's ἐγκράτεια and σωφροσύνη (especially over the captive women) as against the indulgence of the other Macedonians in the wealth and soft living of Persia (24.2). It is in the story of the arduous journey to the temple of Ammon in Egypt that Plutarch finally comments: ἥ τε γὰρ τύχη ταῖς ἐπιβολαῖς ὑπείκουσα τὴν γνώμην ἰσχυρὰν ἐποίει, καὶ τὸ θυμοειδὲς ἄχρι τῶν πραγμάτων ὑπεξέφερε τὴν φιλονεικίαν ἀήττητον (26 fin.). Alexander's apotheosis has now been achieved: son of Ammon, son of Zeus, the king of men stands in a special relation to the king of the gods. But here also may be seen the μεταβολή in the inner history of his spirit. Although not puffed up by the popular belief in his divinity, he uses this as an instrument of power (28 fin.). Darius, believing he has been conquered by a supernatural foe, becomes a mere foil to Alexander, and the new lord of Asia begins to act imperiously towards the Greek cities when he delivers them from their tyrannies by a stroke of the pen (34).

Plutarch however by no means depicts a king who is steadily corrupted by power. Alexander continues to act in a kingly manner; he is μεγαλοδωρότατος, φιλόφρων, and his ἐγκράτεια and μεγαλοφυχία stand in increasing contrast to the extravagance of his lieutenants. Here again, his πρᾳότης and εὔνοια are prominent, and these qualities are strained to the limit in the face of Philotas' treachery. But with the killing of both Parmenio and Philotas, Plutarch depicts the unloosing of the conqueror's ὀργή, which soon leads to the clash with Cleitus and the killing which plunges Alexander into deep remorse. Then, under the flatteries of the philosopher Anaxarchus, his character becomes εἰς πολλὰ χαυνότερον καὶ παρανομώτερον, and there are signs of the end. His ambition to cross the Ganges thwarted, he lies in angry seclusion (62.3), and back in Babylon he begins to doubt the favour of heaven and the fidelity of his friends (74.1), and loses that self-control which has been so remarkable. Plutarch finally introduces the accounts of

Alexander's death with a sombre comment on the excesses of his superstitious fears (75.1). Here is a kind of inner *peripeteia* of the spirit—Alexander of all men the prey of fear! Corresponding to this outwardly is the casting off of all his ἐγκράτεια in sacrifices, feasts and drinking-bouts.

The biographer means his readers to feel a sense of awe at this supreme spectacle of human power, and the setting of eastern despotisms and ancient cults is well-suited to bringing out the drama of Alexander's battles of the soul, which are as real as his military campaigns. As with the *Dion,* there are distinct suggestions of the tragic drama in the latter parts of this *Life,* and the *Alexander* is related to the *Demetrius,* where tragedy is an explicit motif, in rather the same way that the *Caesar* is linked to the *Antony.*

Many of the features of Plutarch's *Alexander* naturally find their counterpart in the *Caesar.* Early instances of Caesar's τόλμη and παρρησία abound, but the soil in which his innate φιλοτιμία is nurtured is very different in Plutarch's view. He openly courts the favour of the common people, who admire his eloquence in the courts and on the public platform: πολλὴ δὲ τῆς περὶ τὰς δεξιώσεις καὶ ὁμιλίας φιλοφροσύνης εὔνοια is Plutarch's early picture, with lavish expenditure as the hallmark of Caesar's first magistracies. On this was built a political strength which few assessed highly enough: all could observe Caesar's δεινότης τοῦ ἤθους, but only Cicero, Plutarch reports, rightly interpreted this as a τυραννικὴ διάνοια (4.4).

Just as Alexander's φιλοτιμία necessitated rivalry and opposition, so Caesar's relentless ambition elicits the fears of the Senate and *nobiles.* The cult of Marius his kinsman and the defeat of Catulus in the elections for Pontifex Maximus conspired to make them fear him for 'his intentions to lead the people on to every extreme of recklessness' (7.3). The pattern thus set is now intensified: Plutarch recalls the Catilinarian Conspiracy, moves on to the clash with Cato, the praetorship, and the Bona Dea trial, and the alliance with Crassus, a man who needed the Καίσαρος ἀκμὴ καὶ θερμότης against Pompey. Plutarch places the well-known incident of Caesar's reading from the *Histories* of Alexander at this point, during the praetorian year in Spain where it has dramatic fitness if not historical.

There is a strong contrast in the narrative between the disciplined, brilliant Gallic campaigns by which Caesar 'like an athlete greatly outdistanced his fellow-runners' and equalled Pompey's fame, and the virtual anarchy in Rome (τὴν πόλιν ὥσπερ ἀκυβέρνητον ναῦν ὑποφερομένην . . . 28.4) which made 'monarchy' the only solution. At the brink of the Civil War Plutarch reinforces his nautical metaphors. Caesar after agonizing hesitations cast himself on the future, but Pompey 'yielded and was swept along by the universal tide' (33.5) and Rome herself 'was the most pitiable spectacle, with so great a storm bearing down upon her, carried onwards like a ship abandoned by her helmsmen' (34.2).

After Pharsalus and the campaigns in Egypt and Asia, Caesar's mildness and clemency appear in sharp contrast to these storms of state. But Plutarch believed a μεταβολή took place in the conqueror's spirit after Thapsus: the speech back in Rome was boastful, the triumphs and spectacles showed a dangerous excess. They were the portents, as it were, of the triumph following Munda into which Plutarch introduces the note of *hybris*—ἀνῃρηκότα ταῖς τῆς πατρίδος ἐπιπομπεύειν συμφοραῖς οὐ κακῶς εἶχεν, ἀγαλλόμενον ἐπὶ τούτοις ὧν μία καὶ πρὸς ἀνθρώπους ἀπολογία τὸ μετ' ἀνάγκης πεπρᾶχθαι (56.4). A verdict on the dictatorship is added: it 'was acknowledged as a tyranny, since the monarchy had added the element of permanence to its irresponsibility' (37.1). The shadow of Fate now casts itself over the narrative, and in spite of numerous generous actions and the revival of Caesar's φιλοτιμία in fresh military plans, it is his passion for the kingly title, and an increasing aloofness, even from the highest magistrates, which seal his doom—humanly speaking. For beyond this Plutarch resorts to the *daemones*. It was they who as it were staged the assassination, and the calculating Caesar is now strangely filled with an ἐνθουσιασμὸς καὶ πάθος (66.2). This theme Plutarch develops in his final assessment. Caesar himself, he concludes, was impelled by his φιλοτιμία, his passion for *gloria,* but only his 'great daemon' made this possible, and lingers beyond his death as the avenger on the tyrannicides (69).

There is an obvious parallelism in the structure of the *Alexander* and *Caesar.* Here Plutarch was attempting the portrayal of two men in whom innate superiority joined with an unswerving φιλοτιμία to make possible the exercise of virtually complete autocracy. This of course has meant considerable manipulation of historical materials, but it has imparted a dramatic unity to the *Lives.* Plutarch felt impelled both by personal and artistic conviction to search for supernatural explanations of the dynamism he has portrayed. Hence the motifs of Τύχη in the *Alexander* and the δαίμων in the *Caesar.* These are a study in themselves as employed in Plutarch's *Lives* and expounded in the Essays,[25] but are mentioned here as elements in two narratives where they have a particular dramatic appropriateness.

Of the two pairs of *Lives* in the Third Series the *Demetrius* and the *Antony* are of exceptional interest for this enquiry. Reference has already been made to Plutarch's professed purpose, stated at the beginning of the *Demetrius*, of selecting some notable characters in whom vices outweighed virtues, so that his readers may be further edified. Plato is properly appealed to on this point,[26] and both Demetrius and Antony are to be painted on a large canvas—powerful personalities, great successes, great vicissitudes and failures. These two *Lives* specially lend themselves to dramatization, as Plutarch says explicitly at the end of the first: Διηγωνισμένου δὲ τοῦ Μακεδονικοῦ δράματος ὥρα τὸ 'Ρωμαϊκὸν ἐπεισαγαγεῖν.

Phillip de Lacy has demonstrated that Plutarch's attitude to the tragic drama itself was closer to Plato's evaluation in ethical terms than to the literary evaluation of Aristotle: and, since allusions to drama are so frequent in the *Demetrius*, he has analysed this narrative to show how Plutarch's views have provided the framework of a biography. It is the story of a man who is by nature humane and generous, but whose φιλοτιμία and φιλονεικία bring him to eventual ruin. There is a close parallel to the degeneration from aristocracy through timocracy to tyranny of the *Republic* viii-ix.[27]

It will suffice here to show that the *Antony* is constructed on very similar lines. Like Demetrius, Antony has exceptional gifts, but they are perverted early in life through Curio and Clodius. His character, like the Asiatic oratory he practised, is 'swash-buckling and boastful, full of empty exultation and of φιλοτιμία ἀνωμάλος'. However, it was some time before the Romans saw him as he really was. First he established a high military reputation in Egypt, and besides having an aristocratic appearance was known for his φιλανθρωπία, εὔνοια, ἐλευθεριότης. But as Antony moves into the orbit of Caesar, the portrait becomes more complex. On the one hand he is the trusted commander of the left wing at Pharsalus, who returns to Rome as Master of the Horse, but he also abuses his power by a life of debauchery which Plutarch believes contributes greatly to the unpopularity of Caesar's regime (6.6, 9.3-6). It is only his marriage with Fulvia which brings a temporary reform.

After Caesar's death, Antony exploits his power: ἔπραττεν αὐτοκρατορικῶς is the key expression. But from this point the conflict with Octavian becomes dominant, and Antony's strangely contrasting qualities are displayed. In flight after Mutina he is an inspiring leader with astonishing resilience (17.2), as a *triumvir* he is cruel and exultant and reverts to his former depravity (20.2, 21.1). In Greece, however, he acts as an enlightened commander and phil-hellene. But this is only the prelude to his entry into Asia, at which point Plutarch sets a distinct though minor μεταβολή in Antony's life.

In the East Antony meets with adulation and the temptation to live as if he is a god. In the *Demetrius* it is the Athenians' flattery which works the fatal change, and father and son both accept the title of king. On this Plutarch comments: 'it excited proud thoughts in the men, inflated their judgments, and made them haughty and oppressive in their manner of life and intercourse with others, just as actors of tragedies, on changing costumes, change also their walk, their speech, their manner of reclining and address' (18). So Antony now reveals his character in actions which will inevitably lead to his doom. Flattered by kings and their queens, surrounded by Asiatic performers, he is 'swept back by his passions into his wonted mode of life' (24.1). He enters Ephesus surrounded by bacchantes and satyrs, hailed as Dionysus the Giver of joys and blessings, a title which Plutarch took as full of irony in view of his exactions and punishments. Thus the dramatic climax, Antony's in-fatuation with Cleopatra and his abject submission, the τελευταῖον κακόν, has been well anticipated. From this point the biography reads more and more like a play.

There are continual interchanges of light and shade in the story. Antony's revels by night in Alexandria are called his 'comic mask', but all the time he is caught in the toils of Cleopatra, and must resume the 'tragic mask' when sombre reports come from Rome (30.1). Octavia, beautiful, dignified and intelligent, becomes the foil in the drama to the Egyptian queen. Again, Antony's bravery and endurance can still win the admiration of his men (43), but his Eastern campaigns are mishandled through Cleopatra's mach-inations. The extravagances of both in Egypt, growing more and more bizarre (54), are matched dramatically by the reading of Antony's will to the Senate in Rome and the declaration of war. Plutarch's narrative of Actium relies on the tension between Antony's residual skills and his subordination to the wishes of Cleopatra, and the climax is reached when, with the queen's ships already in full flight, he makes it clear that he 'is being dragged along by this woman as if he has become part of her very nature and involved in her every movement' (66.4).

Antony's gloom and remorse now becomes the dominant note, and Plutarch pictures him dramatically as seated for three days in silence, head in hands, at the prow of his ship: then at Alexandria he withdraws to the solitude of Pharos and strikes a pose as a second Timon, wronged by his friends and hating all mankind. The sheer unreality of the final residence of Antony and Cleopatra in the city is vividly portrayed in the rest of the *Life*. This is theatre as much as history, and Plutarch's skill is undeniable. Cleopatra displays more and more of the flamboyance of an eastern ruler in her preparations for death—the poisons, the tomb, the excesses of grief over the dying Antony, the speech over his urn, the prostrations before Octavian whose attempts to deceive her succeeded no more than Cleopatra's to deceive him. If it is her εὐγένεια which still excites Octavian's admiration after her death (86.4), it is the innate manliness of Antony that Plutarch invites us still to respect: ἐπιφανέστατος ἀνθρώπων γενόμενος καὶ πλεῖστον ἰσχύσας καὶ νῦν οὐκ ἀγεννῶς 'Ρωμαῖος ὑπὸ 'Ρωμαίου κρατηθείς (77.4). It was perhaps an empty claim for the historical Antony, but in the setting of this elaborate narrative it has a certain dramatic truth.

We have remarked that the vocabulary of tragedy is more noticeable in the *Demetrius*, and the portrayal of a disastrous decline in character and power clearly suggests the mould of an actual play. Demetrius, who at first possessed βασιλικὴ σεμνότης and is generous, just and humane, dies a drunken captive who perhaps now really believes he has found what he missed in his folly and ambition (52). But in the *Antony* the tragic framework is no less present, and Antony more closely approaches the tragic hero of Aristotle's analysis. The reader's pity for him is enlisted, and the domination of Cleopatra seems not so much the reward of his wickedness as the crowning evil sent by the gods, as Antony moves to a predetermined end. Thus he surely sustains a truer εὐγένεια in the closing act than does Cleopatra, and he excites a more lively sympathy in us than does Demetrius.[28]

IV

In this review attention has deliberately been focused on Plutarch's literary and dramatic skills rather than on the historicity of these *Lives*. There can be no doubt that the biographer was fascinated by the spectacle of autocratic power, probably more as a human problem than as a political phenomenon. Within the framework of a 'conventional' tyranny of the Persian type he has portrayed the human tensions behind the exercise of dynastic power, and with Greek tyrannies, as we have seen in the *Dion*, he has given added depth to the characterization of individuals by describing the contention between the different systems of which they were symbols. Faced with the supreme examples of human ambition and power in Alexander and Caesar, he has given an unmistakable impression in the narratives of a progress which seems to be irresistible, and as a Greek of religious sensitivity has looked for a supernatural dimension to the story. Has Plutarch really succeeded in picturing κακίαι μεγάλαι with his *Demetrius* and *Antony?* It would seem not, for he possessed a natural humanity which made him draw these characters with that blend of good and evil which we associate with tragedy, and which evokes as much pity as condemnation.

This aspect of the *Lives* helps us to understand Plutarch as a biographer of the particular type he claimed to be. To his genuine historical interest he had added the perception of a moralist and of a literary artist, and the importance of all three elements must be borne in mind in an appreciation of him. On the historical side it is really beside the point to regret that he lacked the understanding of a Thucydides or Polybius. In the Greek tradition of biography and moral philosophy there were undoubtedly, as described above, elements which limited his achievement. There is a certain artificiality about the framework of the *Lives;* the analysis of personality in men of power has not the psychological depth we associate with a great modern historian or historical novelist—virtues and vices are mechanically conceived as ingredients of character, and the μεταβολαί, although legitimate aspects of this group of *Lives,* tend to be schematic. But Plutarch the man attracts us by his own φιλανθρωπία, a quality of which he is among the best ancient examples and also expositors,[29] and this suffuses his biographical writing with life. To the student of Greek literature in the early Roman Empire it is not difficult to see why he is without a rival in this genre.

NOTES

1. For useful bibliographies, see G. T. Griffith 'The Greek Historians' in *Fifty Years (and Twelve) of Classical Scholarship* (2nd ed., Oxford, 1968), pp. 203-4 with notes, also Appendix p. 238; A. Lesky, *History of Greek Literature* (London, 1966), pp. 828-9.

2. *Galba* 2.3. For the most recent discussion of Plutarch, as biographer see J. R. Hamilton, *Plutarch, Alexander: A Commentary* (Oxford, 1969), p. xxxviiff. This book reached the writer too late for fuller consideration in the present essay.

3. *Alexander* 1.3.

4. *Timoleon* 1.1.

5. *Pericles* 1.2-4, 2.3.

6. *Timoleon* Praef. 3, *Demetrius* 1.3.

7. *Cimon* 2.3-5.

8. N.E. ii.1-2.

9. *Tradition and Originality in Roman Poetry* (Oxford, 1968): Excursus—'The Roman view of historical explanation', p. 627.

10. See F. Leo, *Die griechisch-römische Biographie nach ihrer litterarischen Form* (Leipzig, 1901), p. 97ff.; D. R. Stuart, *Epochs of Greek and Roman Biography* (California, 1928), p. 119ff.

11. Cf. A. W. Gomme, *A Historical Commentary on Thucydides* Vol. 1, p. 81ff.; for an earlier criticism, G. H. Stevenson, *JPh,* 1920, 204ff.

12. Op. cit., p. 54ff.

13. Ibid., pp. 82, 84.

14. J. E. Powell, 'The sources of Plutarch's *Alexander*' JHS lix (1939), 229-240: cf. Gomme op. cit., p. 82 n.1.

15. D. A. Russell, 'Plutarch's Life of Coriolanus.' *JRS* liii (1963), 21-28.

16. 780E.

17. See F. E. Adcock, *Roman Political Ideas and Practice* (Michigan, 1959), Ch. VI; Ch. Wirszubski, *Libertas as a political idea at Rome* (Cambridge, 1950), Ch. V; B. F. Harris, *Bithynia under Trajan* (Univ. of Auck. Bulletin 67, 1964), pp. 22-28.

18. *De Fortuna Romanorum* 316E; cf. R. H. Barrow, *Plutarch and his times* (London, 1967), p. 142ff.

19. Cf. Gomme, op. cit., p. 70.

20. *Praec. g.r.p.* 819F-820A. For a treatment of φιλοτιμία as a personal moral quality see H. Martin Jnr., 'The character of Plutarch's Themistocles', TAPA xcii (1961), 331-339.

21. Cf. Gomme, op. cit., p. 66.

22. For the sources, see the discussion in W. H. Porter, *Plutarch's Life of Dion* (Dublin, 1952), p. xviiff.

23. The fifth century Greek *Lives* form a separate group, best studied in another context. The *Timoleon* is a kind of sequel dramatically to the *Dion*. Here is the gentle tyrant, favourite of Fortune and 'common father' of Syracuse. But it is less successful as a biography.

24. For Alexander's portrait, see also Hamilton, op. cit., p. xlff.

25. For Plutarch's *daemones,* see Barrow, op. cit., p. 86ff., Hamilton, op. cit., p. 140.
26. *Rep.* 491 D-E, 495B.
27. P. de Lacy, 'Biography and Tragedy in Plutarch,' *AJP* 73 (1952), 159-171.
28. It is surprising to find the bald statement in *CAH* X. p. 875 that 'in the *Antony* Plutarch is obviously out of sympathy with his protagonist'.
29. See J. Ferguson, *Moral Values in the Ancient World,* Ch. VI: H. Martin Jnr., 'The Concept of *Philanthropia* in Plutarch's *Lives',* *AJP* lxxxii (1961), 164-175.

THE EPISTLES OF CYPRIAN

G. W. Clarke

My title is somewhat of a misnomer. For what I really wish to
deal with are a few aspects of life in Carthage as revealed by an
ecclesiastical writer of the mid-third century, by a man who was
born,[1] lived,[2] and died[3] in Carthage, namely Saint Cyprian, bishop
of Carthage. And the particular works of Cyprian of Carthage
which I wish to place under scrutiny are his surviving letters.

For this period of the mid-third century of the Christian era,
our extant literary sources are notoriously meagre and jejune. Cassius Dio, the consular Greek historian of the Roman Republic and
the Roman Empire, who tended anyhow to become not a little
episodic, and indeed downright scrappy, as he reached that dangerous period of contemporary or near-contemporary events, had left
off his History long ago in the glorious year of his second consulate, when he shared the consular *fasces* with the Emperor Severus
Alexander himself, in A.D. 229.[4] Herodian, another Greek historian, who had himself been writing, for the most part, the history
of his own times, had begun his chronicle—a singularly unfactual
and uninformative chronicle—with the death of Marcus Aurelius
and the accession of Commodus, that is to say, with the year A.D.
180; but even he had left off his feeble exercise in ersatz Thucydides with the portentous year of A.D. 238, the year that witnessed
Pupienus, Balbinus and the three Gordians all Emperors.[5]

Thereafter, for better or for worse, we live with the company of
the *Historia Augusta,* a series of biographies of the Caesars which
are in fact ancient forgeries dating most probably from the late
fourth century A.D.[6] This Augustan History is our only major
guide down to the beginning of the reign of Philip the Arab (A.D.
244), and then even that most peculiar document breaks down entirely, only to begin again with the closing passages of the *uita* of
Valerian.[7] That is to say, for the years A.D. 244 to A.D. 259, cov-

ering the period of the Emperors Philip, Decius, Gallus and Valerian with his son Gallienus, we must rely for the most part, for
our literary accounts of the political history, on those tantalizing
shreds of evidence often shed so unconcernedly by Aurelius Victor,
Zonaras and their allied company of epitomators and chrono-
graphers. One must even have recourse, appropriately enough, to
the *Sibyllina Oracula*, blatant *post euentum* prophetic forgeries, the
thirteenth book of which was composed at this season.[8]

Accordingly, obscurity lies deep over this period, but the gloom
would be all the deeper did there not survive from within precisely
these poorly documented years the writings of Cyprian of Carthage
—some treatises, thirteen in number, a generous volume of *spuria*
(many datable approximately to this age of Cyprian),[9] and most
valuable of all for the historian,[10] a substantial *corpus* of letters,
eighty-two altogether. Most of these letters may be securely dated
between the years 250 and late summer 258, when Cyprian died. A
few may be earlier,[11] and needless to say, none may be later, save
the four additional spurious letters.[12] The epistles span, in other
words, the poorly documented reigns of Decius, Gallus and part of
the principate of Valerian-Gallienus. They are, therefore, precious
historical documents.

Firstly a few general remarks about these epistles as a collection.
Not all the letters are of Cyprian's own hand. As in the correspondence of Cicero, some—but unfortunately only some—of the
letters which prompted Cyprian's replies have also come down to
us, amounting to sixteen letters in all, and providing, incidentally,
some fine examples of ungrammatical and, at times, almost unin-
telligible vulgar Latin.[13] In addition, synodal or collective letters
of the African Church tally six—they bear clearly and not unnaturally, some of the marks of the presiding Metropolitan of the
African synod, Cyprian of Carthage himself. That Metropolitan
presided over the combined dioceses, as Cyprian tells us,[14] of Africa
Proconsularis, Numidia and the Mauretanias, in Cyprian's day a
total of ninety bishoprics at the very least.[15] The remaining sixty
letters are all Cyprian's own work. Excepting synodal letters there
are at least a dozen other letters actually cross-referenced by
Cyprian himself, or referred to by others elsewhere, which are not
extant; and there appear to be a considerable number more which
can be reasonably inferred from Cyprian's text or from his epistolary practice.[17]

For it is quite clear that, on the one hand, there was well established in the very generation after Cyprian's death, the general

corpus of Cyprian's treatises, and that *corpus* survives intact. This we know from Pontius, the biographer and contemporary of Cyprian, whose *uita* of Cyprian survives as our first extant Christian biography; he lists all thirteen treatises.[18] Similarly, in the so-called Cheltenham List of A.D. 359-365, a stichometric list of the contents of a manuscript of that date, the thirteen treatises are all there *cum indiculis uersuum*,[19] as they are also in a sermon of Augustine which was edited for the first time in this century.[20] The general manuscript tradition of the treatises was thus firmly established from the start.[21]

On the other hand, the *corpus* of the epistles appears to have been slow to gather definitive shape. The total of von Soden's list of manuscripts containing at least some works of the pen of Cyprian amounted to the daunting figure of 431[22]—and one can reasonably assume that his list (drawn up in 1904) is not exhaustive— but even so not one manuscript contains the full number of our letters. What manuscripts do have letters, approximately half the total, have them with great diversity of number and of order. Only one—a late, fifteenth century, one—has all but one collected together.[23] The letter missing from that collection was published for the first time as recently as 1944; it survives in but one, fifteenth century, manuscript from Norfolk.[24] The *explicit* only of this letter did, however, turn up in an earlier (eleventh century) collection.[25] One is made to wonder whether further remnants of the Cyprianic correspondence may chance to be disclosed elsewhere.

It is also worth bearing in mind that what we mostly have from Cyprian and his correspondents are not private messages but public letters, written and designed from the start to be encyclical in the full sense, to be circulated and to be copied freely—and indeed Cyprian feels free to insist, gently but firmly, that Pope Cornelius disseminate and have read publicly the letters he sends as intended, and not suppress them.[26] (There was, however, a certain amount of double-think in all this. For Cyprian could also express astonishment at Cornelius for even considering reading publicly in Rome a defamatory letter about Cyprian himself, written by one of Cyprian's disaffected Carthaginian presbyters;[27] elsewhere, Cyprian reminds Cornelius that he did not hesitate about suppressing a letter from Cornelius' rival, the anti-pope Novatian—that letter, he avers, was too improperly unchaste in language to be heard by Christians and in Church.)[28] But generally, Cyprian takes pains to urge that copies are to be taken of his letters both by the clergy present in Carthage and by any visiting clergy who may turn up in the future—even, on one occasion, appointing a *lector* to act as supervisor of the operation,[29] and on another sending already prepared *exemplaria*, apparently intended to facilitate distribution.[30] And he certainly kept old letters, his own as well as others', ready at hand to have copies taken at need to be passed on to other correspondents. At one time such an enclosure amounted to a dossier of no fewer than thirteen letters (all of which, as a result, we still have),[31] others amounted to nine, five, four, two;[32] and there were, similarly, *addenda* attached to letters that he received from others.[33] Such are the sources of the majority of the non-Cyprianic letters.

Paradoxically, the non-survival of letters of Cyprian's correspondents can also be explained by these practices of inclusion, circulation—and suppression. Here is one example. Cyprian had carefully circulated his own objections and answers to Pope Stephen's controversial baptismal policy, but somehow Cyprian did not quite get around to circulating Stephen's reply to that letter. One bishop was bold enough to ask Cyprian for a copy of that reply—he did get his *exemplum* but with a full ten-page covering supplement (of refutation) by Cyprian's own hand. That supplement survives—presumably Cyprian saw that it was circulated independently—but Stephen's letter, clearly generally suppressed, significantly does not.[34] In this maze of copy-keeping and circulating letters one clearly could not be too cautious. The Numidian bishop Antonianus was naive enough, for example, to write to Cyprian one version of his attitude towards the schismatic Novatian (a copy of which was to be forwarded to Pope Cornelius) and later on another and a more sympathetic version, which was passed on to Cyprian through the services of a fellow-bishop Quintus. Cyprian in comparing these two inconsistent versions is spurred on to pen a vigorous twenty-page reply.[35]

After Cyprian's death (in September 258), his devotees would gather dossiers of their hero's epistles for themselves—just as in the preceding century we learn from Polycarp of the Philippians gathering a collection of the correspondence of Ignatius of Antioch[36] or just as Eusebius, early in the following century, collected over a hundred letters written by Cyprian's exact contemporary, Origen.[37] But it would have been no easy task to gather together Cyprian's correspondence, for several of the letters are as long as fully-fledged pamphlets or *libelli* (such as *Ep.* 63 against the practice of celebrating the Eucharist with water unmixed with fermented wine[38] or *Ep.* 69 in defence of the efficacy of 'clinical', or sick-

bed, baptism[39]). And *pace* Bayard, the collection does not seem to
have been complete by the late fourth century, in Augustine's day.

Augustine found a reference by Crescens of Cirta to a letter of
Cyprian to Pope Stephen on the subject of rebaptism:[40] he searched
his copy of Cyprian, found the letter to Stephen, but complains, at
considerable length, that he couldn't find anything on that topic of
rebaptism there. From his description he was clearly looking at our
Ep. 68, and he was right to complain. But we happen to have *two*
letters of Cyprian to Stephen and the second, our *Ep.* 72, is obviously the one Crescens had in mind, but it clearly did not figure
in Augustine's collection. It is ironical to think that despite the
vast volume of imperial literature that we have lost, we are probably
better supplied with Cyprian's epistles than were some of the early
Fathers of the Church.

Bayard[41] bases his case on a complete collection of the epistles
on remarks of Rufinus of Aquileia (at the close of the fourth century).[42] Rufinus observes that '*sancti Cypriani martyris solet omne
epistolarum corpus in uno codice scribi*' and he goes on to note that
at Constantinople heretics were peddling such volumes of the complete *Epistolae* with the heretical (Novatianic) tract *De Trinitate*
surreptitiously interpolated in the *codices,* and they were peddling
them among the poor at bargain prices to entice them to buy the
heresy baited with a generous amount of the orthodox Cyprian.[43]
But here *Epistolae,* as it does in many of the subscriptions to our
manuscripts, could well mean merely *libelli* and it is the complete
collection of Cyprian's treatises which is in all likelihood being
referred to; for these, as we have seen, were published in full.

So much for the letters as a collection. I wish now to examine
some of the letters which throw light upon general attitudes and
circumstances of Cyprian's own period. I have necessarily been
selective in what has been chosen for illustration; the letters are, of
course, rich in other information.

One of the pervasive features of the government of the Roman
Empire was a sense of hierarchy and of service-grades, or if you
like, of career-structures and of corresponding salary-classifications.
It was a period when it was *comme il faut* to have your official
salary as part of your official title (thus we learn from Cyprian that
the renegade Spanish bishop Martialis appeared before the *procurator ducenarius,* i.e. an official with an annual salary of 200,000
sesterces)[44] and to have that salary firmly emblazoned on your

tombstone for posterity to covet or to emulate. And this general attitude of mind was prevalent not merely among Roman citizens in the civil service, but it had spread generally to men of servile class as well.[45]

And we have evidence to show that by now the Church, not unnaturally, exhibits this same attitude of its environment towards its own government and institutions. In Rome, ecclesiastical grades can now be listed almost fully-fledged by Pope Cornelius, Cyprian's exact contemporary and correspondent.[46] In the statistics which Cornelius gives for the Roman Church there were, in addition to the Bishop, forty-six presbyters, seven deacons (that is, one for every two of Rome's fourteen *regiones*?[47]), seven sub-deacons, forty-two acolytes, fifty-two, in all, of exorcists, readers and doorkeepers. All these were supported by the Church funds.

Though we do not have such detailed statistics for the Carthaginian Church we observe from Cyprian's letters that all these grades are to be found as well at Carthage (with the exception of *ostiarii,* doorkeepers) and that each has carefully defined areas of competence. From the correspondence we learn several further points about them. (1) As at Rome, they are fully supported by the Church and they are not permitted to engage in secular business transactions. (Other—perhaps less prosperous—provinces of the empire were not so stringent in their regulations at this stage.)[48] (2) They receive their salary in a regular, monthly stipend.[49] (3) By a very characteristic arrangement each office was graded at a different level of salary.[50] (4) Not only that; there appears to have been operative the Roman notion of *suus annus,* the appropriate age for appointment at each career-grade in the *cursus religionis.* A typical example is that of Celerinus.[51] Just as partisans might be rewarded after a successful bid for imperial power by adlection to office, so Celerinus, for services rendered to the Church as *confessor* in the Decian persecution, was adlected to the post of reader. He was deemed too young for the higher grade of presbyter. However, he was to get some of the prerogatives of that higher office, notably its salary. He would get the actual prestige rank of *presybter* when he reached the appropriate age.[52] Hence, too, when Cyprian wishes to say the kindest things he can about Cornelius' suitability for his high office as bishop of the *ecclesia principalis* of Rome, he does not talk of his piety or of his sanctity or of his theological acumen, but he says that he did not reach his office *subito* but rather he had properly risen *per omnia ecclesiastica officia,* climbing *cunctis religionis gradibus* to the lofty eminence of the Roman episcopacy.[53]

He had worked his way up, as it were, from keeper of the door to keeper of the keys.

Of course, as with the imperial *cursus honorum,* the exception was always there to prove the rules—either as the result of the workings of patronage or of special talent—and equally, as in the civil *cursus honorum,* such side-stepping of the rules might be a scouring source of suspicion and *inuidia.* Cyprian's was one such case. As a convert of very brief standing (*'adhuc neophytus et ut putabatur nouellus'*)[54] he was promptly raised straight to the presbyterate, and then, after a short interval and by popular acclaim, to the episcopacy.[55] For, asks his biographer Pontius, who would not entrust *all* grades of honour to one who trusted the Lord in the way he did? (*'quis enim non omnes honoris gradus crederet tali mente credenti?'*)[56] This by now somewhat irregular appointment[57] (occurring shortly before the outbreak of the Decian persecution) promptly estranged—and as events were to prove, permanently so —what appears to have been the majority of Cyprian's own presbyters.[58]

During the ensuing persecution of Decius, Cyprian took the prudent course and simply ensured that he was not available for the persecuting authorities. This sensible move provided a welcome opportunity for attack, on the charge of pusillanimity, not merely to Cyprian's local, disaffected clergy but to the presbyterate in Rome as well. These presbyters were ruling the Church in Rome— as they were to do for some fourteen months in all—in the interregnum between the death of Pope Fabian (m. 20 January 250) and the election of his successor Cornelius (probably March 251), and they shared in the suspicion of this clerical upstart. They penned a withering, but anonymous, epistle criticizing Cyprian's flight, along with a sermon on the good and the hireling shepherd. This was sent to the presbyters of Carthage, some of whom could be relied upon to see that it was duly passed on to Cyprian in his place of hiding. They slyly, and pointedly, closed their letter to the Carthaginian clergy, with these words of greeting: 'We ask of you, who do have zeal for the Lord, to send a copy of this letter as opportunity may present itself or as you make the opportunity or when you are sending a messenger to whomsoever you are able, so that they may stand with steadfast courage in the Faith. We send you, dearly beloved brethren, every good wish.'[59]

Cyprian, being a man of no little spirit and diplomacy, was equal to the occasion. He wrote back to Rome: 'I have also received another letter in which it was not specifically stated who wrote it or to whom it was written. And the handwriting in this same letter as well as the contents and the actual paper have led me to suspect that something may have either been withdrawn from the genuine version or have been altered in it. And so I am returning to you the original copy of this letter; you will then be able to recognize whether it is the same letter which you gave to the subdeacon Crementius to deliver. For it is an extremely grave matter if the truth of an ecclesiastical letter has been corrupted by any falsehood or fraud. That we may know this, therefore, examine the handwriting and the concluding greetings to see whether they are yours and write back to us what is the truth of the matter. I send you, dearly beloved brethren, every good wish.'[60]

We have not been vouchsafed any details of a sequel[61] but in this ecclesiastical squabble we can trace some of the effects of the increasing firmness of the *cursus religionis;* certainly in the Western Church it was a growing source for tension, disorder—and indeed already of schism.[62]

To match this stability and order in the governmental structure of the Church was a corresponding sophistication in finances. In Rome the ecclesiastical coffers could support, in addition to the 155 clergy that Cornelius listed, 1500 widows and distressed persons.[63] It was in order to discover the whereabouts of these coffers that Lawrence, the Roman archdeacon, was, according to the popular account, grilled only a few years after Cornelius' episcopate, in August 258.[64] This would not have been a surprising move —if it is true— for the somewhat bankrupt government of Valerian.

Carthage, similarly, we learn from Cyprian's letters, had central funds that were to support not only the clergy but also the poor, the sick, and the widowed, and, in the time of Decius' persecution, the imprisoned, and indigent and homeless refugees to Carthage.[65] To meet such demands during that persecution, Cyprian had carefully distributed, before his flight, emergency funds among his clergy.[66] In addition, he had prudently entrusted some of his own personal funds to a Carthaginian cleric which could be drawn upon to meet extra demands and he had taken with him into hiding even further funds which could be sent if all these other resources did not suffice.[67] But his ecclesiastical *congiaria* were not given heedlessly. On Cyprian's orders, even before the persecution of Decius was completely over,[68] an ecclesiastical commission whilst attending financially to the *desideria* and *necessitates* of the Carthaginian flock, at the same time annotated their census with the *aetates, condiciones* and *merita* of the brethren.[69]. The poor clearly had to be deserving—but their plight was at least systematically and efficiently reviewed.

But one point is worth noting. There is no hint of shortage of funds, of difficulties about raising ready cash, nor of the effects of inflation, devaluation, the issuing of untrustworthy coinage by ephemeral emperors, and so on. Closely concerned with fiscal administration as Cyprian was, the imperial financial embarrassments, so heavily emphasized in our modern secondary literature, and in many incidental primary sources, do not appear to have affected, at this stage, the life of the Carthaginians at any great depth. But one must keep perspective here. For the archaeology of Carthage unmistakably reveals signs of growing economic regression; monumental edifices and public buildings are not being constructed and public inscriptions, whereas once multitudinous, are now rare phenomena.[70] The decline in public liquidity in this area seems to date sharply from the revolts of a decade earlier, of the Gordians in A.D. 238 and Sabinianus in 240.[71] The province simply did not possess the economic resilience, at this juncture of stagnating imperial finances, to stage a full and speedy recuperation from the severe depradations resulting from these uprisings.

Cyprian appears to have been on the whole an able and energetic executive and above all a man of a robust common sense spiced with genial humanity and sobriety. Yet there is one note that is discordant with this harmonious characterization, and in this Cyprian shows himself truly a man of his times. This practical administrator appears to act, strangely, but on the testimony of his own words, not infrequently at the behest and monition of visions and dreams—and so it appears, from the Epistles, do others.[72] Sometimes in this one can legitimately suspect literary or biblical convention. Cyprian, for example, can describe his flight in the persecution of Decius as being due to divine monition (after the style, say, of the flight into Egypt or the homeward route of the Three Kings).[73] But elsewhere, in two passages, he lists several very sound and practical considerations which induced him to flee —without any talk of occult inspiration.[74] In talking in terms of divine monition, therefore, he may have been using a 'mythologizing' manner of speaking.

But that this was not always simply a matter of *modus dicendi* is shown by *Ep.* 66. This is one of the comparatively rare occasions in the correspondence when Cyprian permits himself the pleasure of rhetorical vituperation[75] (though he shows he had clearly a good hand for it), and this is the only occasion when he fails to close his letter with a cliché of epistolary *politesse*. And this is precisely when the power and reliability of dreams—and, in particular, of his own dreams—has been attacked. That matter affected him vitally; he firmly adhered to Penelope's doctrine of the gate of horn through which veridical dreams reach mortal men.

This attitude of credulity on Cyprian's part seems to be symptomatic of an age of increasing superstition, of growing fondness for the occult (demonology was all the rage) and indeed of almost hysterical religious adherence generally. This, incidentally, is a consideration which helps to make sense of an age marked by two general religious persecutions—the first two against Christians. Such generalizations are always vulnerable, but here are some substantiating examples.

About the time of Cyprian's birth Cassius Dio could describe, not without literary parallels,[76] how he was commanded by his δαιμόνιον in a dream to write the history of the Severan Civil Wars, and how he was heartened thereafter, by similar somniloquent manifestations, in moments of doubts and weariness in the historical task he subsequently undertook.[77] Characteristically he seems to have opened his literary career with a βιβλίον τι, a pamphlet, on the dreams and portents by which the future emperor Severus learnt that he would ascend the throne;[78] this was of course diplomatic, but it was also a sign of the times. It is not surprising, therefore, that portents loom large even in Dio's account of reigns contemporary with his own lifetime. In the same manner, his earlier coeval Galen, however enlightened a court-physician and open-minded a philosopher, was still even prepared to make diagnoses, apply cures, and actually to perform a surgical operation at the bidding of a dream.[79] And the composition of *oneirocriticae* continued to be as profitable and popular an enterprise as ever. Appropriately, the one great dream book that has survived from antiquity, that of Artemidorus, appears to date from this period.

This, too, not surprisingly, was an age of relic-collecting. Handkerchiefs (*'linteamina et manualia'*) were carefully laid out by the faithful to catch the treasured drops of Cyprian's blood at his beheading in September of 258;[80] just a few months earlier,[81] the faithful in Spain gathered the *disiecta membra* of the martyr Fructuosus after his imperfect combustion and severally took them home. The faithful were, however, all inspired—by a dream—to regather them and bury them properly *uno in loco*.[82] In the next generation we read in Optatus of Milevis of the Carthaginian Lucilla whose engaging habit it was to kiss her favourite martyr's bone before receiving the Eucharist. Her ecclesiastical authorities rebuked her on the grounds that the bone was an unauthenticated relic, and that she was besides deemed thus to be breaking the Eucharistic fast.[83] Nor is it very many years from Cyprian's lifetime until we have Constantine's rather bizarre and frankly superstitious brand of Christianity. It is no wonder, therefore, that Cyprian should share in this respect for and the cultivation of the occult, nor that in later tradition he came to be hopelessly confused with a homonymous Cyprian, the *magus,* viz. Cyprian of Antioch.[84]

All this can have its lighter side. The deacon Pontius composed his biography of his bishop Cyprian consciously in emulation of and, indeed, in rivalry to the extremely popular *Acta* of Perpetua and Felicity, African martyrs of 203—Acts which continued to enjoy such popularity that in his day Augustine felt constrained to remind his readers that they were not canonical writ.[85] Perpetua and Felicity were merely of the catechumenate and of the laity, and so Cyprian is proudly proclaimed by Pontius to be the proto-episcopal martyr of Africa (as indeed he is).[86] In the earlier *Acta* Perpetua in prison is vouchsafed a vision of the coming conflict in the arena she is soon to undergo[87]—a vision in the manner of Stephen, the archetype of Christian martyrdom, and indeed of many another *moriturus,* Jewish or pagan.[88] And so Cyprian, before the time of his execution, is carefully granted in his place of exile a consciously bigger and better vision of his approaching trial.[89] It is palpably a tasteless literary fiction, but it did cater for the taste of the time.

Such are a few aspects, out of many that may be drawn from the extant correspondence, which illuminate Cyprian as a man of his times.

NOTES

1. For full *testimonia* of Cyprian's *uita,* see A. Harnack, *Geschichte der altchristlichen Literatur* vol. 1 (Leipzig, 1893), 701ff. The precise location of Cyprian's birth-place is unknown but Carthage is a fair surmise. The date of his birth is unknown also (cf. Aug. *sermo* 310, *PL* 38, 1413 'quando natus sit, ignoramus'), but the tone of some passages suggests he cannot have been too young at the time of his elevation to the bishopric of Carthage c. 249 (e.g. in a very early episcopal letter he is prepared to address a fellow bishop as 'fili carissime' *Ep.* 2.2.3 ; he clearly

includes himself in a class of bishops variously described in
Ep. 55.24.2 as 'in aetate antiqui, in fide integri, in pressura pro-
bati, in persecutione proscripti').

2. Journeys outside Carthage are unknown save (1) self-imposed
concealment—near Carthage?—during the persecution of Decius,
(2) a visit to Hadrumetum (*Ep.* 48.1), (3) exile in 257-8 at
Curubis, Pont. *Vit. Cyp.* 12.2, *Acta Procons.* 2. A visit to Thi-
baris was planned, but thwarted (*Ep.* 58.1.1. 'cogitaueram . . . ipse
ad uos uenire').

3. Beheaded, 'in agrum Sexti' *Acta Procons.* 5, 14 September 258.

4. See F. Millar, *A Study of Cassius Dio* (Oxford, 1964).

5. The recent translation by E. C. Echols (Berkeley and Los Angeles,
1961), though a welcome venture, is unfortunately untrustworthy.

6. See most recently R. Syme, *Ammianus Marcellinus and the Historia Augusta* (Oxford, 1968).

7. H. Mattingly, 'The religious background of the *Historia Augusta*',
Harv. Theol. Rev. 39 (1946), 213ff. at 214f. surmises the gap is
due to the later suppression of anti-Christian material which these
lives contained (for the good press Valerian enjoys in the *Hist.
Aug.* see also A. D. E. Cameron, *J.R.S.* 55 (1965), 247) ; A. R.
Birley, 'The Augustan History', in *Latin Biography,* ed. T. A.
Dorey (London, 1967), 113ff. at 125f. surmises the lacuna was
deliberately contrived by the writer to avoid offending Christian
sensibilities too blatantly in the accounts of Phillip, Decius and
Valerian. Neither thesis is altogether convincing.

8. See especially A. T. Olmstead, 'The mid-third century of the
Christian era', *C.P.* 37 (1942), 241ff., and esp. 398ff.

9. See J. Quasten, *Patrology,* vol. 2 (Utrecht, 1953), 367ff. for description and bibliography.

10. But very frequently neglected by them, e.g. the debated question
whether the religious edict of Decius applied to all the inhabitants of the Empire or to citizens only ought to be considered
with reference to Cyp. *Epp.* 15.4 and 55.13.2 along with *de laps.*
25 ; these passages suggest non-citizen inhabitants were involved.
See, most recently, T. D. Barnes, 'Legislation against the Christians', *J.R.S.* 58 (1968), 49. See further, G. W. Clarke, 'Some
Observations on the Persecution of Decius', *Antichthon* 3 (1969),
68ff.

11. Notably *Epp.* 1 and 2 but less likely 3 and 4 (on internal evidence
of ideas and attitudes parallel to later, datable epistles).

12. *C.S.E.L.* 3.3.272 (two attributed to Cyprian, one each to Donatus
and Cornelius). The forgers were Donatists who cherished Cyprian's works: 'uos qui scripta Cypriani nobis tamquam firma-
menta canonicae auctoritatis opponitis' Aug. *c. Cresc. Donat.* 1.32
(40). See also H. K. Mengis, *Ein donatistisches Corpus cyprianischer Briefe* (Diss. Freiburg, 1916).

13. Especially *Epp.* 21, 22, 23.

14. *Ep.* 48.3.2: 'sed quoniam latius fusa est nostra prouincia, habet etiam Numidiam et Mauritaniam sibi cohaerentes . . . '

15. In time past ('ante multos fere annos') Privatus of Lambaesis could be condemned by a synod of 90 bishops, *Ep.* 59.10.1. It is sheer conjecture how many more actual sees existed in Cyprian's day—and *contra* Gibbon (ed. Bury) 2.62 too much ought not to be made of 'village-bishoprics' in the African context: see C. H. Turner, *Studies in Early Church History* (Oxford, 1912), 60ff. See also on this question H. von Soden, 'Die Prosographie des afrikanischen Episkopats zur Zeit cyprians', *Königl. Preussischen Historischen Institut in Rom,* Bd. xii (1909), 247ff.

16. For a full discussion and catalogue, A. Harnack, 'Über verlorene Briefe und Aktenstücke, die sich aus der cyprianischen Brief-sammlung ermitteln lassen' *Texte und Untersuchungen* 23.2a (1902), to which add Chronicle of 395 (*M.G.H.* 9.738 ed. Momm-sen): 'hac persecutione Cyprianus hortatus est per epistolas suas Augustinum et Felicitatem, qui passi sunt apud ciuitatem Capuen-sem, metropolim Campaniae' (on this see further H. Delehaye, *Les origines du culte des martyrs,* 2nd ed. (Brussels, 1933), 303 f.).

17. E.g. the tone of letters suggest previous communications with communities in Spain (see *Ep.* 67) and Gaul (see *Ep.* 68), and probably Cappadocia (but observe a hint to the contrary in *Ep.* 75.25.1—'quod nec uos latere confidimus') ; likewise, a con-gratulatory letter on Stephen's election and, similarly, on Xystus' is to be expected (cf. 61.1.1 referring to a lost letter of felicita-tion to Lucius).

18. Pont. *Vit. Cyp.* 7. Some confirmation may also come from some MSS of the *Sent. Episc. LXXVI ;* biographical annotations sug-gest a manuscript tradition dating from well before the close of the third century—before some of the participating bishops were dead (see C. H. Turner, 'Prolegomena to the *Testimonia* and *ad Fortunatum* of St Cyprian', *J.T.S.* 29 (1927-8), 113ff. at 117ff., H. Delehaye, *Les origines du culte des martyrs* (2nd end., Brus-sels, 1933), 381f.).

19. See Th. Mommsen, 'Zur lateinischen Stichometrie', *Hermes* 21 (1886), 142ff.; 25 (1890), 636ff., W. Sanday, 'The Cheltenham List of the Canonical Books of the Old and New Testament and of the Writings of Cyprian', *Studia Biblica et Ecclesiastica* 3 (1891), 217ff. at 274ff., and K. Mengis, 'Ein alles Verzeichnis cyprianischer Schriften', *Ph.W.* 38 (1918), 326ff.

20. See now Migne, *Patrol. Lat. Supplementum* (Paris, 1960), vol. 2, 610f.

21. See in general M. Bévenot, *The tradition of MSS. A study in the transmission of St Cyprian's Treatises* (Oxford, 1961).

22. H. von Soden, 'Die cyprianische Briefsammlung. Geschichte ihrer Entstehung und Überlieferung', *Texte und Untersuchungen* 25 (1904).

23. Turin, Bibl. Naz., E1115 (1459 A.D.). See H. von Soden, op. cit., 151f.

24. M. Bévenot, 'A new Cyprianic fragment', *Bull. John Rylands* 28 (1944), 76ff., exploited, for the unravelling of MS traditions, in op. cit. in n. 21.

25. See H. L. Ramsay, 'Our oldest MSS of St Cyprian. iii. The contents and order of the MSS LNP', *J.T.S.* 3 (1901-2), p. 592.

26. E.g. *Ep.* 45.4.2 'melius autem, frater, facies si etiam exempla litterarum . . . legi illic fratribus iubeas' ; cf. *Ep.* 59.19.1 'Et quanquam sciam . . . plebi legere te semper litteras nostras, tamen nunc et admoneo et peto . . . ut hac epistula lecta . . . ' and Cornelius, *Ep.* 49.3.3 'Has litteras puto te debere, frater carissime, et ad ceteras ecclesias mittere . . . '

27. *Ep.* 59.2.1, cf. 59.14.1, 59.16.1.

28. *Ep.* 45.2 ; this letter (cf. 55.2.1) was written 'discordioso stilo', packed 'acerbationibus criminosis' by those 'uel furori suo uel libidini seruientes': regrettably it does not survive.

29. *Ep.* 32.1.2 'Quamuis et Satyro lectori fratri nostro mandauerim ut singulis desiderantibus describendi faciat potestatem . . . '('singuli' appears to refer here largely to individual laymen ; clerics are to have automatic faculty—'facultatem transcriptionis accipiant').

30. *Ep.* 45.4.3 'Exemplaria autem eadem nunc quoque . . . transmisi.'

31. *Ep.* 20.2.1 (viz. *Epp.* 5-7, 10-19).

32. *Epp.* 27, 25, 32, 73. For a full list of references to enclosures see C. H. Turner, appendix to article by Sanday cited in n. 19, at 323 n. 1.

33. E.g. *Epp.* 30.5.2 (Novatian), 59.2.1 (Cornelius), 73.4.1. (Iubaianus).

34. *Ep.* 74.1.1. The only verbatim report which we have of Stephen's text occurs in the quotation in 74.1.2. Zonaras' note on this letter appears to be studiously vague (12.22 p. 139, vol. 3 ed. Dindorf): οὗ καὶ ἐπιστολὴ περὶ τούτου πρὸς Κυπριανὸν τὸν ἱερομάρτυρα ἀναγράφεται.

35. *Ep.* 55.1.1., 2.1.

36. Polycarp *ad Philip.* 13.2: We are sending to you the letters of Ignatius, which he sent to us, and others which we have in our possession.

37. Euseb. *H.E.* 6.36.3: 'As many of these letters as we have been able to collect, preserved here and there by various people, we arranged in separate roll-cases so that they might no longer be dispersed.' These letters number more than a hundred. 'The col-

lection included letters to Origen, and decrees of synods concerning him.' Lawlor and Oulton ad loc.

38. On this see especially A. von Harnack, 'Brot und Wasser: die eucharistischen Elemente bei Justin', *Texte und Untersuchungen* 7.2 (1891), 117ff, H. Leitzmann, *Mass and Lord's Supper*, E.T. by D. H. G. Reeve (Leiden, 1953+), fasc. 4, 200ff.

39. For the suspicions entertained about such baptism cf. Eusebius *H.E.* 6.43. 14, 17, *de rebapt.* 4ff. (*C.S.E.L.* 3.3. 73ff.), Council Neocaes. *can.* 12, Council Elvira *can.* 24.

40. Aug. *de bapt.* 6.15. 24f. (*C.S.E.L.* 51.1. 313ff.).

41. *Saint Cyprien Correspondence*, vol. 1 (Paris, 1962), xlvii; cf. H.-I. Marrou, 'La technique de l'édition à l'époque patristique', *V.C.* 3 (1949), 216.

42. Rufinus, *de adulteratione liborum Origenis* 41ff., *PL* 17. 628ff. This passage and Jerome's comments on it (esp. *adv. Ruf.* 2.19, *PL* 23. 464) are conveniently collected in Harnack, op. cit., in n. 1, 694f., 706.

43. Rufinus wrongly attributes the tract to Tertullian. On the addition of *spuria* cf. H. L. M. van der Valk, 'On the Edition of Books in Antiquity, *V.C.* 11 (1959), 8: 'The works of Christian authors were particularly liable to falsifications by the insertion of heretical doctrines, a manipulation which is especially known to us from Hieronymus' letters.'

44. *Ep.* 67.6.2. For the *fasti* of known Spanish procurators see H.-G. Pflaum, *Les carrières procuratoriennes équestres sous le Haut-Empire romain*, vol. 3 (Paris, 1960), 1047ff., A. Balil, 'Funcionarios subalternos en Hispania durante el imperio romano', *Emerita* 33 (1965), 297ff. at 305ff. This procurator cannot be identified; he appears to be acting as governor (a *uicarius?*)— see H.-G. Pflaum, *Les procurateurs équestres sous le Haut-Empire romain* (Paris, 1950), 135 no. 16. And generally on *ducenarii*, Pflaum op. cit., 275ff. and idem, 'Histoire et cultes de Thasos', *Journal des Savants*, 1959, 75ff at 83 n. 1 (on 'ducenarius' as an honorific title). The case of Paul of Samosata is notorious ('wishing to be called ducenarius rather than bishop' Euseb. *H.E.* 7.30. 8).

45. Notably in the functionaries of the *familia Caesaris*; see the articles by P. R. C. Weaver, 'Status Nomenclature of imperial Slaves', *C.Q.* 14 (1964), 134ff., 'Slave and freedman "cursus" in the imperial administration', *Proc. Camb. Phil. Soc.* 190 (1964), 74ff., 'Status Nomenclature of imperial Freedman', *C.Q.* 13 (1963), 272ff., 'Social mobility in the early Roman Empire: the evidence of the imperial freedmen and slaves', *Past and Present* 37 (July, 1967), 3ff.

46. Euseb. *H.E.* 6.43.11. The omission is that of *fossor*. But it ought to be observed that in [Cyp.] *Ep.* 8.3.2.—a letter written by the

Roman clergy coeval with Cornelius—a special group of *fossores* may be envisaged; if so, they were clearly not yet elevated to clerical rank ('Et quod maximum est, corpora martyrum aut ceterorum si non sepeliantur, grandis periculus imminet *eis quibus incumbit hoc opus.'*)

47. This would be a natural assumption, but later evidence indicates that the ecclesiastical *regiones* did not correspond, at least at the date of the evidence, to the Augustan, civil *regiones*; see L. Duchesne, *Le Liber Pontificalis,* second ed., vol. 1 (Paris, 1955), 148 n. 3.

48. *Ep.* 1.1.1. 'quando singuli diuino sacerdotio honorati et in clerico ministerio constituti non nisi altari et sacrificiis deseruire et precibus adque orationibus uacare debeant', 1.2 'quae nunc ratio et forma in clero tenetur ut qui in ecclesia Domini in ordinationem clericam promouentur in nullo ab administratione diuina auocentur . . . ' (cf. Cyp. *de laps.* 6, Tert. *de idol.* 11.1f.). Contrast Council *Elvira* can. 19 assuming, but regulating, clerical trading practices or, in the third quarter of the third century, Maximus, the *papas* of Alexandria, along with a lector and other clerical staff, engaged in corn transactions (A. Deissmann, *Light from the Ancient East,* E.T. by L. R. M. Strachan (London, 1910), 192ff.). The documents preserved by Eusebius at *H.E.* 5.18.2 (Apollonius on Montanus) and at H.E. 5.28.10 (Anonymous on Natalius) indicate unmistakably that clerical salaries, at these earlier times, were considered a scandalous innovation.

49. *Ep.* 39.5.1. diuisiones mensurnas cf. *Ep.* 41.2.1 and Tert. *Apol.* 39.5 'modicam unusquisque stipem mentrua die . . . apponit'. Note the temporary suspension of salaries in Cyp. *Ep.* 34.4.2. 'interea se a diuisione mensurna tantum contineant'.

50. Hence Aurelius and Celerinus the *lectores* in *Ep.* 39.5.1 are exceptionally to be presented 'aequatis quantitatibus' with the *presbyteri* cf. *Didas. Apost.* ix, p. 90 (Connolly).

51. On Celerinus see E. W. Benson, *Cyprian, his life, his times, his work* (London, 1897), 69ff. and my article, 'Some observations on the persecution of Decius', *Antichthon* 3 (1969), 63ff.

52. To be marked, symbolically, by a seat in the *presbyterium* ('sessuri nobiscum prouectis et corroboratis annis suis' *Ep.* 39.5.2) cf. on Numidicus *Ep.* 40.1.1. 'nobiscum sedeat in clero' (on the transfer of Numidicus from another see to that of Carthage); on such translations see H. Hess, *The Canons of the Council of Sardica, A.D. 343* (Oxford, 1958), 71ff., 88f.

53. *Ep.* 55.8.2.

54. Pontius *Vit. Cyp.* 5.1.

55. Pontius stresses that the election to episcopal office took place 'iudicio dei et plebis fauore' (5.1). The absence of supporting clergy is significant.

56. Pontius op. cit. 3.1.

57. But note the story of the election of Cornelius' predecessor, Fabian, apparently from the ranks of the laity *H.E.* 6.29.2f. For other, and later, spectacular 'irregular' appointments (e.g. of Ambrose, Augustine, Basil) see H. Hess, op. cit., in n. 52, 105 n. 3.

58. The numbers involved are rather obscure; at least five clerics of the grade of presbyter were openly hostile ('quinque isti presbyteri' *Ep.* 43.3.1, 'ex quinque presbyteris' *Ep.* 59.9.1—names appear to be recorded in *Ep.* 14.4.1)—out of a tally of possibly eight. In *Ep.* 43.1.1 Cyprian appears to indicate he has only three loyal presbyters one of whom had been recently co-opted (*Ep.* 41).

59. *Ep.* 8.3.4.

60. *Ep.* 9.2.1f.

61. In the next correspondence with Rome that survives (*Epp.* 20, 27) relations have been somewhat restored though Cyprian is still rather on the defensive; a reply came from the pen of Novatian (*Ep.* 30).

62. Note, for example, the appointment of the Confessor Callistus over the claims of Hippolytus (Hippol. *Philos.* 9.12).

63. Euseb. *H.E.* 6.43.11. Note the parallel terms used by the Roman clergy in *Ep.* 8.3.1. 'siue uiduae siue thlibomeni'.

64. Such details of Lawrence's manner of execution, suspiciously, do not occur in the earliest accounts.

65. *Epp.* 5.1.1. 7.1.2. 'Viduarum et infirmorum et omnium pauperum curam peto diligenter habeatis. Set et peregrinis si qui indigentes fuerint suggeratis de quantitate mea propria quam apud Rogatianum compresbyterum nostrum dimisi.' 12.2.2, 14.2.1, cf. 30.8.1 (refugee bishops at Rome), 55.13.2 (general refugee movements) etc.

66. *Ep.* 5.1.1 'summula omnis . . . sit apud clericos distributa': note the terms of Cyprian's proscription *Ep.* 66.4.1 'si quis tenet possidet de bonis Caecilii Cypriani episcopi christianorum . . . '

67. E.g. *Ep.* 7.1.2. 'quae quantitas ne forte iam uniuersa erogata sit, misi eidem per Naricum acoluthum aliam portionem . . . '.

68. i.e. before Cyprian's return from voluntary exile which occurred shortly after Easter, 251 (*Ep.* 43.1.2). It remains quite obscure in what way the persecution terminated.

69. *Ep.* 41.1.2. The commission's inquiry also served to solicit possible vocations for Cyprian's depleted clergy. W. Telfer, *The Office of a Bishop* (London, 1962), 172f. takes *Ep.* 41 to refer to clergy only and to the making up of arrears to their monthly *sportulae*. There is room for doubt that this is correct.

70. See R. P. Duncan-Jones, 'Costs, outlays and summae honorariae from Roman Africa', *P.B.S.R.* 30 (1962), 53f.

71. *S.H.A.* Gord. 15f., 23.6, Max. 19, *Herod*, 7.4ff. See also T. Kotula, 'Sources du séparatisme africain au iiième siècle de notre ère,' *Travaux de la Société des sciences et des lettres de Wroclaw*, ser. A, 74 (1961), 1ff.

72. E.g. Celerinus 'hortatu in uisione per noctem compulsus' in *Ep.* 39.1.1. See generally on this question A. von Harnack, 'Cyprian als Enthusiast', *Z.N.W.* 1902, 177ff. and compare Dionysius of Alexandria ap. Euseb. *H.E.* 7.7.2f. inspired by a dream to read heretical literature, and Augustine's uice *Conf.* 7.12 'tolle lege, tolle lege' and Jerome's dream *Ep.* 22.30 'Ciceronianus es, non Christianus'.

73. *Ep.* 16.4.1. Note there the presence of what appear to be the Christian equivalent of child mediums ('praeter nocturnas uisiones per dies quoque impletur apud nos Spiritu Sancto puerorum innocens aetas quae in ecstasi uidet oculis . . . '). On such youthful mediums see E. R. Dodds, *The Greeks and the Irrational* (Berkeley and Los Angeles, 1964), 263 n. 70, 309 n. 115.

74. *Epp.* 14.2.1, 20.1.2.

75. But note also Cyprian on Novatianists *Ep.* 55.16ff.

76. Cf. Pliny *Ep.* 3.5.4 (Pliny the Elder began his twenty books on the German Wars 'somnio monitus').

77. Dio 72.23.2ff. For the rôle played by dreams in Dio's life see F. Millar, op. cit., 179ff.

78. 72.23.1.

79. Galen xvi. 219ff. (Kühn) and compare Marc. Aurelius *in se ipsum* 1.17.8 'by the agency of dreams I was given antidotes especially against the spitting of blood and vertigo': for such addiction to dreams cf. E. R. Dodds, op. cit. in n. 73, 120f. and G. W. Bowersock, *Greek Sophists in the Roman Empire* (Oxford, 1969), 73f.

80. *Acta Cyp.* 5. Relics and the like were, of course, a feature of even the most primitive Christianity; compare, for example, Acts. 19.12—σουδάρια ἢ σιμικίνθια impregnated with the virtue of Paul and used for curative and exorcistic purposes.

81. Date, January 259: for the *Acta*, Knopf-Krüger-Ruhback, *Ausgewählte Märtyrerakten* (Tübingen, 1965), 83ff. and for a commentary P. Franchi de' Cavalieri, 'Gli Atti di S. Fructuoso di Tarragona', *Studi e Testi* 65 (1935), 129ff.

82. *Acta Fruct.* 6.

83. Optatus *De Schismate* 1.16 (C.S.E.L. 26.18f.) ; on the passage see H. Delehaye, *Sanctus. Essai sur le culte des saints dans l'antiquité*, Subs. Hag. 17 (Brussels, 1927), 162f.

84. On the confusion see J. Coman, 'Les deux Cypriens de saint Grégorie de Nazianze', *Stud. Patrist.* 4 (1961), 363ff., H. Delehaye, *Les origines du culte des martyrs,* 2nd ed. (Brussels, 1933), 91ff., A. D. Nock, 'Hagiographica', *J.T.S.* 28 (1926-7), 409ff. at 411ff.
85. Aug. *de anima* 1.12 (*PL* 44.481) cf. *de anima* 3.9 (*PL* 44.517). For the dating see now T. D. Barnes, 'Pre-Decian *Acta Martyrum',* *J.T.S.* 19 (1968), 509ff. at 521ff.
86. *Vita Cyp.* 19 'sic consummata passione perfectum est, ut Cyprianus . . . etiam sacerdotales coronas in Africa primus imbueret . . . numquam aliquis quamuis ex bonis et sacerdotibus ad passionem uenisse memoratur' etc. For the ecclesiastical status of Perpetua and Felicity, *Acta Perp. et Felic.* 2f.
87. Ibid., 4.2ff.
88. Stephen, Acts 7.55 ; for pagan parallels in multitude see A. S. Pease on Cic. *de. div.* 1.63f. (on 'adpropinquante morte multo est diuinior [animus]' and 'facilius euenit adpropinquante morte ut animi futura augurentur') and for Jewish, H. A. Fischel, 'Martyr and Prophet', *Jewish Quarterly Review* 37 (1947), 363ff.
89. Pontius *Vit. Cyp.* 12. On this rhetorical aspect of Pontius' biography see H. Delehaye, *Les passions des martyrs et les genres littéraires* (Brussels, 1921), 94ff.

M